GW00715911

WHY I SUPPORTED THE EMERGENCY

WHY I SUPPORTED THE EMERGENCY
Essays and Profiles

KHUSHWANT SINGH

Compiled and Edited by
Sheela Reddy

PENGUIN
VIKING

VIKING
Published by the Penguin Group
Penguin Books India Pvt. Ltd, 11 Community Centre, Panchsheel Park, New Delhi 110 017, India
Penguin Group (USA) Inc., 375 Hudson Street, New York, New York 10014, USA
Penguin Group (Canada), 90 Eglinton Avenue East, Suite 700, Toronto, Ontario, M4P 2Y3, Canada (a division of Pearson Penguin Canada Inc.)
Penguin Books Ltd, 80 Strand, London WC2R 0RL, England
Penguin, Ireland, 25 St Stephen's Green, Dublin 2, Ireland (a division of Penguin Books Ltd)
Penguin Group (Australia), 250 Camberwell Road, Camberwell, Victoria 3124, Australia (a division of Pearson Australia Group Pty Ltd)
Penguin Group (NZ), 67 Apollo Drive, Rosedale, North Shore 0632, New Zealand (a division of Pearson New Zealand Ltd)
Penguin Group (South Africa) (Pty) Ltd, 24 Sturdee Avenue, Rosebank, Johannesburg 2196, South Africa

Penguin Books Ltd, Registered Offices: 80 Strand, London WC2R 0RL, England

First published in Viking by Penguin Books India 2009
Copyright © Khushwant Singh 2009
Introduction copyright © Sheela Reddy 2009

These essays have appeared in different form in the columns 'With Malice Towards One and All . . .' and '. . . This Above All' in *Hindustan Times* and the *Tribune* respectively, and in *Outlook*, the *Telegraph* and the *Taj Magazine*.

ISBN 9780670083244

Typeset in Minion by Inosoft Systems, Noida
Printed at Gopsons Papers Ltd, Noida

CONTENTS

Editor's Acknowledgements

There are so many people I want to thank for making this book possible: Vinod Mehta, editor of *Outlook*, for his generosity and for turning a blind eye as I scurried to meet deadlines not of his making; Diya Kar Hazra, for making it look so easy, and Mekhala Moorthy for her painstaking editing; Sashidharan Kollery for his moral support and for cheerfully rushing to my aid to retrieve and send the manuscript back and forth; Lachhman Das for meticulously filing away years of newspaper clippings; and not least, Penguin's trusty Auto Ravi for ferrying mountains of pages from my office to Penguin's.

INTRODUCTION

Fourteen years ago, when I was a reporter for the *Asian Age*, my editor, M.J. Akbar, sent me to interview Khushwant Singh. I had met Khushwant once years ago when I was trying to make a precarious living as a young freelance journalist. At that time I had duly pounded the pavements of Bahadur Shah Zafar Marg, better known in my circle of freshly arrived immigrants to Delhi as the Fleet Street of India. The first editor's door that I could get past was that of an unknown tabloid called the *Sun*. I had an article with me—on Barbara Cartland's visit to Hyderabad—that I had written and typed out. It was accepted and the editor asked me if I could also interview Khushwant Singh for the *Sun*. I had no idea why he wanted a feature on Khushwant Singh after Barbara Cartland, but I accepted the assignment with alacrity.

Khushwant was certainly easier to meet than Barbara Cartland, whose gatekeepers included a five-star hotel staff, the organizers of her event in Hyderabad and finally her husband's cold voice on the phone. Khushwant's number was listed in the telephone directory and he answered the phone himself. 'Come at four o'clock today,' he said briskly, without even asking which newspaper I was reporting for. It brought him down a little in my young rank-conscious eyes. He was already a legend by then, churning out his two weekly columns for over a dozen English and fifteen language dailies across the country. And these columns were collected into books almost as fast as he wrote them. Then, as now, you couldn't go to a single railway station, no matter how small, and not find a paperback written by him at the

A.H. Wheeler stall. Another reason for my disdain was that my father, a retired railway engineer who read only newspapers, the *Illustrated Weekly* before it folded up and Perry Mason thrillers by Erle Stanley Gardner, read him religiously every week.

Khushwant opened the door himself, a barefoot, sloppy, bespectacled sardar with a beard dyed jet black, in shorts and a T-shirt that was once white but was now stained with what looked like ketchup but turned out to be the Pan Parag he chewed all day. He led me into his little den, which made me a little nervous: he had a reputation and I couldn't see if anyone else was in the house besides him. All four walls of the study were lined with books. Just as we settled down, he in a comfortably worn black leather sofa, his bare feet up on a moda, a servant arrived with a tray carrying two large mugs of tea and two or three generous slices of fruit cake. The cake was for me, Khushwant said, and deftly led me into my interview without wasting time on further preambles. I've forgotten now what the interview was about, but I recall being lulled by his avuncular kindness into asking questions I wouldn't have dared to ask anyone else of his age and stature. He answered in very simple, plain words, with an openness I had rarely encountered, considering each question I put to him with a gravity that made me feel as if I was a veteran journalist instead of a cub reporter for an unknown tabloid, which, incidentally, closed down very soon after this incident. He waited till I'd finished, before starting his own grilling: where was I from? Was I single or married? What did my parents do? And my husband? But his probing was very skilful, disguised under the cover of many amusing anecdotes and stories about people whom I'd vaguely heard of even though they were from Hyderabad, the city where I grew up. I got the impression even then that behind his benign gaze, he didn't miss a thing. And I left feeling flattered by his rapt attention. I was convinced I had made a lasting impression on him.

Of course, when I interviewed him again, he had no memory of that meeting. He had changed very little in the twelve or thirteen years since I had last met him. He still answered his phone on the first ring, briskly saying, 'Come at four o'clock,' and he opened the front door himself for the photographer and me, offering us tea and biscuits before answering any questions. This time I was there to ask him his view on Rabindranath Tagore's writings. It was, to say the least, interesting—what an overrated writer the Nobel Laureate was, how underwhelmed he was by Tagore's poetry and novels, and how he was a mere songwriter, but no one dared to say so because Bengalis immediately took umbrage. He spoke in the unconcerned way I remembered from our first meeting, one bare foot up on the moda, as if he was saying something quite commonplace. He has this gift, even now, of saying something outrageous with the utmost sincerity. Nor did he look nervous, as politicians sometimes did when I noted down everything they said, wondering if they had been too outspoken. He was either too naïve to know the effect his words would have when they made the headlines, or he couldn't give a damn.

The next morning there was an uproar in Calcutta about what Khushwant had said, and angry letters poured in. My delighted editor sent me back for a follow-up, to try and squeeze the last drops out of the controversy. I was doubtful: surely, by now Khushwant would be repenting his off the cuff answers. Perhaps he would turn his rage on me for his own heedlessly uttered words, accusing me of misquoting him. But he was as genial as ever, unrepentant at the storm he had unleashed with his words. It made it easier to ask him for another interview that would rake over the coals. He rose gallantly to the challenge, pointing out that Tagore was among the four holy cows among Bengalis—the others being Subhas Chandra Bose, Bengali cuisine and I forget the last one, possibly Rabindrasangeet. To criticize any of these four holy Cs, he said, was to whip up a storm among Bengalis. I began to admire this curious old man: he had known all the time, while I was diligently taking down his words, the effect he would have in Bengal the next day and yet he didn't back off; he just strolled into battle with a careless laugh.

This time the impression I'd made on him was less fleeting. When I called him again in a few weeks, he could not only recall my name but he also invited me to come at 7 p.m. Everyone in Delhi—or rather, everyone who read his columns—knew that 7 p.m. at E-49, Sujan Singh Park was his charmed hour when the high and mighty, famous and infamous, godmen and godless, writers, both aspiring and renowned, painters, dancers, scholars, visiting journalists from abroad and, of course, pretty women, rang the bell under the now famous signboard. This board has travelled with him since his paying guest days in Bombay: Please Do Not Ring the Bell Unless You Are Expected. They were invited in for a round or two of Scotch and soda and some conversation, both flowing generously until exactly an hour later, they were ejected rather peremptorily by his wife, Kaval, so that he could have an early dinner and go to bed. An invitation to his daily soirée was a prized thing then, as it is now. For most, it was their ticket to instant fame in those pre page 3 days.

I arrived dressed for the occasion. But Khushwant hadn't bothered to change—the same grey, stained pathan shirt and salwar, the same bare foot propped up on a moda, his long white hair untidily bundled in a yellow muslin cloth—the informal turban, safa, that sardars wear at home, as he later explained to me. There were four or five visitors whom he had already engaged, almost miraculously, in a conversation. I say miraculous because none of the visitors knew each other—nor did they care to find out. They were the most disparate group of strangers I'd ever seen sit down together for a drink. That evening, there was a senior police officer from Chandigarh, a retired army general, a woman tour operator from Germany whom Khushwant had befriended on one of his visits to Berlin, two quiet men from Bangalore who had come to seek his permission to translate and use his columns for a newspaper they were starting, and a pretty, young anchor from Doordarshan who wanted him to appear on her show. What I didn't know then was that Khushwant regularly arms himself for these evening soirées with a variety of conversational gambits—from abusive postcards he's received, the amusing anecdotes he's collected over a lifetime of travelling and meeting people, and from his wide reading—which he then deftly uses to keep the conversation from flagging. If there is anything he's afraid of, it must be the chilling silences that occasionally descend upon his random guests.

'You are late,' were his first words of greeting when I arrived. I was to hear these words, spoken without rancour, being repeated thousands of times in the years to come. I have never met a man who lives so rigidly by the clock and yet prospers so joyously. Khushwant has that rare thing in a punctual person: he doesn't lose his temper if someone is late for a meeting. He has a little clock tucked away on the bookshelf facing his chair. No one can see it except him, but it is there to enable him to decide when to give that last call: 'Achcha, last drink. Time for the buddha.' But he rarely needs to even glance at the little clock to know the time, night or day. Unerringly, the pen stops moving on the yellow legal pad that he scribbles on all day a few minutes before 7 p.m., and he's up on his feet, shuffling off to the bathroom to rinse his mouth for the Sacred Hour devoted to Scotch whisky. Unerringly, too, he seems to know when visiting hour is up. Nor does he need an alarm clock to wake him up at the crack of dawn, so he can get down to work undisturbed. I suspect there is a little clock embedded deep in his brain, which will only stop ticking when he goes to meet his Maker. He has little use for the many clocks and watches he receives as gifts from his admirers. And in those early years of our friendship, he loved to offload them on me as gifts, no doubt in the hope that I'd mend my unpunctual ways, but then he eventually gave up.

I soon became what his family called 'Papa's Latest', their code word for the scores of women, usually half his age or younger, whom he befriended in serial order, turning on the full power of his attention; he gently drew them out, helped them up whichever ladder they chose to climb and, his job done, as gently withdrew. By the end of it, he discovered whatever there was to discover in each of them. And all this was done with such tact—or perhaps it was his deep sense of loyalty, I can't decide which—that none of his serial favourites seemed to resent the consequent ones. His 'harem', as he jokingly describes it, is a warm, friendly and ever-widening circle of female friends. Beauty is an asset that might help while joining the 'harem' but the only two reasons for disqualification are possibly insincerity and ill temper. Khushwant seems to have an in-built detector for humbug and soon grows bored with anyone, man or woman, who doesn't level with him. And bad temper is perhaps the only thing he can never forgive.

I was invited to attend his at-homes two or three evenings a week. His wife, Kaval, had just been diagnosed with Alzheimer's disease, and while no one knew as yet what this meant, she sat moodily in front of him all day and stared into space. Khushwant moved out of his den and into the living room so that he could keep an eye on her as he worked. She had stopped drinking and usually disappeared into the bedroom as soon as his visitors started to arrive. He needed someone to keep the sanctity of his Sacred Hour intact, to pour the drinks and to tell his guests when to leave. I was only too glad to play High Priestess, considering the rich dividends: the company was invariably interesting and I now had the chance to meet some of the best minds from around the world. Besides, I wanted to be a writer like him: to blur the distinctions between journalism and literature, to be gloriously prolific, have a hundred books to my name, and be recognized wherever I went, sought after by Presidents and butchers alike. He made it look so easy. I wanted to apprentice myself to him, and what better way of getting started than at his evening mehfils?

Occasionally Khushwant took me along with him when he had to attend art shows, dance performances, book launches or dinners with ambassadors and ministers. I often accompanied him on his walks in Lodhi Gardens, Talkatora Gardens or Khan Market. He drove us everywhere in his battered Fiat Premier. Wherever we went, he was recognized. People came up to him for autographs, to share jokes, to take photographs. It was like stepping out with a Father Christmas version of Amitabh Bachchan. I basked in the reflected glory and came away more impressed each time by the person behind the mask of the Dirty Old Man and the clown—the depth of his reading, which he hid behind his humour, his curiosity about how other people lived, his keen observation that never missed a thing, absorbing every detail and quirk, his unshakeable courage to be himself on all occasions, and, above all, his complete lack of vanity. One evening, for example, I had accompanied him to Khan Market where he wanted to buy himself a new notebook to start off yet another book. I needed to go to the butcher's for meat and suggested that I meet him outside. But Khushwant followed me in, not wanting to miss peeping into a butcher's shop. I think it was the first time he had ever entered one in his long and privileged life. He began to peer at the shelves of meat and the butcher's block and then shuffled over to examine the pictures of Mecca with verses from the Quran on the tiled walls. But inconspicuous as he was trying to be, his presence had a startling effect on the butchers: they rose, awestruck, their knives paused over wooden blocks. 'We read your column every week in the Urdu papers,' said the one at the cash box, and recounted, almost word for word, an article by Khushwant that he'd read years ago about a visit to a swimming pool in London when his long hair unwound itself from his cap to the consternation of the other swimmers in the pool. Khushwant laughed and, changing the subject, pointed to the verses from the Quran, asking if he could read them aloud. When we were outside, he said: 'It's something, isn't it, when even the butcher reads you?' and then promptly dismissed it from his mind forever. But I still get the best and fastest service from the butcher, thanks to that one visit with Khushwant.

A new phase began when I joined *Outlook* magazine. By now Khushwant was in his mid-eighties, he had sold his beloved Fiat and had decided not to stir out of his home, except for his bi-annual visits to his home in Kasauli. What hadn't changed, however, was his killing schedule: up by 4 a.m. and working almost non-stop till 7 p.m. to keep pace with his nightmarish deadlines—two weekly columns, besides a couple of books or more a year. And the soirées—his attempt to cut down on socializing and focus on his writing only swelled the crowd that turned up at 7 p.m., turning his evening drinking hour into what he described sometimes as 'a sultan's nightmare'. I turned to him more than ever in my new job as a books editor. He was not only the best sounding board I could ever hope to find, but everything about him—his straightforwardness, his refusal to fudge or be intimidated, his discipline in delivering on deadlines, his long familiarity with Indian writing and writers, and his ability to read a book from cover to cover and reduce it to its basics—made him an ideal reviewer. I began to increasingly rely on him to review books that others dared not take on. Moreover, he was unique in the world of letters for combining his forty years' experience as an unbiased political observer with an enviable readability. That made him an obvious choice whenever *Outlook* needed an essayist who could cover a broad sweep of history in a few hundred words, or assess the worth of national heroes with a judgement unclouded by idolatry or bias. Then, of course, who better than Khushwant when it came to writing about the people he had encountered in his life. With his keen eye for quirks and eccentricities he could literally raise a person from the dead. Again, I couldn't think of anyone better to examine the various reports over the years, including the Nanavati Commission's on the '84 riots against the Sikhs. He was a Sikh who was far more objective about the Sikhs than any non-Sikh would ever dare to be. He became one of *Outlook*'s familiar by-lines. He often grumbled about being overworked, but was too loyal a friend to turn me down. Some of the portraits and essays in this book are a result of that arm-twisting.

Even at ninety-three, he can deliver on deadlines that would probably send a reporter quarter his age to the loony bin. No matter how tight the deadline, he beats it by several hours, and sometimes even days. I am invariably summoned to pick it up earlier than even I had anticipated. His review, overview, essay or obituary, whatever—it's hard to pin down the genre that Khushwant writes, which is possibly why he likes to call them 'pieces'—is never longer than one or two sheets of a yellow legal pad, no matter how complex the subject. And his thoughts seem to flow with such practiced ease that there's rarely a word deleted or rewritten. My role after this is very similar to that of his other 'slave driver', his secretary Lachhman Das. Younger than Khushwant, but with his knees already giving way, Das is the other half of this remarkable writing industry. His job, for close to forty years, has been to collect the sheets of crabbed handwriting when they're done, type them out and push them into dozens of brown paper envelopes, which will be collected later in the day by various newspapers across the country. I, too, type out the pages, push them into an envelope, but I take them right back to him so that he can edit his own copy. The whole process was more educative than I expected. As his stenographer there were things I was learning about writing that I missed as his reader.

Khushwant always rallies his points. The ease with which he writes, rarely pausing to delete or revise, is deceptive. He begins by pondering over the issue, and then makes notes and sticks to the structure he has outlined for himself. His mind is forever making order of the chaos and clutter in which life comes to us; and then he valiantly, diligently, reduces the incomprehensible until his sentences stand in orderly rows, like schoolboys in the morning assembly.

He does his homework thoroughly before sitting down to write. Information is the altar at which he worships. According to him, a writer, be he an essayist or novelist, is reneging on one of his key responsibilities if he doesn't inform his reader even as he provokes and entertains him. For Khushwant, playing with words is the worst form of self-indulgence. Instead, what he demands of a book he reads is: tell me something I don't know. As a result, most of his essays are based on a breathtaking array of sources. His essay 'A Hosanna to the Monsoons', for instance, cites from the religious scriptures of the Sikhs, the Bible, literature, both Sanskrit and English, and even the agricultural report, besides quoting proverbs from regional languages. Even the memorable description of the coming of the monsoons is based on years of observation. For over half a century now, Khushwant has kept a diary where he maintains a daily record of the exact time of sunrise and sunset, the temperature, what trees are budding and when, and of every bug and bird he sees and the time of the year he sees them. Fidelity to facts, however, is not a licence to be a bore. Or to duck tough issues.

At ninety-three, Khushwant is still the most avid reader I've ever met. On an average, he reads around forty new books a year. He meticulously marks the date and time he starts and finishes reading a book, usually taking two or three days over each. Then there is the reading he doesn't count: the dozens of manuscripts people bring him in the hope of getting them published through him, or merely to say a few words about them that can be used as a blurb on the book jacket. As far as I know, I don't think he has turned away any aspiring writer who reached out for help. Besides, he is forever dipping into his perennials—the Bible, the Quran, the Guru Granth Sahib, the Oxford dictionary, books on nature, poets from the classical to the contemporary of English, Urdu and Punjabi. When asked once by a newspaper which poems he could recite by heart, Khushwant was quoted as saying: the Psalms, Wordsworth, Tennyson, Keats, Shelly, Arnold, Omar Khayyam, Iqbal, T.S. Eliot. The list could probably go on and on. Even now, in the early hours of the day, sitting on his chair in the dark, the poetry rises almost unbidden to his mind: Ghalib, Shakespeare, Vedic hymns, limericks, a joyous mix of the sublime and the ribald—verses he has made no effort to memorize, just stuck in his head, the product of a long life spent celebrating the written word.

Khushwant doesn't believe in wearing his erudition on his sleeve. The temptation to show off one's eclectic reading is usually irresistible, but no one knows better than him how suicidal it is for a writer. In his essay 'Qurratullain Hyder—Aunty Subjantiwalli', Khushwant points out just this flaw. For him, to be a good writer one has to pluck out all conceit, verbal or otherwise. If his sentences seem bald, shorn of all adjectives, there is a reason: Khushwant works very hard at rooting out any sign of vanity that may creep into his writing. He once wrote in his column: 'I call myself simple minded because I have no patience with complicated words—I get bamboozled by words like "politico-socio-economics". Words like "spiritual", "soul", "cosmic power" mean nothing to me. I shy off them.' He is the best example of the writing style that Naipaul once recommended: no adjectives, except those of colour, size, height and shape. Short sentences of not more than four or five words. Even complex subjects can be broken down this way.

Khushwant wins over the reader by confessing his weakness. Not since Gandhi perhaps do we have a writer who disarms you so completely by confessing his every small, humiliating weakness in a newspaper. It could be something like dripping soup, dal and curry on his beard and shirt—'People around me find it repulsive. I could not care less,' he writes in his essay on old age. Or worse, wetting his pants because of an enlarged prostate—'It is best to pretend carelessness. Others know the truth but maintain a polite silence.'

Khushwant deliberately inserts a few jokes even in his more scholarly essays, though he knows that the humour will result in him being dismissed as a lightweight. He is possibly the only historian who can write an essay on the history of his community ('The Sikhs: Poets of Enterprise') and dare to put in his favourite jokes about them, even if it subverts his own gravitas. But those who dismiss him as a joker don't know that there is a long tradition of using humour in serious works. He points this out in his portrait of Mir Taqi Mir and observes in 'Of Godmen and Their Legacies' that Osho, too, 'often ended his sermons with a dirty joke' despite being one of the world's most erudite religious philosophers.

He always levels with the reader. He believes the only way not to talk down to your reader is to be transparently honest, which is more painful than you can imagine. For most people, the struggle for true openness and intimacy is a lifelong one. But in Khushwant's case, he seems to have long ago clobbered the mental cop that resides in each one of us into pulp. He can write about farting and fornicating on the same page as a verse by Adi Shankara or an Urdu couplet by Iqbal, and make it all appear as the most ordinary thing to do.

Khushwant isn't afraid to be himself. His writing is very much like him. Just as it is a matter of honour for him to stay uncompromisingly himself, no matter where or with whom, he refuses to dress up his writing—or his thoughts, even—to suit the occasion. He says exactly what comes to his mind, and doesn't give a damn what others think. It takes courage to write in this exposed way. He has also mastered the art of capturing the many stray thoughts that the rest of us reject even before we are conscious of them.

Above all, Khushwant believes there's no difference between journalism and literature. There's nothing too big or too small to write about, there's only good and bad writing. There is a reason why everything he writes, be it his ubiquitous columns, a middle, an essay in a hotel magazine or even his jokes, has such a long shelf life. He considers each of them to be of equal worth. Which is probably why publishers have long recognized that Khushwant is possibly the only writer in India who can sell anything he writes.

He has been accused of writing rubbish, but what neither his admirers nor his detractors have ever understood is that for this most incisive and fearless writer that India has ever produced there is no distinction between high and low subjects. 'I have never thought in those terms,' he once confessed. 'If something occurred to me in the morning, I put it down on paper and if it was a short piece, I sent it in as a middle. If it was long, it went as an article . . . I had no distinctions between what was journalism and what was literature—none at all.' Blurring that distinction is harder than it seems. As Khushwant once told a detractor who accused him of 'turning bullshit into an art form', 'Just try it and see.'

Many of the essays and portraits in this collection are his stock-taking of a long and colourful life of letters. There is possibly no other man or woman alive who has known so many of India's brightest and best and at such close quarters. And certainly no one who can examine them with such clear-eyed honesty, unadulterated by idolatry or humbug. Be it Jawaharlal Nehru, Indira Gandhi, Rajiv Gandhi, Sanjay Gandhi, Jayaprakash Narayan, writers from the early pioneering days of Indian English or today's superstars, he brings to each his own unique way of seeing, never letting his affection or admiration get in the way of his judgement. When he writes of his old friend, Mulk Raj Anand, as a great name-dropper and a 'crashing bore', he says it with the confidence of someone who is resolved not to go that way. He spares no one, whether it is Nehru and his cantankerous temper, his conceit and his habit of talking down to Indians, or Indira's vindictiveness, and her son Sanjay's bullying of his mother, or R.K. Narayan's quirky habit of bringing his ambling walk to a stop when he wanted to complete a sentence, or his sitting implacably through a blue film. And yet, he is still able to see the sterling qualities of each.

Khushwant refuses to draws a distinction between who and what is worth his contemplation. Curiously enough, that is also his strength. Torn between his inability to refuse a person's request to be promoted in his columns and his own professional instinct to keep the reader's interest from flagging, Khushwant rises to the challenge by turning the piece into a self-confession or provides his own insight into the subject.

He has always had a lively curiosity about the world and its inhabitants. When he was still travelling, everything was grist for his mill. Even a drive from the airport in Kolkata could spark off an essay on Nazrul Islam. How many of us have driven down roads named after vaguely familiar people and actually bothered to find out more? And having done that, have the courage to say what one really thought of them?

It's that same mix of healthy scepticism and lively curiosity leavened by humour that he brings to exploring the new country he now finds himself in—old age, approaching death and meeting his Maker, if indeed there is one. Khushwant has had ample time to thoroughly examine the subject of death in a few of his essays. His advice to the aged (in 'On Old Age') contains a few gems that a reader of any age can profit from.

His travelling days may be behind him, but he has not given up his habitual curiosity. Last week, for instance, I found him surrounded by a sea of books, including over a hundred books that he has written so far. His bookshelves, he said, had been infested with termites and had to be replaced. And while the carpenters were busy building the new shelves, Khushwant pored over his books on bugs: he wanted to find out what kind of creatures these bookworms were. I could see the next column being born before my eyes. It reminded me of the motto he has chosen for himself: 'I mean to keep reading books, all kinds of books, till my eyes give up on me. And I mean to keep writing till the pen drops out of my hand.'

SHEELA REDDY

WHY I SUPPORTED THE EMERGENCY

The Emergency has become a synonym for obscenity. Even men and women who were pillars of Emergency rule and misused their positions to harass innocent people against whom they had personal grudges try to distance themselves from their past in the hope that it will fade out of public memory forever. We must not allow them to get away with it. Because of them many mistakes were made which must be avoided the next time conditions require the suspension of democratic norms for the preservation of law and order.

With some reservations I supported the Emergency proclaimed by Mrs Indira Gandhi on 25 June 1975. Let me explain why. I concede that the right to protest is integral to democracy. You can have public meetings to criticize or condemn government actions. You can take out processions, call for strikes and closure of businesses. But there must not be any coercion or violence. If there is any, it is the duty of the government to suppress it by force, if necessary. By May 1975, public protests against Mrs Gandhi's government had assumed nationwide dimensions and often turned violent. With my own eyes I saw slogan-chanting processions go down Bombay's thoroughfares, smashing cars parked on the roadsides and breaking shop windows as they went along. The local police was unable to contend with them because they were too few, the protesters too many. The leaders of Opposition parties watched the country sliding into chaos as bemused spectators, hoping that the mounting chaos would force Mrs Gandhi to resign.

The unquestioned leader of the anti-Mrs Gandhi movement was Jayaprakash Narayan, a man for whom I had enormous respect and admiration. He had become the conscience keeper of the nation. But it was Lok Nayak, as he came to be known, who crossed the Lakshmana rekha of democratic protest. His call for 'total revolution' included preventing elected members of state legislatives from entering Vidhan Sabha buildings. He announced his intention to gherao Parliament house and even asked the police and the army to revolt against the government. I wrote to Jayaprakash protesting that what he was advocating was wrong and undemocratic. He wrote back justifying his stand. I published both my letter and his much-longer reply in the *Illustrated Weekly of India* which I then happened to be editing. I believe, and still believe, freedom to speak one's mind is the basic principle of democracy.

Early June I was attending a conference in Mexico City. I arrived back in Bombay the day the Emergency was declared. The night before, all the Opposition leaders had been picked up from their homes and put in jails across the country. The *Times of India* offices were in pandemonium. We were told that censorship had been imposed on the press: we had to toe the line or get out. I was determined to resist and thought if editors of other papers published by Bennett, Coleman & Co. would form a united front against censorship we would succeed in making the government change its mind against the press. I expected Sham Lal, editor of the *Times of India*, to become our leader. He bluntly refused to do so. Sham Lal's number two, Girilal Jain, resident editor in Delhi, went one better by lauding the emergence of Sanjay Gandhi as the new leader. Not one other editor was willing to risk his job. Editors of the *Navbharat Times, Maharashtra Times, Dharmyug, Filmfare, Femina, Sarika* decided to stay away from the protest meeting we organized. Inder Malhotra's behaviour was enigmatic. He kept going up and down the floors greeting everyone with 'jai ho' and moving on. He never looked anyone in the eye. To this day I don't know whether he was for or against the Emergency. For three weeks I refused to publish the *Illustrated Weekly*. My friend from my college years in England, Rajni Patel, who became the dominant voice on the board of directors, told me bluntly: 'My friend, if you are looking for martyrdom, we'll give it to you.' The board chairman, Justice (retd) K.T. Desai, was gentler. 'You don't realize how serious the government is about censorship on the press. If you refuse to publish the journal we will have no option but to find another editor. Why not give it a try to see how it goes?' I agreed to give it a try. After all, I had criticized Jayaprakash Narayan's call for a 'total revolution' as undemocratic. The Allahabad high court judgement declaring Mrs Gandhi's membership of Parliament invalid weakened her position and she was persuaded by her closest advisers to strike out.

The Emergency, when first imposed, was generally welcomed by the people. There were no strikes or hartals, schools and colleges re-opened, business picked up, buses and trains began to run on time. People are under the impression that the Emergency administrators were very efficient. They were not. A few days after it was promulgated I got a call from H.Y. Sharada Prasad asking me to come over to see the prime minister. I was not to tell anyone about the appointment. The next day I met her in her South Block office. I pleaded with her to withdraw censorship on the press. 'Editors like me who support you have lost credibility. Nobody will believe that we are doing so of our free will and not being dictated to,' I argued. She remained adamant. 'There cannot be any Emergency without censorship on the press,' she maintained. I returned to Bombay disappointed. Back in the office, I found in my mail a letter reading, 'How did your meeting with Madame Dictator go?' Signed George. George Fernandes had gone underground but someone (obviously in the PMO) had informed him about my meeting. The same afternoon four leading members of the RSS, against whom warrants of arrest had been issued, boldly walked into my office and for half an hour questioned me about what had passed between the PM and me. And then, as boldly, walked out.

The censorship was also selective and eccentric. Some papers like the *Indian Express* were made targets of Mrs Gandhi's ire. Others like the *Times of India* and *Hindustan Times* were left alone. As was the weekly *Blitz*, owned by the most unprincipled editor of our times, Rusi Karanjia, who enthusiastically supported Mrs Gandhi. Kuldip Nayar was arrested. For no reason whatsoever, so was his eighty-two-year-old father-in-law, Bhim Sain Sachar, once chief minister of Punjab. Ramesh Thapar, once very close to Mrs Gandhi, closed down his *Seminar*. His sister, Dr Romila Thapar, who kept her distance from politics, was harassed by income-tax sleuths for many days. Mrs Gandhi could be very vindictive against people she had once been close to.

In Bombay, censorship had its lighter sides. Vinod Mehta, who edited the sleazy girlie magazine *Debonair*, was asked to have his articles and pictures cleared before they were sent to the printer. The censor looked over the pages. 'Porn? *Theek hai!* Politics, no.' Most of it was soft porn. It was quickly cleared. I was not subjected to the indignity of pre-censorship except for a few hours. I happened to be at a luncheon reception given by Governor Ali Yavar Jang in honour of President Fakhruddin Ali Ahmed. Out of the blue the President turned to me and said loudly, 'What is all this you keep publishing in your journal? Don't you know there is an Emergency?' I didn't know what he was referring to. Nor did S.B. Chavan, chief minister of Maharashtra, who overheard the President's remark. When I returned to my office I found a pre-censorship order slapped under the CM's authorization on the *Illustrated Weekly*. The offending article had in fact appeared in *Femina* and not in my journal. I rang up Sharada Prasad. Mrs Gandhi was due to go abroad the next day. Chavan was told to withdraw the censorship order immediately. He did so as tamely as the braggadocio with which he had imposed it.

During the Emergency I was frequently in Delhi to help out Maneka Gandhi and her mother, Amtesh, with their magazine

Surya. I saw something of the caucus which was running the government. Siddhartha Shankar Ray had drafted the regulations; Sanjay was the kingpin. Besides his kitchen cabinet comprising his wife and mother-in-law, there was the old family retainer, Mohammed Yunus (Chacha); civil servant Navin Chawla; Kishan Chand, Lt Governor of Delhi, who later ended his life by jumping into a well; and Jagmohan, who was put in charge of clearing slums which he did with ruthless zeal. There was the Rasputin figure of Dhirendra Brahmachari, swamiji to the royal household; and two pretty women, Ambika Soni and Rukhsana Sultana—Sanjay had an eye for pretty women. He also had an enthusiastic supporter in Bansi Lal who had allotted him land in Haryana where he was CM on the rustic truism '*bachda pakad lo toh ma toh peechey chali ayegee*'—catch the calf and its mother is bound to follow you. He had I.K. Gujral packed off to Moscow and replaced by the more amenable Vidya Charan Shukla as information and broadcasting minister.

Because of my frequent visits to Delhi to monitor the progress of *Surya*, I saw quite a bit of the Gandhi family, particularly Sanjay and his in-laws. He was more relaxed with Maneka's family than with his own. He was a man of few words but with enormous zest for work. He was a strict teetotaller and even avoided drinking tea, coffee, aerated drinks and iced water. In some ways he epitomized the slogan he had coined: *Kaam ziyaada, baatein kum*—work more, talk less. He was a young man in a hurry to get things done. He had no patience with tedious democratic processes and red tape, no time for long-winded politicians or bureaucrats. The fact that he had no legitimacy for imposing his fiats on the country, besides being the son of the prime minister, was of little consequence to him. Unlike Maneka, he never used strong language and was extremely courteous towards elder people like me. In his younger days he was known to have stolen cars—he had a passion for cars. He had been in many brawls: despite his modest size he rippled with muscles. I took to him as a loveable goonda.

For many months this coterie ruled the country. Anyone who crossed their paths was promptly put behind bars. There was not a squeak of protest. Virtually, the only party which kept a passive resistance movement throughout the period were the Akalis. Long before the Emergency was lifted, it had lost public support. Arbitrary arrests, the ruthless way Jagmohan bulldozed slums in Delhi, made people believe the wildest canards, of the way men were picked up from bus and cinema queues to be forcibly sterilized, as true. Nobody ever verified the facts but most people lent willing ears to stories of Sanjay's excesses. The Emergency, which was well received when it was imposed, and even justified by a sage like Acharya Vinoba Bhave, was distorted into an abominated monster which had to be destroyed for ever. There may be other occasions to impose an Emergency in the country. If we do not make the mistakes of 1975–77, we would be able to keep the country on the right track when it begins to wobble.

ON IWE FICTION

The story of Indians writing fiction in English goes back to a few decades before our Independence. The pioneers were a trio comprising Mulk Raj Anand, Raja Rao and R.K. Narayan. Their impact was limited. Mulk Raj Anand roused the consciousness of the British and upper-class Indians to the exploitation of poor Indians; he was a Marxist propagandist, and used his pen like a sledgehammer to drive his point home. Raja Rao, who began promisingly with some delightfully humorous short stories, turned back to exploiting the mystical and spiritual aspects of India. R.K. Narayan remained a simple storyteller. None of his novels or stories has the ingredients I consider integral to fiction: sex, violence or pithy turns of phrase. It was the patronage of *The Hindu* that turned him into an icon of South Indians. He remains to this day the most widely read Indian of his times.

Not surprisingly, none of the three pioneers really made any significant impact on the English literary world. That was left to G.V. Desani with *All About H. Hatterr* which created quite a stir in London's literary circles, and as a result, back home as well. It was a refreshing departure from the quaintly charming works of the pioneers. His model was James Joyce's *Ulysses*. Like Joyce's classic, one needed an explanatory guide to read *Hatterr*.

It is surprising there was no major work in fiction to come out of the momentous events in the history of India's freedom movement. Nor about the partition of the country, particularly in blood-soaked Punjab. The best novel on partition came from

7

the comparatively peaceful division of Bengal: Amitav Ghosh's *The Shadow Lines*, which I regard as a masterpiece.

Once the ground was broken, dozens of Indian English writers began to surface: Manohar Malgonkar, Kamala Markandaya, Ruth Prawer Jhabvala, Anita Desai, Nayantara Sahgal, Sasthi Brata, Bharati Mukherjee. They made some impact on the English and American literary scenes. There were also a few Parsi writers who carved a niche of their own. These writers—Farrukh Dhondy, Firdaus Kanga, Rohinton Mistry—confined themselves to what they knew best: their own Parsi community, poking fun at it, and, in the process, infused much-needed humour into Indian English fiction.

The man who smashed the wall of resistance in the literary world abroad was Salman Rushdie. His *Midnight's Children* not only won the Booker but also opened the floodgates for other Indian writers. Soon after, two more superstars appeared in the Western skies: Vikram Seth and Amitav Ghosh. After them came the deluge: Amit Chaudhuri, I. Allan Sealy, Upamanyu Chatterjee, Pankaj Mishra, Vikram Chandra, Shashi Tharoor. With Arundhati Roy, too, winning the Booker and Jhumpa Lahiri the Pulitzer, Indian English was no longer on the fringes, growing by leaps and bounds until it is now treated on par with translations of Latin American novelists like Gabriel García Márquez.

Though more than half of the writers whom I regard as significant and rate as the best in the last sixty years are now foreign nationals, their themes are Indian and the applause they get abroad resonates in India. They return to India periodically to be garlanded and to get fresh material, and now also earn handsome royalties in rupees.

ON BEING BUGGERED

It all started during my recent summer vacation in Kasauli. I woke up one night with a queasy feeling in my stomach. Half asleep, I tottered to the loo to rid myself of my sleep breaker. When I got up from the lavatory seat to flush out the contents, I was shocked to see I had passed a lot of blood with my stool. 'Shit!' I said to myself, suddenly wide awake. The rest of the night was wasted in contemplation of the end. I had had a reasonable innings, close to scoring a century, so no regrets on that score. Was I creating a self-image of heroism in the face of death? That vanished on the following day as more blood flowed out of my belly.

I asked my friend Dr Santosh Kutty of the Central Research Institute (CRI) to drop in for a drink in the evening. Over a glass of Scotch, he heard me out. When I finished, he asked me: 'Have you been eating chukandar?' I admitted I'd had beetroot salad the day before.

'It could be that,' he suggested. 'It is the same colour as human blood. Or it could be nature's way of reducing high blood pressure—bleeding through the nose or arse. Or it could be a polyp, or piles, or . . .' He did not use the word but I understood he meant cancer. 'Let me examine your rectum.'

'You'll do no such thing,' I rasped. 'I'd rather die than show my rectum to anyone.' He paused and continued, 'It would be wise to have an enteroscopy. It will clear all doubts. We don't have the facility in Kasauli. You can have it done at PGI in Chandigarh or in Delhi. The sooner the better.'

I opted for Delhi, to be with my family. And rang up my friend Nanak Kohli to send up his Mercedes Benz to take me down.

I looked up my dictionary to find out exactly what polyp and enteroscopy meant. One is a kind of sea urchin-like growth in the lower part of the intestine, the other an instrumental examination of one's innards. I spent the rest of the day drafting in my mind farewell letters to my near and dear ones. Nothing mawkish or sentimental, but in the tone of one who couldn't care less about his fate, something they could quote in my obituaries: he went like a man, with a smile on his face, etc., etc.

The next morning, my son, Rahul, and I drove back to Delhi. The first thing I did was to ask Dr I.P.S. Kalra, who lives in the neighbouring block, to come over. Dr Kalra is a devout believer in miracles performed by Wahe Guru. He has been our doctor for over half a century and has treated several members of my extended family in their last days on earth, until their journey to the electric crematorium. Since I am a lot older than him, he addresses me as Veerjee (elder brother). He took my blood pressure, it was higher than normal. He heard my bloody tale and straightaway fixed an appointment with Dr S.K. Jain, Delhi's leading endoscopist.

The next evening, accompanied by Kalra, Rahul and my daughter, Mala, I presented myself at Dr Jain's swanky clinic in Hauz Khas Enclave. All white marble, spotlessly clean, and with the obligatory statuette of Lord Ganapati, with a garland of fresh marigold flowers around his neck, sitting above the receptionist's desk. Since I was the first patient of the many he had to examine that evening, I was conducted immediately to his operating room.

I can tell you that enteroscopy strips your self-esteem and any dignity you may have. I was ordered to take off my salwar kameez, given an overall to wear, and ordered to lie down. Dr Jain took my BP and proceeded to insert an endoscope up my rectum. At times the pain was excruciating. It went on for an hour. When it was over, Dr Kalra ordered me, 'Veerji, pudd maro—kill a fart, you'll feel easier.' I refused to oblige and instead went to the lavatory to get rid of the wind the nervous tension had created inside me.

Dr Jain pronounced the verdict: 'No polyp, no cancer, only internal piles which bleed because of high BP. It is nature's way of bringing it down.' As a parting gift, he gave Mala a filmed version of all that had transpired—from my bottom being bared to the muck inside my belly. As if that was not enough, when asked about his father's health, Rahul told everyone, 'Pop has piles.' There is something romantic about cancer; polyp is like a plop sound produced by a frog leaping into a stagnant pool; but haemorrhoids have no romance attached to them; they are simply a miserable man's piles. Many well-wishers called to enquire how my enteroscopy had gone and how I felt about the whole exercise. My reply was standard: 'I feel buggered.'

ON THE LAST MOGUL

The rebellion of 1857 lasted only a few months—from May to September 1857—but it shook the whole of India like a severe earthquake, taking a toll of thousands of lives. Its epicentre was Delhi, the capital of the Mogul empire founded by Babar in 1526. By the time it struck, the empire had shrunk to a few square miles around the city. As the adage went: *Sultanat Shah Alam az Dilli ta Palam*—the kingdom of Shah Alam extends from Delhi to Palam. By the time the last of the emperors ascended the throne, it had shrunk further and was confined to the Red Fort; his subjects comprised his vast harem of begums, concubines, their offspring, maidservants and manservants, most of them living in hovels without much to eat. The fort was guarded by an English officer; the so-called emperor received a living allowance from the British Resident and had little to do with governance. He spent his time composing poetry, practising calligraphy, watching his elephants being bathed in the Yamuna, and praying. Once in a while, he rode on his favourite elephant to the royal mosque, Jama Masjid, amid bursts of fireworks, or visited his wife's relations in the city. What he most looked forward to was holding poetic symposia (mushairas) in the Red Fort or in Delhi College outside Ajmeri Gate where his latest composition was read out first, followed by recitals of other poets, both Indian and European. The mushairas usually ended in the early hours of the morning with recitals by masters like poet laureate Zauq and the greatest of them all, Mirza Asadullah Ghalib. As Ghalib put it, the candle burns brightest before it flickers and dies out.

A few decades before the outbreak, relations between Indians and Britons were reasonably amicable. Quite a few Britishers acquired Indian customs and styles of living, spoke Persian and Urdu; some married native women. Sir David Ochterlony had thirteen bibis in his harem, James Skinner (Sikander Sahib) had fourteen. Besides building St James' Church at Kashmere Gate, Colonel Skinner built a mosque for his Muslim wives and a temple for the Hindus. They wore Indian clothes, ate Indian food and smoked hookahs. It was one-way matrimonial traffic. Nubile English girls who came to India were not willing to share their nuptial beds with rival wives. But there was the Kashmiri dancing girl, Farzana Zebunnissa, who converted to Catholicism, cohabited with Whites and carved out a principality of her own and became Begum Samru of Sardana near Meerut.

Relations between Whites and natives began to sour with the aggressive evangelical zeal of clerics who attempted to convert Indians to Christianity. The Christian missionaries were confronted by jehadi elements from madrassas who looked down on both Christians and Hindus as infidels. However, the English topped the jehadis' hate list. The British had already annexed Satara, Jhansi and Nagpur on the grounds that they had no male heirs. Then, without any excuse, they incorporated the Muslim state of Avadh as well. There was no doubt in anyone's mind that their next victim would be whatever remained of the Mogul kingdom of Delhi.

In the suspicion-laden atmosphere came the issue of new cartridges which had to be greased with the fat of cows and pigs. Sepoys who were largely upper-caste Hindus from Uttar Pradesh and Bihar and Muslims who were lesser in number saw this clearly as a deliberate attack on their religions. The fat then was really in the fire. The first shot was fired by Mangal Pandey on 29 March at Barrackpore. He was promptly hanged. A little under two months later, sepoys in the Meerut Cantonment refused to obey orders, killed their English officers and marched to Delhi to reinstate Zafar as the badshah of Bharat. So did thousands of jehadis, including women, from Delhi and outlying towns, in a desperate attempt to restore Islamic rule in Hindustan.

In his book, *The Last Mughal*, William Dalrymple explains why Indians looked up to Bahadur Shah Zafar as their leader against foreign rulers: 'The dramatic way in which both Hindus and Muslims had rallied to the Mughal capital at the outbreak of the uprising had demonstrated the degree to which the mystique of the dynasty was still very much alive more than a century after the Mughals had ceased to exercise any real political, economic or military power. Contrary to all expectations, the idea of the Mughal Emperor as the divinely ordained axis mundi, the universal sovereign and Padshah, Lord of the World, still had resonance across Hindustan at this time.'

Bahadur Shah Zafar proved to be a reluctant and inept leader, bullied in turn by the rebellious sepoys and nagged by his principal begum, Zeenat Mahal, forty-two years younger than him, whose only ambition was to see her son, Jawan Bakht, recognized as the heir apparent in preference to his elder stepbrothers. She kept in constant touch with the British. Zafar's diktat did not hold even in the Red Fort. A few days after the mutineers had taken control, they slaughtered all the English men, women and children to whom Zafar had given shelter in the palace, as well as every white person and Indian Christian they could lay their hands on. Their nemesis was not long in coming.

The British swore dire vengeance. Led by men like General John Nicholson, Captain William Hodson and Theophilus Metcalfe who looked down on Indians with loathing and contempt, they descended on Delhi with their new mercenary forces comprising Gurkhas, Sikhs and Pathans. They pillaged every town and village, setting them on fire and hanging every able-bodied man they could find on their way. For three months, the defenders fought back heroically. After the northern city wall had been breached, they retreated and continued their resistance till they could resist no more. The city was subjected to a general massacre. Women and children were spared but men hanged or shot in hundreds every day. Large parts of the city were levelled to the ground, and the Jama Masjid converted into a stable for the Sikh cavalry.

Bahadur Shah Zafar turned to the Quran for portents. He opened the holy book at random (faal). The message did not give any hope. It read: 'Neither you nor your army, but those who were before.' On 18 September, there was a solar eclipse. For superstitious Indians, it portended more evil to come.

Knowing the struggle was over, one night Zafar slipped out of the Red Fort and sought refuge in Humayun's tomb. A few days later, Hodson brought him, his wife and favourite son back as prisoners on the undertaking that their lives would be spared. A couple of days later, he got Zafar's three other sons and stripped them naked before shooting them. Ghalib wrote to a friend: 'The light has gone out of India.'

Zafar was put on trial, convicted and sent to exile in Rangoon with Zeenat Mahal, their son, Jawan Bakht, a couple of other wives and servants. He died at 5 a.m. on 7 November 1862. He was buried in an anonymous grave at the back of a walled prison enclosure. Thus ended the story of the great Moguls.

F*** ALL EDITORS

There was a time, not very long ago, when our dailies derived credit from the stature of the men who edited them. During the British Raj, editors of British-owned national papers like the *Times of India* and the *Statesman* had knighthoods conferred on them. Even after India gained Independence and Indians took over as editors, they enjoyed considerable prestige in society. Names like Frank Moraes, Chalapathi Rau, Kasturi Ranga Iyengar, Pothen Joseph and Prem Bhatia were known to readers. Dilip Padgaonkar, editor of the *Times of India* in the 'eighties, was not far wrong in asserting that next to the prime minister he had the most important job in the country. Constructive criticism of the ruling party came not from the Opposition political parties but from the free press edited by able, responsible men.

The scenario changed with the spread of TV. People who saw events take place before their own eyes could not be bothered to read about them in the papers the next morning. Fewer and fewer people read editorials. Proprietors of newspapers sensed that editors were dispensable as they and their business managers could better meet the challenges posed by the electronic media. All that was needed was to fill their pages with pictures of scantily clad starlets or models, recipes for exotic foods, vintage wines and gossip. The formula could be summed up in four Fs: films, fashion, food and fuck editors. Many notable pen-pushers fell victim to the fourth F: Frank Moraes, Girilal Jain, B.G. Verghese (Magsaysay award winner), Arun Shourie (another Magsaysay awardee), Vinod Mehta, Inder Malhotra, Prem Shankar Jha.

16

Today if you ask people who is the editor of the *Times of India*, *Hindustan Times*, the *Telegraph* and the *Statesman*, nine out of ten will plead ignorance. As for Dilip Padgaonkar, you may well get a reply with a counter-question: 'Dilip who?'

The hard truth about Indian journalism is that proprietors matter, editors do not; money counts, talent does not. The latest instance of money trashing ability and experience is the unceremonious sacking of M.J. Akbar, founder–editor of the *Asian Age*. He is perhaps the most distinguished living member of his tribe. He started the weekly *Sunday* and the *Telegraph* for the Ananda Bazaar group of papers based in Calcutta. He has been elected member of the Lok Sabha and is the author of half a dozen books, all of which have gone into several editions. In 1993, with a set of friends, he launched the *Asian Age*. It was a bold venture as the *Asian Age* came out in all the metropolitan cities of India as well as in London. It had little advertising but had a lot more readable material, taken from leading British and American journals, than any other Indian daily. It was as close to being a complete newspaper as any could be. Besides having these unique qualities it also published articles by writers critical of the government and the ruling party. It was probably this aspect of the journal that irked Akbar's latest partner in the venture; he had political ambitions of his own and wished to stay on the right side of the government. So without a word of warning, on the morning of 1 March 2008, while he was on his way to his office, Akbar learnt that his name was no longer on the *Asian Age* masthead as its editor-in-chief. It was an unpardonable act of discourtesy committed by someone with less breeding and more money.

It is difficult to forecast what Akbar will, or can, do to settle scores with the people who wronged him and the profession of journalism. The episode will rankle in his mind. He is only fifty-seven years old and is a man who never forgets, nor forgives.

Akbar was one of the small team of editors who helped me take the circulation of the *Illustrated Weekly of India* from a measly

60,000 to well above 4,00,000. It is ironical that I was sacked in much the same way in 1978 as Akbar was thirty years later. The journal, like all others published by Bennet Coleman, including the *Times of India*, had been restored by the government to the Jain family. As soon as they took over, they started meddling in my business. My contract was terminated and my successor appointed. I had one week to go. I wrote a tearful piece of farewell, wishing the *Illustrated Weekly* future prosperity. It was never published. When I arrived at the office in the morning to tidy up my desk, I was handed a letter asking me to quit immediately. I picked up my umbrella and walked back home.

It was an undeserved, deliberate insult. It still rankles in my mind. The Jain vendetta continues to this day. Even functions held in my honour, presided over by people like Amitabh Bachchan, Maharani Gayatri Devi and Prime Minister Manmohan Singh, while reported in the *Times of India*, never carry my name or photograph. That is how small-minded people with pots of money and power can be.

On the Maharajas

The action begins on the morning of 12 December 1911 in Delhi where King George V and Queen Mary are to grace the coronation durbar being held in their honour. Word's gone around to all the maharajas that they are expected to pay homage to their sovereign. They are to be dressed in their regalia and follow a prescribed routine: approach their majesties on foot, stand at a respectable distance, bow their heads thrice, retreat three steps before they turn around to go back. Or else!

The princes do not like to be humiliated in this manner. But only one of them has the guts to show his resentment: Sayaji Rao Gaikwad III, Maharaja of Baroda, the fourth richest princely state of India. Instead of carrying his bejewelled sword, he carries his walking stick; instead of bowing three times, he bows only once; instead of retreating three steps, he turns around and walks away. His demeanour is noted by the hawk-eyed Viceroy. The maharaja of Baroda is already on the blacklist of the British rulers for hobnobbing with nationalist leaders. So is his maharani, Chimnabai, a powerful woman in her own right. The Gaikwad is asked to explain his conduct. The threat of being deposed hangs over his head. He makes an abject apology and assures the rulers of his unflinching loyalty to their Britannic Majesties.

The story of the princes goes back in history. As the British expanded their empire, one after the other ruling princes came to terms with them. At the end of the Maratha Wars in 1818, all the Maratha rulers including Baroda's accepted British suzerainty.

19

Punjab's ruling families did so even before the Sikh kingdom was annexed in 1849.

Nevertheless, some princes harboured illusions of sovereignty. The British thought it wise to periodically squash their pretensions to royalty. How the three states of Baroda, Jaipur and Cooch Behar entered into matrimonial alliances reads like an Indian fairy tale. Princess Indira Raje of Baroda, engaged to marry an older, pot-bellied Scindia of Gwalior, meets the handsome Jitendra of Cooch Behar, responds to his overtures and much to the chagrin of her parents, elopes with her lover and marries him. In due course, her daughter, Gayatri Devi, who has inherited her mother's looks, falls in love with Maharaja Mansingh of Jaipur and agrees to become his third—and favourite—wife.

Another thing the princely families had in common was plenty of time for shikar, racing, gambling in casinos, throwing lavish parties with caviar and champagne. Though they had to get the British government's permission to go abroad, they often managed to get away. The dividing line between their states' exchequers and what they spent on their pleasures is blurred. The Gaikwads, despite great shows of concern for their subjects, took abroad with them an entourage of fifty-five, including a pandit, a tailor, a doctor, cooks carrying groceries and two cows. And once out of surveillance, all the royals threw huge parties. They bought whatever met their fancy. Their womenfolk let down their hair and went to town: amongst them, the exotic Indira who, after she lost her husband, became the toast of British aristocracy. The incidence of liquor-related deaths among them was extremely high. The only apt word for their squandermania is 'obscene'.

The outstanding figure in maharanis is Gayatri Devi, Dowager Rajmata of Jaipur. She was once listed among the ten most beautiful women of the century. At eighty-nine, she still retains her youthful charm combined with regal snobbery. She has seen her world change beyond recognition. Starting in Cooch Behar as a bit of a tomboy, she adjusted herself to what was expected of the maharani of Jaipur. She shared her husband's passion for polo. After he died by being crushed under his polo pony, she devoted herself to opening a chain of schools. Perhaps the most dramatic period of her life was winning her way to the Lok Sabha as the leader of the Swatantra Party. She fell foul of Prime Minister Indira Gandhi whom she had known since their short period together in Santiniketan. Indira could not stomach a woman more good-looking than herself and insulted her in Parliament, calling her a bitch and a glass doll. Gayatri Devi brought the worst out in Indira Gandhi: her petty, vindictive side. When she declared the Emergency, Gayatri Devi was among her first victims. Indira Gandhi had her Jaipur palaces ransacked by income-tax inspectors. All they found was petty cash. Nevertheless, Indira had her locked up in Tihar Jail. When Sanjay Gandhi was killed in a plane crash, Gayatri rang up Indira to offer her condolences. Indira refused to take her call.

Most Indian rulers regarded themselves above common rules and conventions. Without exception, they swore loyalty to the Sarkar-e-Inglishia and were allowed to build large palaces and stock them with wives, concubines and maidservants-cum-mistresses and sired scores of children through them. They owned elephants, thoroughbred horses and kennels of dogs of high pedigree and celebrated the matings of dogs and bitches with lavish parties; they amassed jewellery, periodically went to Europe taking large staffs of servants with them. They ran into heavy debts and had to be bailed out by the government.

They enjoyed the powers of life and death over their subjects and had no qualms about having people they didn't like bumped off, their estates confiscated, their wives or daughters forced into their seraglios. They did not find it too difficult to host Viceroys, Governors, Residents and visiting English aristocracy, arranging tiger or duck shoots, pig-sticking, polo matches, nautch and loading them with expensive parting gifts.

The prime example of the princely order at its worst was Bhupinder Singh of Patiala. He was a headstrong bully, a debauch, drunkard, womanizer and philanderer. Nevertheless, he became chancellor of the Chamber of Princes, represented India at the Imperial War Council during World War I and the Sikhs at the First Round Table Conference. He also put Indian cricket on a firm wicket, encouraged wrestling with handsome stipends to the families of wrestlers like Gama Rustam-i-Hind and patronized classical music under Ustad Bade Ghulam Ali Khan of the Patiala gharana.

In the summer of 1926, Maharaja Bhupinder Singh drove from Patiala to Srinagar to attend the investiture of Maharaja Hari Singh of Kashmir. Amongst the things he brought back to Patiala which, according to the author of his biography, Natwar Singh, caused much 'consternation and surprise', was a hookah made of gold and silver for smoking cigarettes and cigars. 'As Sikhs are forbidden to smoke, it was a mystery as to what the Maharaja wanted such a gadget for.'

I could solve the mystery of the hookah. One morning in March 1931 when I was a school-going boy of sixteen, I saw a conclave of maharajas standing in the circle adjoining Parliament house on Sansad Marg. There was no mistaking Bhupinder Singh of Patiala. He was the only Sikh in the circle. He was very portly, turbaned and bedecked in jewelled regalia. And he was smoking a massive cheroot. I was taken aback. In later years I discovered that many members of the Patiala ruling family, including Bhupinder Singh's son and successor, Yadevendra Singh, Natwar Singh's father-in-law, were not averse to smoking. Only, they avoided doing so when in company of Sikhs. Quite a few Sikhs were, and are, bathroom smokers. In Patiala they don't bother with such niceties. On any evening in the Patiala Club you can see sardars at their card tables puffing cigarettes as they down Patiala pegs of whisky.

Bhupinder Singh was a complex character, an excellent subject for a psychiatrist or a writer of fiction. He had many traducers. To cite *Freedom at Midnight*: 'Until the end of the century, it had been the custom of the Maharaja to appear once a year before his subjects naked except for his diamond breastplate, his organ in full and glorious erection. His performance was judged as a kind of temporal manifestation of the Shivalinga. As the Maharaja walked about, his subjects gleefully applauded, their cheers acknowledging both the dimensions of the princely organ and the fact that it was supposed to be radiating magic powers to drive evil spirits from the land.'

Earlier, John Gunther in his *Inside Asia* had this to say: 'If the Nizam of Hyderabad is known as His Exalted Highness, the old Maharaja of Patiala was called his Exhausted Highness. He had a prodigious harem and a considerable part of his activity was the acquisition of young ladies to freshen it. In 1930 the Patiala Enquiry Committee appointed by the All India States Peoples Conference wrote a strong report charging the old Maharaja with most crimes and sins in the calendar, from lechery to murder.'

Though Bhupinder Singh was exonerated of these charges by a one-man committee of his choice, there was nothing loveable about His Highness. He supported General Dyer's killing of 379 innocent men at Jallianwala Bagh, he wormed his way into the top echelons of the Akali party only to sow seeds of discord and to keep the government informed of their plans. All he wanted in return was to have the seventeen-gun salute given to him to be raised to nineteen, a few more medals and titles to go with his name. He ended by being Lt Gen., His Highness, Farzand-i-Khas, Daulat-i-Inglishia, Mansur-i-Zaman Amir-ul-Umra, Maharajadhiraj Raj Rajeshwar Sri Maharaj-i-Rajgan Sir Bhupinder Singh Mahinder Bahadur GCSI, GCIE, GBE, ADC, Maharaja of Patiala.

His acknowledged progeny numbered over eighty. But any healthy man given the same opportunities to service as many women could have easily matched this.

Utterly Butterly Verghese Kurien

A favourite game some of my close friends and I indulge in periodically is to draw up lists of men and women who should have got, or deserve today, the Bharat Ratna. The names on our lists vary from the late H.D. Shourie, Satyajit Ray and Baba Amte to Anna Hazare, Atal Bihari Vajpayee, Ela Bhatt, Mahasweta Devi and a few others. One name that appears on everyone's list is that of Verghese Kurien. He has already got a Padma Shri (1965), Padma Bhushan (1966), Padma Vibhushan (1999), Magasaysay Award (1963), Wateler Peace Prize (1986), the World Food Prize (1989) and honorary doctorates from many universities.

Kurien was born in 1921 to a well-to-do Syrian Christian family in Calicut. A bright student, he was with the Tatas after graduating in science and engineering from Madras University. He applied for a government scholarship for higher studies abroad, hoping to return to his job with added qualifications. One question, put to him by a member of the selection panel, changed his entire career. He was asked, 'What is pasteurization?' He answered correctly that it was processing milk to make it last longer. He was told he'd be sent to Michigan State University in the US to study dairy farming and milk production. He was flabbergasted but accepted the offer. If he changed his mind after he returned to India, he would have to repay the government Rs 30,000. He did not have that kind of money. So a very sulky young lad found himself in a dusty little town—Anand—in Gujarat to ensure continuance of milk supply to Bombay. He could not speak Gujarati, was a beef-eating Christian and a bachelor. No family in Anand was willing to have him as a paying guest. He converted an empty garage into his home.

It did not take him very long to befriend locals, chiefly farmers who owned buffaloes and sold milk to earn their livelihood. He found two stalwarts to support him: Tribhuvan Patel and Miraben, the daughter of Sardar Patel. He formed the Kaira District Cooperative Milk Producers' Union, better known after its butter, Amul.

Luck was on his side, or so he believed. Professing to be an unbeliever in the occult, he had his fortune read by the length of his shadow at noontime. The shadow reader told him his future accurately: he did not like his job and would leave it in a month. Also, 'your career is set for a phenomenal rise—the kind you can never imagine'. Kurien told his biographer, 'In hindsight, it could not be truer.' He quit the government creamery and joined the Kaira cooperative. The rest is history.

The Anand milk cooperative was modernized. When President Rajendra Prasad came to lay its foundation stone, a mouse came out from nowhere and jumped on to the stove. 'The entire gathering was overcome with joy,' says Kurien, 'because the mouse is seen as Lord Ganesha's vehicle.' So, with the blessings of Ganesha, the lord of auspicious beginnings, began Kurien's meteoric rise to dazzling heights.

Soon Bombay was getting its fresh milk supply from Anand by train with specially designed wagons rather than the local doodhwala. It began to produce butter and knocked Polson from the market. Dairy specialists from New Zealand, Switzerland and Holland were of the considered opinion that milk powder and condensed milk could not be produced from buffalo's milk. Kurien's team produced both without a drop of cow's milk added to it. Whenever government babus or ministers created hindrances, Kurien had the backing of all the Gujarati MPs and ministers, from Sardar Patel, Morarji Desai and H.M. Patel to

Manubhai Shah, to back him up. So did a succession of PMs, from Nehru, Shastri, Indira Gandhi and Morarji Desai to Rajiv Gandhi. Once when Agriculture Minister Rao Birendra Singh wanted to remove Kurien from his post, he was dropped from the cabinet. Another time when Babu Jagjivan Ram wanted to do the same, he was sternly told: 'Don't touch Kurien.'

Kurien was asked to replicate the Anand model in India's other metros—Delhi, Calcutta, Madras—and he did so with equal success. 'Operation Flood' made the country self-sufficient in milk and its by-products. He used the best ad firms. Even the Pakistani government invited him over to perform the same miracle in their country.

Kurien has much to pat himself on the back. Regrettably, buffalo's milk, butter, milk powder, condensed milk, ice cream, dahi and ghee do not make scintillating topics for conversation. And it was usually heavy going when he occasionally came to visit me.

R.K. NARAYAN

It must be over forty years ago that I first met R.K. Narayan in his hometown, Mysore. I had read some of his short stories and novels. I marvelled at how a storyteller of modern times could hold a reader's interest without injecting sex or violence in his narratives. I found them too slow-moving, without any sparkling sentences or memorable descriptions of nature or of his characters. Nevertheless, the one-horse town of his invention, Malgudi, had etched itself on my mind. And all my South Indian friends raved about him as the greatest of Indians writing in English. He certainly was among the pioneers comprising Raja Rao, Govind Desani and Mulk Raj Anand. Whether or not he was the best of them is a matter of opinion.

Being with Narayan on his afternoon strolls was an experience. He did not go to a park but preferred walking up to the bazaar. He walked very slowly and after every few steps he would halt abruptly to complete what he was saying. He would stop briefly at shops to exchange namaskaras with the owners, introduce me and exchange gossip with them in Kannada or Tamil, neither of which I understood. I could sense these gentle strolls in crowded bazaars gave him material for his novels and stories. I found him very likeable and extremely modest despite his achievements.

We saw a lot more of each other during a literary seminar organized by the East-West Centre in Hawaii. Having said our pieces and sat through discussions that followed, we went out for our evening walks, looking for a place to eat. It was the same kind of stroll as we had taken in Mysore, punctuated by abrupt halts in the middle of crowded pavements till he was ready to resume walking. Finding a suitable eatery posed quite a problem. Narayan was a strict teetotaller and a vegetarian; I was neither. We would stop at a grocery store where he bought himself a carton of yoghurt. Then we would go from one eatery to another with R.K. Narayan asking, 'Have you got boiled rice?' Ultimately we could find one. Narayan would empty his carton of yoghurt on the mound of boiled rice. The only compromise he made was to eat it with a spoon instead of his fingers which he would have preferred. Such eateries had very second-rate food and no wines. Dining out was no fun for me.

One evening I decided to shake off Narayan and have a ball on my own. 'I am going to see a blue movie. I don't think you will like it,' I told him. 'I'll come along with you, if you don't mind,' he replied. So we found ourselves in a sleazy suburb of Honolulu watching an extremely obscene film depicting all kinds of sexual deviations. I thought Narayan would walk out, or throw up. He sat stiffly without showing any emotion. It was I who said, 'Let's go.' He turned to me and asked kindly: 'Have you had enough?'

We should get Narayan in the proper perspective. He would not have gone very far but for the patronage of Graham Greene who also became a kind of literary agent. He also got the enthusiastic patronage of *The Hindu* of Madras. N. Ram and his former English wife, Susan, wrote an excellent biography of Narayan. Greene made Narayan known to the English world of letters; *The Hindu* made him a household name in India.

Narayan was a very loveable man, but his humility was deceptive. Once when All India Radio invited a group of Indian writers to give talks and offered them fees far in excess of their usual rates, while all others accepted the offer, Narayan made it a condition that he should be paid at least one rupee more than the others. In his travelogue, *My Dateless Diary*, he writes about a dialogue at a luncheon party given in his honour. 'I blush to record this, but do it for documentary purposes. After the discussions (between two publishers declaring which of Narayan's novels is their favourite one, and rank him with Hemingway and Faulkner as the world's three greatest living writers) have continued on these lines for a while, I feel I ought to assert my modesty—I interrupt them to say, "Thank you, but not yet . . ." They brush me aside and repeat, "Hemingway, Faulkner and Narayan, the three greatest living . . ."' Narayan goes on at some length about the argument between the publishers over whether to include Greene or Hemingway, besides Narayan himself, among the three greatest.

I was foolish enough to write about this in my column. Narayan never spoke to me again.

My Last Days in Lahore

It was one day in mid-June 1947. Hot, still and silent. People were rudely shaken out of their siestas by shouts and exploding crackers. Since March, their nights had been disturbed by sporadic gunfire and mobs yelling in the streets, hurling slogans like missiles. From one end Muslims armed with knives and lathis shouted *Naara-e-Takbeer* followed by full-throated *Allah-O-Akbars*. From the other end came the reply: *Har Har Mahadev* and *Boley-se-Nihal Sat Sri Akal*. Stones were thrown, abuses exchanged, and unwary pedestrians stabbed to death. The police fired to disperse mobs, a few people were killed before peace was restored. The next morning, the papers reported the casualties like Muslims vs the Rest cricket scores. The score was invariably in favour of the Muslims. The chief reason for the Muslims having the upper hand was that the umpires were Muslims. Over 80 per cent of the Punjab Police was Muslim; the state government was Muslim-dominated. It was the same story all over western Punjab. Hindus and Sikhs had begun pulling out of Muslim-dominated towns to Lahore. And finding Lahore equally unsafe, trudged on to Amritsar and the towns of eastern Punjab where Hindus and Sikhs outnumbered Muslims.

That June afternoon of 1947 remains etched in my mind. I had returned from the high court when I heard the uproar. I ran up to the roof of my apartment. The sun burnt down fiercely over the city. From the centre billowed out a huge cloud of dense, black smoke. I did not have to make guesses; the Hindu–Sikh mohalla of Shahalmi was going up in flames. Muslim goondas had broken

30

the back of the non-Muslim resistance. After Shahalmi, the fight went out of the Hindus and Sikhs of Lahore. We remained mute spectators to Muslim League supporters marching in disciplined phalanxes chanting: *Pakistan ka naara kya, La-ilaha-il-lal-lah.*

The turmoil had little impact on the well-to-do who lived around Lawrence Gardens (today's Bagh-e-Jinnah), and on either side of the canal which ran on the eastern end of Lahore. We went about in our cars to our offices, spent evenings playing tennis at the Cosmopolitan or the Gymkhana Club, had dinner parties where Scotch which cost Rs 11 per bottle flowed like the waters of the Ravi. In elite residential areas, the old bonhomie of Hindu–Muslim bhai bhai-ism continued. We placed a lot of faith in the Unionist government of Khizr Hayat Tiwana who had Hindus and Sikhs in his cabinet and was strongly opposed to a separate Muslim state. League leaders turned their ire on him. Processionists chanted: *Taazi khabar, mar gaya Khizr.* Then he threw in the sponge. Overnight he became the hero of Muslim sloganeers: *Taazi khabar aayee hai, Khizr hamara bhai hai.*

The juggernaut gathered speed. Hindus and Sikhs began to sell properties and slip out towards eastern Punjab. One day I found my immediate neighbour had painted in large Urdu calligraphy: *Parsee ka makaan.* Another, on the other side, had a huge cross painted in white. Unmarked Hindu and Sikh houses were thus marked out. We were within walking distance of Mozang, a centre for Muslim goondas. I did not see anyone being killed but, unknown to me, escaped being murdered myself. I had gone on a case to Abbotabad. I decided to walk down to Taxila to catch a train to Lahore. I was surprised to see the road deserted. Suddenly, a lorryload of Sikh soldiers pulled up and a lieutenant ordered me to get in. 'Are you crazy?' he shouted. 'They have killed all Sikhs in the neighbouring villages and you are strolling along unconcerned.' At Taxila station, I noticed the train halt at a signal. Sikhs were dragged out and killed. At Badami Bagh, there was another massacre. Locked in my first-class bogey, I neither saw nor heard anything. At Lahore, my friend, Manzur

Qadir (later foreign minister of Pakistan), was on the platform to take me home.

By July 1947, stories of violence against Muslims in east Punjab circulated in Lahore, and a trickle of Muslim refugees flew westwards. This further roused Muslim fury. The last time I went to the high court I saw a dozen Sikh students from National College in handcuffs. They were charged with the murder of two Muslims on Grand Trunk Road, running in front of their college. Among them was Ganga Singh Dhillon, later pioneer of the demand for Khalistan. They were produced before Justice Teja Singh, the only Sikh judge. He freed them on bail. That had become the pattern of justice.

A week before Independence, Chris Everett, head of the CID in Punjab, who had studied law with me in London, advised me to get out of Lahore. Escorted by six Baluch constables, my wife and I took a train to Kalka to join our two children who had been sent ahead to their grandparents in Kasauli. By arrangement, I met Manzur Qadir coming down from Simla and handed him the keys of my house.

Then, I drove down to Delhi. There wasn't a soul on the 200-mile stretch. I arrived in Delhi on 13 August 1947. The next night I was among the crowd outside Parliament house chanting *Bharat mata ki jai*. We heard Sucheta Kripalani's voice over loudspeakers singing *Vande mataram*. Then Nehru's 'Tryst with Destiny' speech. What a tryst it was! And what destiny.

On Sting Operations

Spying on those in public life has always been the business of journalists; now, the means and doings have become more sophisticated. As far back as the 'seventies, I can recall how a minister was caught on tape demanding a bribe. This was done by Vasant Seth, the owner of the biggest shipping company in India. Seth had applied to the government for a licence to buy some ships. An official from the shipping ministry called on him a few days later and mentioned in passing the sum of money that he would be required to shell out for the licence. Seth protested, saying he didn't have that kind of money. A month later, the official was back at Seth's home; he said the sum was now double of what he'd quoted earlier. Seth repeated his protest; the official asked him to deal directly with the minister. When Seth eventually went to meet the minister, Chand Ram, he took care to slip a tiny tape recorder—a gadget that had recently been introduced—into his pocket. Chand Ram repeated the offer once again, doubling the amount he wanted as a bribe. Seth took the tape to the then prime minister Morarji Desai. He refused to listen to the tape. 'Do you think you are Raja Harishchandra?' Morarji asked. Seth then came to see me and I asked him to give me the tape. The next time I met Sanjay Gandhi, I gave it to him suggesting he make use of it to embarrass the ruling party in Parliament. But that was the last I heard of the tape, although a few months later when the government fell and elections were called, Chand Ram was contesting on a Congress ticket.

I believe a journalist is justified in using whatever means he can to expose those who profess one thing and do something entirely different. There is far too much skulduggery going on and it's the duty of journalists to expose it. It needn't be just politicians but anyone—civil servants, holy men and women. Of course, the criterion is that the journalist must be strictly above board—there have been instances in the past where journalists have ended up as blackmailers. On the whole, I think journalists have been playing a very positive role, whether it is exposing Sanjay Joshi whom they caught with his pants down, or the Kanchipuram seer making passes at women despite his vows of celibacy. They had to be exposed for the sake of public morality. Think about it: the MPs who were caught red-handed taking money for raising questions in Parliament would never have been exposed except for this new, sophisticated technology.

I wish this technology had existed at the time when I was the editor of the *Illustrated Weekly of India*. By the time the infamous photographs of Jagjivan Ram's son, Suresh, were out, I was no longer with the *Weekly* and was editing the *National Herald*. Suresh was not only a womanizer, he was something of a narcissistic voyeur as well. It was well known that he used to have himself photographed with almost all the women he slept with. The photographs came to light by sheer accident—a gang of Jat boys, enraged that he was carrying on with a Jat girl, abducted him in order to give him a sound thrashing. After they'd done that, one of the boys opened the compartment in the front of the car in search of a light for his cigarette and found instead an envelope containing these pictures. They made several dozen copies of them and delivered them to every editor in Delhi. No one dared to publish the pictures. As the editor of the *National Herald*, I, too, received the lot. I took them to Mrs Indira Gandhi to ask if she wanted them published in the *Herald*. But she didn't think the *Herald* was the right place for them. A few days later, Jagjivan Ram, who was defence minister in Morarji's government, sent feelers to Mrs G indicating his willingness to switch over to her camp. Mrs Gandhi's response was typical: ask him to switch first, then the photographs will be returned to him. He took his own time and the photographs appeared in *Surya* magazine that Maneka was running at that time. Of course, we had to stick black tape at the appropriate places.

It's not just the technology that has changed, it's also the attitude of the news media. Even if a newspaper or magazine editor had access to these sophisticated means, few would have dared to publish the results. It meant taking a huge risk which no proprietor would be willing to agree to. But it's quite a different matter in these days of dozens of TV channels and newspapers all vying with each other for scoops. In these circulation-conscious times, few editors would think of self-censorship. Except perhaps a very conservative newspaper like *The Hindu*. And that is as it should be: you are after all exposing people who deserve to be exposed because their pretensions don't match their practices.

Every citizen has the right to privacy and anyone who invades it deserves to be punished. Thus the use of hidden cameras in hotel rooms and bridal suites should be punished by cancelling the hotelier's licence, imposing a heavy fine and sending the person to jail. However, a distinction should be drawn between a private citizen and people in public life like politicians, civil servants, defence personnel, members of the judiciary, leaders of religious organizations and others who preach public morality. If what they profess in public does not tally with what they indulge in themselves, exposing them in their nakedness is wholly justified.

A Hosanna to the Monsoons

'Monsoon' is not another word for rain. As its original Arabic name (mausam) indicates, it is a season. There is a summer monsoon as well as a winter monsoon, but it is only the nimbus south-west winds of summer that make a mausam—the season of rains. The winter monsoon is like a quick shower on a cold and frosty morning. It leaves one chilled and shivering. Although it is good for the crops, people pray for it to end. Fortunately, it does not last very long.

The summer monsoon is quite another affair. It is preceded by several months of working up a thirst so that when the waters come they are drunk deep and with relish. From the end of February, the sun starts getting hotter and spring gives way to summer. Garden flowers wither. Wild flowering trees take their place. Then the trees lose their flowers as well as their leaves. Their bare branches stretch up to the sky as if begging for water; but there is no water. The sun rises earlier than before and licks up the drops of dew before the fevered earth can moisten its lips. It sears the grass and thorny scrub till they catch fire. These fires spread and dry jungles burn like matchwood.

The sun goes on, day after day, from east to west, scorching relentlessly. The earth cracks up and deep fissures open their gaping mouths, asking for water; but there is no water—only the shimmering haze at noon, making mirage lakes of quicksilver. Poor villagers take their thirsty cattle out to drink, both man and beast are struck dead. The rich wear sunglasses and hide behind curtains of khus fibre on which their servants pour water.

The sun makes an ally of the breeze. It heats the air till it becomes the loo and sends it on its errand. Even in the intense heat, the loo's warm caresses are sensuous and pleasant. It causes prickly heat. It produces a numbness which makes the head nod and the eyes heavy with sleep. It brings on a stroke which takes its victims as gently as the breeze bears a fluff of thistle down.

Then comes a period of false hope. The temperature drops. The air becomes still. From the southern horizon a black wall begins to advance. Hundreds of kites and crows fly ahead. Can it be . . .? No, it is a dust storm. A fine powder begins to fall. A solid mass of locusts covers the sun. They devour whatever is left on the trees and in the fields. Then comes the storm itself. In furious sweeps it smacks open doors and windows, banging them forward and backward, smashing their glass panes. Thatched roofs and corrugated iron sheets are borne aloft like bits of paper. Trees are torn up by the roots and they fall across power lines. The tangled wires electrocute people and set fire to houses. All this happens in a few seconds. Before you can say Chakravarti Rajagopalachari, the gale is gone. The dust hanging in the air settles on your books, furniture and food; it gets into your eyes and ears and throat and nose.

This happens over and over again until people lose all hope. They are disillusioned, dejected, thirsty and sweating. The prickly heat on the back of their necks is like emery paper. There is another lull. A hot petrified silence prevails. Then comes the shrill, strange call of a bird. Why has it left its cool dusky shade and come out in the sun? People look up wearily at the lifeless sky. Yes, there it is with its mate! They are like large black-and-white bulbuls with perky crests and long tails. They are Pied Crested Cuckoos (*Clamator jacobinus*) who have flown all the way from Africa ahead of the monsoon.

Isn't there a gentle breeze blowing? And hasn't it a damp smell? And wasn't the rumble which drowned the bird's anguished cry the sound of thunder? People hurry to the roofs to see. An ebony wall is again coming up from the east. A flock of herons flies across. There is a flash of lightning which outshines the daylight. The wind fills the black sail of the cloud and it billows out across the sun. A profound shadow falls on the earth. There is another clap of thunder. Big drops of rain fall and dry up in the dust. A fragrant smell rises from the earth. Another flash of lightning and another crack of thunder like the roar of a hungry tiger.

It has come! Sheets of water, wave after wave. The people lift their faces to the clouds and let the abundance of water cover them. Schools and offices close. All work stops. Men, women and children run madly about the streets, waving their arms and shouting 'ho, ho'—hosannas to the miracle of the monsoon.

The monsoon is not like ordinary rain which comes and goes. Once it is on, it stays for three to four months. Its advent is greeted with joy. Parties set out for picnics and litter the countryside with the skins and stones of mangoes. Women and children make swings on the branches of trees and spend the day in sport and song. Peacocks spread their tails and strut about with their mates; the woods echo with their shrill cries.

After a few days the flash of enthusiasm is gone. The earth becomes a big stretch of swamp and mud. Wells and lakes fill up and burst their bounds. In towns, gutters get clogged and streets become turbid streams. In villages, the mud walls of huts melt in the water and thatched roofs sag and descend on the inhabitants. Rivers, which keep rising steadily from the time the summer's heat starts melting the snows, suddenly turn to floods as the monsoon spends itself on the mountains. Roads, railway tracks and bridges go under water. Houses near the river banks are swept down to the sea.

With the monsoon the tempo of life and death increases. Almost overnight grass begins to grow and leafless trees turn green. Snakes, centipedes and scorpions are born out of nothing. At night, myriads of moths flutter around lamps. They fall into everybody's food and water. Geckos dart about filling themselves with insects till they get heavy and fall off ceilings. Inside rooms, the hum of mosquitoes is maddening. People spray clouds of insecticide and the floor becomes a layer of wriggling bodies and wings. The next evening, there are many more fluttering around the lampshades and burning themselves in the flames. The monsoon has its own music. Apart from the thunder, the rumble of storm clouds and the pitter-patter of rain drops, there is the constant accompaniment of frogs croaking. Aristophanes captured their sound: 'Brek-ek-ek-ek, Koax. Koax!'

While the monsoon lasts, the showers start and stop without warning. The clouds fly across, dropping their rain on the plains as it pleases them, till they reach the Himalayas. They climb up the mountain sides. Then the cold squeezes the last drops of water out of them. Lightning and thunder never cease.

Then the season of the rains gives way to autumn.

It is not surprising that much of India's art, music and literature is concerned with the summer monsoon. Innumerable paintings depict people on rooftops looking eagerly at the dark clouds billowing out from over the horizon with flocks of herons flying in front. Of the many melodies of Indian music, Raga Megha Malhar is the most popular because it brings to mind the distant echoes of thunder and the falling of raindrops. It brings the odour of the earth and green vegetation to the nostrils; the cry of the peacock and the call of the koel to the ear. The commonest theme in Indian songs is the longing of lovers for each other when the rains are in full swing. There is no joy greater than union during monsoon time, there is no sorrow deeper than separation during the season of the rains.

The Indian's attitude towards clouds and rain remains fundamentally different from that of the Westerner's. To the one, clouds are symbols of hope; to the other, of despair. The Indian scans the heavens and if nimbus clouds blot out the sun, his heart fills with joy. The Westerner looks up and if there is no silver lining edging the clouds, his depression deepens. The Indian talks of someone he respects and looks up to as a great shadow, like the one cast by the clouds when they cover the sun. The Westerner, on the other hand, looks on a shadow as something evil and refers to people of dubious character as shady types. For him, his beloved is like the sunshine and her smile a sunny smile. An Indian's notion of a beautiful woman is one whose hair is as black as monsoon clouds and whose eyes flash like lightning. The Westerner escapes clouds and rain whenever he can to seek sunnier climes. An Indian, when the rains come, runs out into the street shouting with joy and lets himself be soaked to the skin.

The monsoon has exercised the minds of Indian writers (as well as painters and musicians) over the centuries. Some of the best pieces of descriptive verse were composed by India's classical poets writing in Sanskrit. Amaru (date uncertain, but earlier than 9 century AD) describes the heat of the summer and the arrival of the monsoon:

The summer sun, who robbed the pleasant nights,
And plundered all the water of the rivers,
And burned the earth, and scorched the forest-trees,
Is now in hiding; and the autumn clouds,
Spread thick across the sky to track him down,
Hunt for the criminal with lightning-flashes.
(*Poems from the Sanskrit.* Translated by John Brough; Penguin Books)

To be away from one's wife or sweetheart during the season of rains can be torture:

At night the rain came, and the thunder deep
Rolled in the distance; and he could not sleep,
But tossed and turned, with long and frequent sighs.
And as he listened, tears came to his eyes;
And thinking of his young wife left alone,
He sobbed and wept aloud until the dawn.
And from that time on
The villagers made it a strict rule that no traveller
Should be allowed to take a room for the night in the village.
(*Poems from the Sanskrit.* Translated by John Brough; Penguin Books)

Literary conceit and facetiousness have always been practised by Indian poets. Thus Sudraka (probably 3 or 4 century AD) has a girl taunt a cloud:

Thundercloud, I think you are wicked.
You know I'm going to meet my own lover.
And yet you first scare me with your thunder,
And now you're trying to caress me
With your rain-hands!
(*Poems from the Sanskrit*. Translated by John Brough; Penguin Books)

Bhartrihari (500 AD or a little earlier) went into erotic ecstasies combining descriptions of the monsoon with dalliance:

Flashing streaks of lightning
Drifting fragrance of tropical pines,
Thunder sounding from gathering clouds,
Peacocks crying in amorous tones—
How will long-lashed maids pass
These emotion-laden days in their lovers' absence?
(*Bhartrihari Poems*. Translated by Barbara Stoler Miller; Columbia University Press)

While the downpour lasts there is little that lovers can do besides staying in bed and making love:

Heavy rains keep lovers
Trapped in their mansions;
In the shivering cold a lord
Is embraced by his long-eyed maid,
And winds bearing cool mists
Allay their fatigue after amorous play.
Even a dreary day is fair
For favoured men who nestle in love's arms.
(*Bhartrihari Poems*. Translated by Barbara Stoler Miller; Columbia University Press)

Monsoon is not only trysting time for humans but also for animals and birds, above all the national bird—the peacock. Yogesvara (circa 800 AD) describes the courtship dance in these beautiful lines:

> With tail-fans spread, and undulating wings
> With whose vibrating pulse the air now sings,
> Their voices lifted and their beaks stretched wide,
> Treading the rhythmic dance from side to side,
> Eyeing the raincloud's dark, majestic hue,
> Richer in colour than their own throats' blue,
> With necks upraised, to which their tails advance,
> Now in the rains the screaming peacocks dance.
> (*Poems from the Sanskrit*. Translated by John Brough; Pengiun Books)

Subandhu (late 6 century AD) in his *Vasavadatta* is exuberant in his welcome of the monsoon:

> The rainy season had arrived. Rivers overflowed their banks. Peacocks danced at eventide. The rain quelled the expanse of dust as a great ascetic quells the tide of passion. The chataka birds were happy. Lightning shone like a bejewelled boat of love in the pleasure pool of the sky; it was like a garland for the gate of the palace of paradise; like a lustrous girdle for some heavenly beauty; like a row of nail-marks left upon the cloud by its lover, the departing day.
>
> The rain was like a chess player, while yellow and green frogs were like chessmen jumping in the enclosures of the irrigated fields. Hailstones flashed like pearls from the necklaces of heavenly birds. By and by, the rainy season yielded to autumn, the season of bright dawns; of parrots rummaging among rice-stalks; of fugitive clouds. In autumn the lakes echoed with the sound of herons. The frogs were silent and the snakes shrivelled up. At night the stars were unusually bright; the moon was like a pale beauty.

The prolonged monsoon can become tiresome for some people. The Maithili poet Vidyapan (1352–1448) writes about their predicament:

Clouds break.
Arrows of water fall
Like the last blows
That end the world.
The night is thick
With lamp-black for the eyes.
Who keep so late a tryst?
The earth is a pool of mud
With dreaded snakes at large.
Darkness is everywhere,
Save where your feet
Flash with lighting.

Another body of literature where many references to monsoons can be found is the baramasis (twelve monthly) composed by the poets of northern India. We are not sure when the tradition of composing baramasis began but by the sixteenth century it had become well established and most poets tried their hand at describing the changing panorama of nature through the year. The Sikhs' holy scripture, the Granth Sahib, has two baramahs (the Punjabi version of the baramasis) of which the one composed by the founder of the faith, Guru Nanak (1469–1539), in Raga Tukhari has some memorable depictions of the weather. Since the monsoons in the Punjab break sometime after mid-July, Nanak first describes the summer's heat in his verse on Asadh (June–July):

In Asadh the sun scorches
Skies are hot
The earth burns like an oven
Water gives up their vapours
It burns and scorches relentlessly
Thus the land fails not
To fulfil its destiny
The sun's chariot passes the mountain tops;
Long shadows stretch across the land
And the cicada calls from the glades.
The beloved seeks the cool of the evening.

If the comfort she seeks be in falsehood,
There will be sorrow in store for her.

Asadh is followed by Savan (July–August) when the monsoons break in northern India.

O my heart rejoice! It's Savan
The season of nimbus clouds and rain
My body and soul yearn for my lord.
But my lord is gone to foreign lands.
If he returns not, I shall die pining for him.

Since the monsoon is the time for lovers' trysts and thus engrossed they tend to forget their Maker, Nanak admonishes them in his verse on Bhadon (August–September):

In the month of Bhadon
I lose myself in a maze of falsehood
I waste my wanton youth
River and land are one endless expanse of water
For it is the monsoon, the season of merry-making.
It rains.
The nights are dark,
What comfort is it to the wife left alone?
Frogs croak
Peacocks scream
The papeeha calls 'peeoh, peeoh',
The fangs of serpents that crawl,
The stings of mosquitoes that fly
Are full of venom.
The seas have burst their bounds in the ecstasy
Of fulfilment
Without the Lord I alone am bereft of joy
Whither shall I go?
Says Nanak, ask the guru the way
He knoweth the path which leads to the Lord.

The poetic tradition has continued to the present times. India's only Nobel laureate in literature, Rabindranath Tagore

(1861–1941), has a beautiful piece in his most celebrated work, *Gitanjali*:

> Clouds heap upon clouds and it darkens
> Ah, love, why dost thou let me wait
> Outside at the door all alone?
> In the busy moments of the noontide
> Work I am with the crowd,
> But on this dark lonely day
> It is only for thee I hope
> If thou showest one not thy face, if thou leavest me
> Wholly aside. I know not how I am to pass these
> Long, rainy hours.
> I keep gazing on the far-away gloom of the sky and
> My heart wanders wailing with the restless wind.

These are but a few examples from Sanskrit and the languages of northern India illustrating the impact the monsoons make on the sensitive minds of poets and men of letters. Similar examples are available in all the other languages and dialects spoken in the rest of the country.

Many foreign writers have given vivid descriptions of the monsoon as well. Of these there is a memorable one by L.H. Niblett in his *India in Fable, Verse and Story*, published in 1938:

> The sky was grey and laden: the monsoon was dull and pale
> Suspended high, the dust-clouds, in canopying veil.
> Overlooked wide fields and hamlets of India's arid plains
> Sun-baked and scorch'd and yellow-athirsting, for the Rains.
> The atmosphere was stifling; the air was still as death,
> As the parched jheels emitted their foul and charnel breath;
> Storm clouded the horizon; a flash across the sky;
> A boom of far-off thunder, and a breeze like a distant sigh,
> 'Tis the dirge of a dying summer, the music of the gods;
> Dead leaves rise up and caper; the Melancolia nods:
> Tall trees to life awaken: the top-most branches sway
> And the long grass is waving along the zephyr way.
> A mantle of red shadow envelops all around

The trees, the grass, the hamlets, as the storm-clouds forward
bound.
Of a sudden, comes a whirl wind, dancing, spinning rapidly;
Then gust on gust bursts quick, incessant, mad, rushing
furiously.
A crash—and the Monsoon's on us, in torrents everywhere,
With the bellowing roar of thunder, and lightning, flare on flare.
The tempest's now abated; a hush falls o'er the scene;
The myriad birds start chatt'ring and the grass again is green.
The fields like vast, still mirrors, in sheets of water lie.
The frogs, in droning chorus, sing coarse their lullaby
Each tank and pool is flooded; great rivers burst their banks
King summer's reign is ended, the monsoon sovereign ranks.

E.M. Forster, the celebrated author of *A Passage to India*, has
an equally vivid portrayal of the rainy season in his *The Hill of
Devi* (published by Edwin Arnold, 1953).

'The first shower was smelly and undramatic. Now there is a
new India—damp and grey, and but for the unusual animals I
might think myself in England. The full Monsoon broke violently
and upon my undefended form. I was under a little shelter in
the garden, waving seeds in boxes with the assistance of two
aged men and a little boy. I saw black clouds and felt some spots
of rain. This went on for a quarter of an hour, so that I got
accustomed to it, and then a wheel of water swept horizontally
over the ground. The aged men clung to each other for support.
I don't know what happened to the boy. I bowed this way and
that as the torrent veered, wet through of course, but anxious
not to be blown away like the roof of palm leaves over our head.
When the storm decreased or rather became perpendicular, I set
out for the Palace, large boats of mud forming on either foot.
A rescue expedition, consisting of an umbrella and a servant,
set out to meet me. But the umbrella blew inside out and the
servant fell down.'

In every part of India peasants have their own way of predicting
the monsoon. There is a general belief that the more intense the
heat during April, May and June, the heavier will be the rains

that follow. In northern India, some varieties of thorny bushes like the karwand and keekhar break into tiny leaf a month before the rains break. The Papeeha (the hawk cuckoo or the brain-fever bird) is loudest during the hot days. The Pied Crested Cuckoo (*Clamator jacobinus*) also known as Megha Papeeha—the song bird of the clouds—has its natural habitat in East Africa. Taking advantage of the monsoon winds it flies across the Indian Ocean and the Arabian Sea to arrive on the western coast of India a day or so ahead of the rain-bearing clouds. It is rightly regarded as the monsoon herald. It flies at a more leisurely pace over land and is usually sighted in Delhi about fifteen days after the monsoon has broken over the Western Ghats.

Indians divide the few months of the summer monsoons into eight periods of fifteen days each, depending on the signs of the zodiac known as nakshatras. There are twenty-seven nakshatras: Ashwini, Bharni, Krittika, Rohini, Mrigshira, Ardra, Punarvasu, Pushya, Ashlesha, Megha, Purva Phalguni, Uttara Phalguni, Hasta, Chitra, Swati, Vishakh, Anuradha, Jyestha, Mool, Purvasharha, Uttarasharha, Sharvan, Ghanistha, Shatbhisha, Purva Bhadrapada, Uttara Bhadrapada and Revati.

Of the twenty-seven nakshatras the fifteenth, known as Swati, is considered the most auspicious. According to poets, the mythical bird Chatak drinks only of the Swati rain. And it is only the drops of the Swati rain that turn to pearls when they fall into oysters. The Swati falling on bamboo trees produces vanslochan, a precious medicament of Ayurveda, the indigenous system of medicine.

The test of a good monsoon in Maharashtra is when the gunny sacks that the peasants drape over their heads and shoulders as they go out in the rain remain damp long enough to breed insects.

All Indian languages have innumerable proverbs stressing the importance of rains in their particular regions. As far as the Punjab is concerned, comprehensive compilation has been made by the director, public relations, Punjab, in *Agricultural Proverbs of the*

Punjab, 1962. They are largely variations of the single theme: 'If the rains are good, there will be no famine.'

There are also proverbs about the distribution of rains during the year. 'Four months do not need even a rain of gold—Magghar (mid-November to mid-December), Chet (mid-March to mid-April), Vaisakh (mid-April to mid-May) and Jeth (mid-May to mid-June). Except for these four months, rain is desirable in all the other months of the year.'

Despite the summer rains being the real monsoon, it is the short winter rains that the Punjabi farmer prizes more. 'Winter rain is gold, Harh rain, silver and Savan–Bhadon mere copper,' says a proverb. There are parallel proverbs instructing farmers what to do during the monsoon months: 'If you do not plough your land in Harh you will be like a dry Savan and a child who learnt nothing at school.'

The onset of the winter rain is calculated as following 100 days after the end of the summer monsoon. 'If it rains on Diwali the sluggard will be as well off as a conscientious tiller, except that the tiller's crop will be more abundant.' And, 'If there is a spell of rain in Magghar (mid-November to mid-December) the wheat will have healthy colour.'

Most of the Hindi proverbs on rain are ascribed to Ghagh (17 century), a learned Brahmin poet-astrologer, and his even more learned wife, Bhaddari, a low-caste girl he married because of her learning. Says Bhaddari: 'When clouds appear like partridge feathers and are spread across the sky they will not go without shedding rain.' (A similar proverb in Punjabi says exactly the opposite.) Ghagh predicts, 'When lightning flashes in the northern sky and the wind blows from the east, bring oxen under shelter because it is sure to rain.' He also says: 'When water in the pitcher does not cool, when sparrows bathe in dust and the ants take their eggs to a safer place, you can be sure of a heavy downpour.'

Ghagh's forecasts are, 'If the southern wind flows in the months of Magh and Poos (i.e. January and February), the summer monsoon is bound to be good.' And 'Dark clouds in the sky may thunder without shedding a drop; where white clouds may be pregnant with rain,' is another of his sayings. However, some of their proverbs seemed to have been designed to keep hope alive: 'If the clouds appear on Friday and stay till Saturday,' Ghagh tells Bhaddari, 'be sure that it will rain.' The Ghagh-Bhaddari proverbs are on the lips of peasant folks in the Hindi-speaking belt stretching from Haryana and Rajasthan, across Uttar Pradesh and Madhya Pradesh, to the eastern boundaries of Bihar.

Despite the Green Revolution and our self-sufficiency in food, even today it is not far wrong to say that in India 'scarcity is only a missed monsoon away'.

PHOOLAN DEVI: AN OBITUARY

Sometime in 1982, I got a call from the commissioner of police of Lucknow who asked if I would like to send a reporter to cover the arrest of Phoolan Devi. She was reported to be sick and likely to come to her parents living in the village Gur-ka-Purwa to tie a rakhi on the hand of her only brother. Instead of sending a reporter, I decided to go myself: it was too good a story to miss. I was then the editor of *Hindustan Times*. I asked my correspondent in Lucknow, Lakhan Naqvi, to accompany me as I didn't understand the dialect spoken by the villagers.

From Lucknow we drove over dusty, snake-infested scrub country. We arrived at the dak bungalow on top of a hill. I spent much of the morning going through the police files on Phoolan's past. The first and only time she had been arrested was 6 January 1979 in connection with a robbery in her cousin's home. Her father had some dispute over land with him. Some stolen goods were found in their home and she spent a fortnight in police custody.

Her statement was prefaced by a note from the police officer who described her as 'about twenty years old; wheatish complexion, oval face; short but sturdily built'. Phoolan's statement read: 'I am the second daughter of a family of six consisting of five girls. The youngest is a boy, Shiv Narain Singh. We belong to the Mallah caste . . . At the age of twelve, I was given away in marriage to a forty-five-year-old widower, Putti Lal.' Then she talks of her second 'marriage' to Kailash in Kanpur. Later in the afternoon I got the rest of her story from her mother, Muli.

'Phoolan Devi was too young to consummate her marriage and came back to us after a few days. A year or two later, we sent her back to her husband. This time she stayed with him for a few months but was unhappy. She came away without her husband's permission, determined not to go back to him.' It would appear that she had been deflowered. Her mother describes her as being 'filled up'—a rustic expression for a girl whose bosom and behind indicate that she has had sex. It would appear that she had developed an appetite for sex which her ageing husband could not fulfil. Her parents were distraught: a girl leaving her husband was a disgrace.

Phoolan picked up a liaison with the son of a village headman. The headman's son invited his friends to partake of the feast. Phoolan Devi had no choice but to give in. The village gossip mill ground out stories of Phoolan Devi being available to anyone who wanted to lay her. Her mother admitted: 'The family's pojeesun (position) was compromised; our noses were cut. We decided to send her away to her sister, Ramkali, who lived in village Teonga across the river.'

It did not take long for Phoolan Devi to find another lover in Teonga. This was a distant cousin, Kailash, married and with four children. He gives a vivid account of how he was seduced by Phoolan: 'One day I was washing my clothes on the banks of the Yamuna. This girl brought her sister's buffaloes to wallow in the shallows of the river. We got talking. She asked me to lend her my cake of soap so that she could bathe herself. I gave her what remained of the soap. She stripped before my eyes. While she splashed water on herself and soaped her bosom and buttocks she kept talking to me. I got very excited watching her. After she was dressed, I followed her into the lentil fields. We made love many times. But it was never enough. She started playing hard to get. "If you want me, you must marry me. Then I'll give you all you want," she said. I told her I had a wife and children and could only keep her as my mistress. She would not let me touch her unless I agreed to marry her. I became desperate. I took her with me to Kanpur. A lawyer took fifty rupees from me, wrote something on a piece of paper and told us that we were man and wife. When we returned to Teonga, my parents refused to take us in. The next day I told Phoolan to go back to her parents as I had decided to return to my wife and children. She swore she would kill me. I have not seen her since then. But I am afraid one of these days she will get me.'

Phoolan's initiation into dacoity came soon after Vikram Mallah, deputy leader of a gang led by Babu Gujjar, met her. Both Mallah and Gujjar took a fancy to her. She agreed to join them if they spared her younger brother whom she loved dearly. Babu Gujjar was an uncouth and rough man. He liked having sex in the open with his gang watching them. Phoolan complained to Vikram who killed Babu while he was asleep. Phoolan became Vikram's mistress. She had a rubber stamp made for herself which she used as a letterhead: *Dasyu* (dacoit) *sundri* (beauty), *Dasyu Samrat Vikram ki premika* (beloved of Vikram, emperor of dacoits).

The inspector general of police showed me a sheaf of letters written by Phoolan. 'Honourable and respected Inspector General sahib, I learn from several Hindi journals that you have been making speeches saying that you will have us dacoits shot like pye-dogs. I hereby give you notice that if you do not stop bakwas (nonsense) of this kind, I will have your revered mother abducted and so thoroughly raped by my men that she will need medical attention. So take heed.'

The honeymoon with Vikram Mallah did not last long. Thakurs Lal Ram Singh and Shri Ram killed Vikram on 13 August 1980. They took Phoolan with them to Behmai, kept her locked in a room, raped her repeatedly and marched her naked through the streets. On the excuse of relieving herself one night, Phoolan disappeared into the dark.

Phoolan joined another gang led by a Muslim, Baba Mustaqeem. She was not interested in loot; she thirsted for the blood of the Thakurs of Behmai who had murdered her lover and humiliated her. She persuaded Mustaqeem to help her quench her thirst. That's what brought her to Behmai on 14 February 1981. They surrounded the village. Phoolan stood on the parapet of a well in the centre of the village and, through a megaphone, summoned the villagers to her presence. She addressed them in the foulest language and asked them about the whereabouts of the two Thakurs. They swore they had not seen them in Behmai. She marched two dozen men to an open space and lined them against a wall. She gave them a final chance to disclose where the two men were. They denied any knowledge. She ordered them to turn around and face the wall and opened fire, leaving twenty dead and two injured. When the news of the massacre broke, Phoolan's name made headlines in the world media. A gangster's moll became a 'symbol of women's pent-up hatred against women's maltreatment by men'.

Phoolan spent thirteen years in jail. She had her story, *The Bandit Queen*, written by Mala Sen. Thus the poor Mallahin of Gur-ka-Purwa became rich and famous. Mulayam Singh, the chief minister of Uttar Pradesh, withdrew all cases pending against her, had her elected to the Lok Sabha twice and, by honouring her, garnered the votes of the lower castes. She has become proof of the saying, 'Those who live by the gun, die by the gun.' Even though dead, Phoolan will never be forgotten.

A Sardarji in Phoren

In the 'thirties, when I first went to England, Sardarjis were a rare sight in Europe. Despite their long association with the English as soldiers and policemen, few were to be seen in England. They had one gurudwara, Bhupendra Dharamsala, in Shepherds Bush (London) where even on the Gurus' birthdays the congregation rarely exceeded three dozen, half of them clean-shaven, hence indistinguishable from the other Indians. The number of such students in British universities could be counted on one's fingertips. The only such sub-group seen occasionally cycling round the countryside were the Bhatra pedlars. They carried attaché cases full of trinkets: ties, scarfs, Indian perfumes, hairclips to sell to memsahibs living in distant villages. They did not sell very much but whenever they rang the doorbell, kindly old ladies invited them in, gave them tea, cakes and biscuits. They had no problem keeping their bodies and souls together.

Even in England, the man on the street did not know who a Sikh was. Every time I told them I was a Sikh, the usual response was, 'Ah yes, a sheikh from Araby.' Often, when I passed by a family out for a stroll, some child, bewitched by my appearance, would ask, 'Mummy, what was that?' Some people took me to be an itinerant maharaja; I did not mind that. Others thought I was a magician; that left me puzzled. More amusing was when I boarded a tram or a bus to return home to my digs and encountered parties of excited schoolchildren returning home. They played a game to be the first to spot a man with a beard. No sooner one saw me, he would shout, 'Beaver, I saw him first.'

54

After Independence, the number of Sikhs from India and East Africa went up by the thousands across Europe, Canada and the US. Gurudwaras sprang up even in small towns. In 1948, I was posted in the Indian high commission in Canada. A sizeable community of Sikhs had been in existence on the west coast in British Columbia. They had endured many insults by being called 'ragheads' (because of their turbans). All Indians, including Muslims, were known as 'Hindoos'. Despite persecution, the Sikhs had prospered as lumbermen and farmers. Some had become millionaires.

My first experience of mistaken identity came a few days after I arrived in Ottawa. I was staying in one of the capital's largest hotels, Chateau Laurier. It was mid-winter with snow many feet deep. I was waiting on the kerb for the lights to change so I could cross the road to get to my office. There was snow on my turban and all over my beard. A very tall man, evidently an American on a visit, could not make out who I could be. After looking me up and down, he addressed me in quaint old English: 'Sir, by your deportment and demeanour, you look to be a foreigner to these parts.' I admitted I was indeed an alien.

'Sir, may I ask where you are from?'

'I am an Indian,' I replied.

He looked disappointed. 'Are you from a reservation?'

I did not know then that a reservation was an area exclusively meant for Red Indians. 'No, I replied, 'I am staying in Château Laurier.'

The mix-up of Indians with American and Canadian Red Indians landed me in another amusing episode. In the year I was in Canada, I did not come across even one man wearing feathers on his head. I happened to be in Montreal, strolling along the road outside my hotel, when I saw a brown man with high cheekbones walking in my direction on the other side of the road. I was sure that at long last, I had sighted a Red Indian. I smiled at him. He returned my smile. I crossed the road. We shook hands. 'When I saw you, I guessed immediately you were an Indian,' I said.

'Indeed, I am,' he replied, shaking my hand a second time.

'Where are you from?' I asked.

'From Madras,' he replied.

Much the most amusing encounter I had as a Sikh was on my first visit to Israel. I was dining alone in the King David Hotel. Sitting at the adjoining table was an American Jewish couple on a pilgrimage to the Holy Land. They could not make out where I had landed from in Jerusalem. After huddled whispers, the man turned to me. 'Excuse me, do you speak English?'

'Yes, I do.'

'My wife, Ruth, and I were discussing where you might be from. Could you tell us?'

'You make three guesses,' I replied with a broad smile. That got them into a fix. The wife made the first guess. 'Would you be Jewish?'

'No, I am not a Jew,' I replied.

'How could he be a Jew?' burst in her husband. 'Does he look like one?' He made the second guess. 'Would you be a muscleman?'

'No,' I replied, 'I am not a Mussulman.'

They again got into a huddle. After consulting each other they made their third guess. 'Then you must be a Buddhist.'

'No, I am not a Buddhist.'

They had run out of options. 'We give up. Please tell us who you are.'

'I am a Sikh,' I replied.

They had never heard of a Sikh. 'That's the same as "sheikh", isn't it? Aren't sheikhs musclemen?'

'Not sheikh, but Sikh,' I replied.

'Ah,' said the man triumphantly, 'then you must be from Sikkim.'

I gave up. We got talking. I asked them what they did. 'We have a little laundry business in Noo Yok,' he replied.

I could not blame them for not knowing anything about the Sikhs. What would an Indian dhobi know about Israel or the Jews?

Qurratulain Hyder—Aunty Subjantiwalli

Ask anyone who is knowledgeable about Urdu literature who he or she thinks was the best writer of fiction in the language, chances are that nine out of ten will reply: Qurratulain Hyder. If you probe them further on what they think her best work was, without hesitation they will answer: *Aag ka Darya* (*River of Fire*). The novel earned her the Sahitya Akademi award and the Jnanpith award. It is, deservedly, described as something of a trailblazer in Urdu fiction.

Qurratulain Hyder, or Annie Appa as she was known to her friends, was about the most erudite woman around. She wore her erudition on her sleeve and offloaded it in large dollops in her novels and short stories with didactic zeal. While regaling her readers with episodes from the past and the present, she wanted to educate them on subjects like history, geography, religion (Buddhism, Jainism, Hinduism, Islam), mysticism (both Sufi and Bhakti), rituals, Eastern and Western classical music as well as modern pop, poetry (Hindi, Urdu, English), flora and fauna. There was nothing in the world that Aunty Annie did not know and she wanted to make sure that her readers were impressed with her vast fund of knowledge. Most were.

River of Fire was Annie at her best. She spreads a vast canvas to paint on. She starts with Chandragupta and his minister Chanakya, deals with the conflicts between the established Buddhism and the resurgent Hinduism, the advent of Islam, establishment of

Muslim dynasties, arrival of European traders, dominance of the East India Company, English nabobs with harems of Indian bibis and their Eurasian offspring, the consolidation of British rule, upsurge of Indian nationalism, the mutiny of 1857, the First and Second World Wars, the Congress party, the Muslim League, the Partition of India and Pakistan, the post-Independence era up to 1956. It leaves the reader breathless. Hundreds of characters come and vanish from the scene. What stays in the reader's mind are Hindu and Muslim families of Lucknow, Jaunpur, Moradabad and Varanasi, bound by similar backgrounds and bonds of affection. 'In Lucknow history is yesterday,' asserts the author. It overtakes them and splits them apart. Some flee to England, some to Pakistan, some stay on in India where they cannot come to terms with the changed atmosphere; they cry in anguish, 'Why did you forsake me, India!'

A melancholic strain of nostalgia for the days gone by runs like a refrain throughout the novel. It is aptly summed up by Toru Dutt's lines:

O echo whose repose I mar
With my regrets and mournful cries
He comes...
I hear his voice afar,
Or is it thine that thus replied?
Peace: hark he calls!—in vain, in vain.
The loved & lost, comes not again.

River of Fire could have been the most powerful historical novel of India but for some minor, avoidable flaws. There are far too many passages which sound like so many words devoid of meaning. To wit:

The picture of the world was merely the Self which had been painted on the canvas of the Self. This was that pure existence, pure perception, pure life, the studio of the heart which contained all pictures, all imagination, where all images became one, where the same light kept passing through myriad-coloured glasses and all that which had been made with beauty and truth was a complete art-piece and a path, both for the creator and the beholder. And those who knew could understand.

This may be overlooked as expounding some abstruse aspect of Buddhist philosophy, but Hyder's penchant for depicting scenes was far too often stereotyped. She was not as close to nature as she set herself out to be. Her dhak (flame of the forest) flowers in Bhadon (the season of rains) when in fact it flowers for a few days around Holi. She put the battlefield of Plassey in a mango orchard; it was in a forest of palas (another name for flame of the forest). Her fair maidens sporting by river banks have magnolia petals dropping on their heads; there are very few magnolias in India and, unlike American and European trees of the species, have very sparse blossoms. Her hill partridges 'coo'; in fact, hill partridges make calls that grate on the ears.

Hyder insisted on translating her works into English herself: she was convinced she knew it as well as Urdu. So we have thees, thous along with yeah, yep, omigosh and get lost. But no one dared tell Annie Appa that she should allow someone else to handle her fiction. She was the Subjantiwalli. If *River of Fire* did not become the rage in English that it was in Urdu, she had only herself to blame.

Nehru the Man

Pandit Nehru should have been the role model for the prime ministers of India. He was adored by the masses as much as Mahatma Gandhi was. No other prime minister enjoyed the same public esteem. He was above prejudices of any kind: racial, religious or of caste. Being an agnostic, he refused to compromise his secular beliefs by indulging in ritual to gain acceptance. Though the Ganga meant much to him ('I see in its waters the story of India . . . the Ganga is a part of my life,' he wrote), he refused to bathe at the Sangam at the Kumbh Mela. He visited a few temples but only to admire their architecture and refused to worship any deities or accept prasad. He was convinced that religion had played a very negative role in Indian society. His successors exploited religious sentiment to gain political yardage. He was a visionary with precise notions on the India of the future. Being a leader in the true sense of the term he forced Indians to accept, at times unwillingly, his ideas of modernizing the country. He was the father of Indian constitutional democracy, of universal adult franchise, the five-year plans, giving equal rights to women and much else. This was largely due to the fact that he was better educated than any of his successors, with the exception of Manmohan Singh, and spent nine years in jail reading and writing and thinking about his country's tomorrows. He worked hard from early morning to well past midnight. He coined the slogan 'aaraam haraam hai'—to laze about is a sin. His name will go down in history among the greatest rulers of India.

61

Being human, Nehru had his human failings. K.F. Rustamji of the police service, who was for six years his special security officer and as close to him as his shadow, noted them down in his personal diary day after day. He donated his diaries to the Nehru Museum library and let his friend P.V. Rajagopal examine, select and publish them in book form. There is little in it that is not common knowledge but there are some observations about the foibles and eccentricities of the great man which make interesting reading. I was also for a brief period Nehru's shadow. When he came to London to attend the Commonwealth Prime Ministers' Conference, I was attached to him as his press officer. My observations tally with Rustamji's. The only difference is that while Rustamji adored him, I only admired him.

Rustamji saw more of the women in Nehru's life than I did. He mentions four: his sister Vijayalakshmi Pandit, Edwina Mountbatten, Padmaja Naidu and Mridula Sarabhai. Vijayalakshmi took pains to see that she appeared beside her brother in photographs published in papers. Padmaja, who was the plainest of the lot, was more vivacious than the others and enjoyed reading pornography. Mridula—known in the family as 'Boss' and who played a heroic role in rescuing abducted women from Pakistan and India during the Partition riots—tried to boss over Nehru. He had his own way of freeing himself from their possessiveness. Vijayalakshmi was appointed as an ambassador, Padmaja sent off as Governor of West Bengal, poor Mridula locked up in jail. Edwina could not claim exclusive rights on him as she was mostly in England. Of these ladies, the only one I did not meet was Padmaja Naidu.

Rustamji notes that Nehru was vain about his looks. He wore his Gandhi cap at a rakish angle and was never seen without it. He was bald as an egg. I noted that he insisted that every photograph taken by our photographers be shown to him before being released to the press. If one had caught him yawning, asleep or picking his nose, he tore it up with his own hands.

Rustamji has a lot to say about Nehru's unpredictable temper. If his breakfast was late, he stormed into the kitchen or the servants' quarters to berate his cook. Once, on a visit to Sira (in Mysore), 'he barged into the kitchen in a temper, like Jesus among the moneychangers, and almost chased out all the cooks from there,' Rustamji notes in his journal. At almost every public meeting, he found something wrong about the police bandobast to control the crowds lining his route and the distance at which milling crowds surrounded the platform. And he let everyone have it. Even before he became prime minister, he slapped the president of the Punjab Pradesh Congress Committee in full view of the crowd because the microphone went dead while he was speaking. Lashing out at unruly mobs became a habit. During a visit of the prime minister of Pakistan, Mohammed Ali, in 1953, Nehru was furious at the inadequate arrangements for containing the crowds: 'JN got angrier and angrier. He flung about—pushing people, running after cameramen, shouting, firing. I had never seen him so angry. Somebody opened the door of a car for him; he banged the door and beat people with a large, dishevelled bouquet,' Rustamji noted. However, his vocabulary of abuse was limited and the worst he could yell was badtameez or bewakoof. I was at the receiving end on two occasions. Once he arrived in London past midnight. I asked him if he would like me to accompany him to his hotel. 'Don't be silly; go home and sleep,' he ordered. Instead of going to his hotel, he drove to Lady Mountbatten's residence. The next morning one of the papers had a photograph of him with Lady Mountbatten in her negligee opening the door for him. He was furious. On another occasion he took Lady M out for a quiet dinner to a Greek restaurant. The proprietor recognized them and informed the press. Their photographs were in many papers. I was summoned to his presence. He gave me a withering look and said: 'You have a strange notion of publicity.' I thought it best not to say anything in my defence.

Like most Indians, Nehru treated Whites with more courtesy than his countrymen: he spoke on the same level with Whites but tended to talk down to Indians. At times he could forget his manners. Once I had to host a lunch for the editors of leading British newspapers to meet him. Halfway through the meal he fell silent. When a couple of questions were put to him, he simply looked up at the ceiling and did not reply. The questions froze in the air. As if to lend the air some warmth, he lit a cigarette while the others were still eating. To add to my discomfiture, Krishna Menon fell asleep. It was a disastrous attempt at public relations.

Rustamji noted that his idol was a tireless talker. He would start talking to men and women in the car taking him to the venue of his meeting. His rambling speeches would at times go on and on for over an hour while many in his audience dozed. In England his audiences were limited. I noted that even during musical performances Nehru, sitting in the middle of the front row, kept talking to the men and women sitting beside him. However, he did not indulge in gossip and small talk. When he met U Nu, the prime minister of Burma, his host tried to show off how interested he was in India. 'Panditji, I like your Vyjanthimala very much,' he said. Panditji turned to his 'shadow' and asked in Hindustani, '*Kaun hai yeh* Vyjanthimala?' U Nu also advised Nehru not to lose his temper at the conference. 'I will try my best,' Nehru replied. 'But if I do, U Nu, you must kick me hard under the table.'

While for the most part Rustamji bends over backwards to make allowances for his idol, he confesses that Nehru had his share of 'littleness': 'It would be difficult for a person who has not known JN from close to imagine what a petty, cantankerous man he could be at times. How rude and arrogant and full of prima donna tantrums—how irascible and selfish in small things! How childish and unbearably inconsiderate he was, not only to me but to those who were supposed to be his trusted advisers!

And more than anything else, how impossibly sure he could be of himself and his dictums.'

After six years of devoted service, Rustamji was replaced by another man as chief security officer. I was luckier. When Panditji came for the next Commonwealth meet I was no longer in government service.

SIR VIDIA

When I got the news of V.S. Naipaul being awarded the Nobel Prize for Literature, I was delighted and felt that I had been vindicated. I was delighted because I have known him as a friend for over thirty-five years. I have met his first wife, who was English, and get on famously with his charming, vivacious present wife, Nadira, who is Pakistani Punjabi. I met his late brother, Shiva, and saw quite a lot of his mother when she visited Delhi. Whether it was in Delhi or Bombay, throwing a party for Vidia was a must. I took him with me wherever I went. He liked being entertained and meeting new people. He never returned hospitality. That did not matter as everyone felt privileged to have him in their house and to be able to drop his name.

I feel vindicated because every time I wrote about him, I said he deserved the Nobel Prize for Literature as he was a much better writer than many other Nobel laureates. He handled the English language with greater finesse than any contemporary writer and his range of interests was wider: humour, history, travelogues, religion, the clash of civilizations, personal profiles. Why the coveted prize eluded him for so long I could only attribute to some kind of deep-seated prejudice against writers who did not write in their mother tongue or to political considerations. Although Naipaul is a Trinidad-born Hindu, English is his mother tongue and he is essentially an objective observer of political movements, bold enough to come to his own conclusions.

When I first met Naipaul, I had only read his *A House for Mr Biswas*. I sensed then that a new star had risen in the literary firmament. That book has remained my top favourite. I can't recall exactly how we met. Perhaps he rang me up from his hotel and I invited him and his English wife over to my home. I became his escort in Delhi. He was a shy man of few words. His wife was even shyer and hardly spoke. It was evident that they were not enjoying their visit to the land of his forefathers. She was under the weather, bothered by the heat, dust and pestilence of flies. One early morning I took them to Surajkund. We stood on a ridge, looking at the rock-strewn valley ablaze with flame of the forest in flower. Vidia looked at the scene for a long time. I thought I would read a memorable description of it in his next book. Then I took him to Tughlaqabad. I had brought sandwiches and coffee. As we sat munching our sandwiches, village urchins gathered around us. They had nothing but loincloths to cover their nakedness. Their eyes and noses were running and they had flies all over their faces. In *An Area of Darkness*, Naipaul dismissed the bewitching scene of the flame of the forest trees in flower in a couple of lines but had more to say about the semi-naked urchins with flies around their eyes. It was the same with his visit to Kashmir. He visited Pamposh on a moonlit night. He had less to say about the autumn crocus (saffron) scent pervading the atmosphere and more about Kashmiri women lifting their pherans and squatting to defecate. Squalor and stench attracted his attention more than scenic beauty and fragrance.

Naipaul could be very edgy. Once when I invited him to my flat to meet a few friends over drinks, he seemed to be getting on famously with an attractive Parsi lady. But as soon as she fished out a camera from her bag and asked, 'Do you mind if I take a photograph?' Vidia snapped back sourly: 'As a matter of fact, I do mind.' The poor woman was squashed. It took some time for the others to resume conversation.

At another time the owner of a big industrial house invited me to a cocktail reception at the Taj in Bombay. I took Naipaul and my son, Rahul, who had become closer to him than I was. When we entered the ballroom on time, there were very few guests who had arrived. But seated in a row were a few attractive girls. We made a beeline for them. I introduced Vidia and my son to them. None of them spoke English, nor were they related to our hosts. It transpired that they were call girls, invited for the amusement of the guests. For Naipaul, it was an insight into the methods adopted to promote business here.

Naipaul's *Among the Believers: An Islamic Journey* caused a lot of uneasiness among Muslims. Even Salman Rushdie accused him of harbouring anti-Muslim feelings. What Naipaul, in fact, wrote cannot be faulted. He observed that people who accepted Islam wrote off their pre-Islamic past. This phenomenon can be verified in Muslim countries today. In Egypt, the Pharaonic period which produced the pyramids, the Sphinx and many beautiful temples is only of historic interest, bringing in tourists and foreign exchange. It is the same in Pakistan. They have consigned their Hindu and Buddhist past to archives, museums and history books. Even the period of Sikh dominance is brushed aside as of little consequence. The destruction of the Buddhas in Bamiyan is a recent example of erasing a pre-Islamic past. This can be seen in all Muslim nations, including the most westernized like Turkey, Morocco and Tunisia. Naipaul did not invent this fact of history; he only exposed it.

I had the opportunity of interviewing Naipaul with Bhaichand Patel on 8 May 2000. He doesn't relish being interviewed. Patel and I were very exercised over the destruction of the Babri Masjid and heckled him for what was widely believed to be the Sangh Parivar's view of the act of vandalism. Naipaul stood his ground. He was an outside observer not concerned with the rights or wrongs of destroying a mosque. The phrase he used was explanatory: 'It was a balancing of history.' I interpreted this to imply that deep in the Hindu psyche was the resentment that Muslim invaders had destroyed hundreds of their temples. So what was so devilish about destroying a dilapidated old mosque?

Ever since Naipaul married the highly animated and attractive Nadira, he has mellowed a great deal. He is not as gruff and edgy as he was. And for good reason is writing about sex with remarkable candour and erotic artistry. For instance, *Half a Life: A Novel* has a few memorable episodes of lusty, adulterous encounters.

Half a Life is largely about people of mixed racial descent—half-castes, mestizos, mulattos, Euro-Africans and others—half-whites, half-browns or blacks. However physically desirable they may be, they remain socially unacceptable to the majority which prides itself on being pure-blooded. In a prefatory note, Naipaul describes his novel as 'an invention. It is not exact about the countries, periods or situations it appears to describe'. In fact, his story begins in India, travels to England and ends in a Portuguese colony on the west coast of Africa. The main theme in every country is miscegenation. In India, a Brahmin boy, instead of marrying a Brahmin girl approved of by his parents, takes a fancy to the plainest looking Harijan girl in his college. There is no way out because the girl's uncle is a powerful trade union leader. His niece's reputation has been compromised by the two being seen sitting together in the college classrooms and in a café. They marry and lose their castes. They have a son and a daughter who find it comfortable to pose as Christians. Meanwhile, the outcaste Brahmin, who is by now in deep trouble because of charges of corruption, seeks sanctuary in a temple, takes a vow of silence and becomes a minor godman. Amongst the celebrities who come for his darshan is Somerset Maugham. The father inserts Maugham's first name in the middle of his son's—Willie Somerset Chandran, the hero of Naipaul's story.

Willie Chandran gets a scholarship to study in a London college. He is armed with a letter from Somerset Maugham. His sister marries a middle-aged German with a family of his own and moves to Berlin with her husband. She covers revolutions with ethnic backgrounds in Cuba and the Latin American countries.

Willie Chandran has a shaky start but soon picks up a set of friends, English and coloured. He has no experience of sex and makes a hash of bedding the English girlfriend of his closest pal.

He also consorts with sundry prostitutes before falling in love with Ana, the daughter of a Portuguese man and a black African. Ana is light-skinned, very lovely and understanding. When Chandran's scholarship comes to an end, he has no job, little money and nowhere to go. He accepts Ana's proposal to accompany her to Africa where she has a large house and estate left to her by her father. It is a solitary existence in the wilderness, punctuated by Sunday luncheon parties in the homes of other estate owners. Ana stays faithful to Chandran; Chandran finds living with one woman somewhat boring and picks up liaisons with Graca, the wife of an estate manager. Naipaul has an inimitable way of analysing the genesis of desire in people's expressions. He writes: 'The first thing I noticed about her was her light-coloured eyes: disturbed eyes; they made me think again about her husband. And the second thing I noticed was that, for a second or two, no more, those eyes had looked at me in a way that no woman had looked at me before. I had the absolute certainty, in that second, that those eyes had taken me in not as Ana's husband or a man of unusual origin, but as a man who had spent many hours in the warm cubicles of the places of pleasure. Sex comes to us in different ways; it alters us; and I suppose in the end we carry the nature of our experience on our faces. The moment lasted a second. It might have been fantasy, that reading of the woman's eyes, but it was a discovery for me, something about women, something to be added to my sensual education.'

Chandran throws all caution to the winds and seeks Graca with insatiable lust as if his nirvana lay between the grey-eyed woman's thighs. 'The long drive had been a strain. Graca's need matched my own. That was new to me. Everything I had known before—the furtiveness of London, the awful provincial prostitute, the paid black girls of the places of pleasure here, who had yet satisfied me for so long, and for whom for almost a year I had felt such gratitude, and poor Ana, still in my mind the trusting girl who had sat on the settee in my college room in London and allowed herself to be kissed, Ana still so gentle and generous—over the next half-hour everything fell away, and I thought how terrible it would have been if, as could so easily have happened, I had died without knowing this depth of satisfaction, this other person that I had just discovered within myself. It was worth any price, any consequence.'

There are two things about all books written by V.S. Naipaul: they are eminently readable and each one has something new to say. He is an outstanding master-craftsman of letters with varied interests. Once you start reading a Naipaul book, you can't put it down till you have finished it. This cannot be said about many writers of today.

Amrita Sher-Gil

I met Amrita Sher-Gil twice and we wrote to each other a couple of times. I was among the handful of mourners present at her cremation in Lahore on 7 December 1941. She was only twenty-eight. I can hardly claim to have known her. However, she left a lasting impression on my mind—not because she came to be recognized as a great painter but because she was the most unusual woman I'd met.

Amrita was the elder of two daughters of a part-Jewish Hungarian mother, Marie Antoinette Gottesmann, and a Sikh father, Umrao Singh Sher-Gil, a widower with children from his first wife. He came from a distinguished, aristocratic family owning farmland, many houses and a large sugar mill at Saraya (UP). But Marie, a hard-headed, eccentric woman interested in the fine arts and music, went wrong in her calculations. She readily espoused the long-bearded and beturbaned sardar under the impression that he was a very wealthy landowner, only to find that he in fact drew a measly pension from his family and was deeply involved in studying ancient Sanskrit and Persian texts and spent long hours watching stars at night. It was a misalliance from the start: she cheated on him, having affairs that came her way. It remained so till she shot herself in the head with his shotgun in their Simla home on 31 July 1948.

Both Amrita and her sister, Indira, were born in Budapest, were baptized as Roman Catholics and spent the first years of their lives there. At a very early age, Amrita took to drawing pictures, and Indira to playing the piano. The family moved to

Paris where the sisters pursued their studies, one in painting, the other in music. Amrita won recognition at École des Beaux-Arts. She grew conscious of her good looks. Marie encouraged her daughter using her charms to snare well-to-do men with a view to matrimony. An early suitor was Yusuf Ali Khan, the son of the Nawab of Akbarpur. He made her pregnant and infected her with venereal disease as well. She turned to her cousin, Victor Egan, a medical student, to get rid of the unwanted foetus and the disease. Amrita remained reckless in her affairs with men and women throughout her short life. One of her lovers, Malcolm Muggeridge, wrote 'that she was really a virgin because she'd never experienced the spiritual equivalent of copulation: she had many lovers but they'd left no scar. I'll leave a scar'. He failed to leave any scar but noted Amrita's obsession with herself and boasting about her lovers.

Back home in India, Amrita was eager to win recognition. She found two champions: Karl Khandalavala, a noted art critic in Bombay, and fellow Hungarian, Charles Fabri, who lived in Lahore. Both acclaimed her as, perhaps, the greatest painter of the century. Despite the build-up, she found few buyers. She travelled across India with her canvases. Nawab Salar Jung of Hyderabad kept her paintings for a few days but returned them. She tried the maharaja of Mysore but he preferred Ravi Varma's calendar art to hers.

Amrita was not as beautiful as she fancied herself and depicted in her self-portraits. She was fair, petite, with large, searching eyes and full lips. She wore bright-coloured saris and large beaded jewellery. She was liberal in the use of cosmetics and doused herself in perfume. Amrita attracted attention by her flamboyance wherever she went. Amongst her admirers was Pandit Nehru. She had countless lovers: her ravenous appetite for sex was legendary. She did not waste time in preliminaries. If her lover took too long to make the first move, she simply stripped and lay down on the carpet, naked. Badruddin Tyabji gave a vivid description of his encounter with her one winter's night in Simla.

Controversy pursued Amrita to her last and continues to this day. When she was taken ill, she put it down to food poisoning. The other and more reliable version is that she was pregnant and her cousin-husband, Victor, botched up the abortion. After her death, her mother accused Victor of having murdered her. He was lucky as the day after Amrita died England declared war on Hungary and Victor was put in jail as an enemy national.

ME AND MY FILTHY LUCRE

I did not know why money is called filthy lucre. There is nothing filthy about a wad of crisp, new currency notes; nor shining silver rupee or five-rupee coins. Now I know. At the first World Punjabi Conference in Chandigarh, the convenors gave me a copy of the citation stating why I had been among the chosen Punjabis of the millennium, a silver plaque with two coins of the earliest Sikh currency with inscriptions in Persian on both sides and a blue velvet pouch with a golden string. It contained the prize money of Rs 1,00,000. I expected it to be a crossed cheque; it was cash, a bundle of five-hundred-rupee notes.

My troubles began. I hurried back to Hotel Shivalik View, I had invited A.S. Deepak and Vandana Shukla to join me for lunch. I put the velvet bag containing the notes on the table so that I could keep my eyes on it.

'You want me to count them?' asked Deepak. 'It may be more than one lakh.'

I declined his offer. 'It will take you all afternoon to do so. It may be less than the promised one lakh.'

After lunch, I went to my room to have a siesta. I locked the door from the inside, put my things in my bag but held the velvet bag under my pillow and dozed off. I woke up to make sure the bag was still there. And then dozed off again.

The room bell rang. I opened the door to let in two janitors. They said they had come to check if all the light bulbs were functioning. I had not complained about any having fused. They changed one bulb. I became suspicious.

I had to go to dine with the Kaushiks—Anil, who was in the Indian police service, and his wife, Sharda. I took the money with me. I could not put all of it in my pockets and so gave some of it to Deepak, who had come to fetch me, to put in his coat pocket.

In the Kaushiks' home, I mentioned the problem of having so much cash on my person. 'Let's have a look,' said Anil. He felt the wad of currency notes. 'Have you counted them?' he asked.

'No,' I replied, 'I will do that in Delhi.'

Back in my hotel room, I bolted the door from the inside, put the velvet pouch under my pillow and switched off the lights. I slept fitfully. Every little noise outside woke me up. I switched on the lights to make sure no one had broken into my room. I felt under my pillow to make sure the velvet pouch was still there. I must have got up at least four times that night, the longest of the year. I was finally woken up by the operator announcing it was 6 a.m. and the room bearer bringing in a tray with a glass of fresh orange juice and coffee. My throat was sore. I went down with a heavy cold. It was the one lakh rupees in cash which brought it on.

On the train to Delhi, I hugged the pouch against my chest. It was very awkward with a running nose and streaming eyes. However, I managed to get the money safely home. I dumped the pouch in my granddaughter's lap and said, 'Take the bloody lucre as a New Year gift.' And soon my nose stopped dripping and my eyes stopped watering. That proves how filthy lucre can be.

Mrs G: The Wonder that Was Indira

Indira Gandhi was a very good-looking woman, not of the pin-up kind but an indescribable aristocratic type. She reminded me of Hilaire Belloc's lines:

Her face was like the King's command
When all the swords are drawn.

Amongst the many men who were bowled over by her looks was President Lyndon Johnson of the United States. Just before a dinner hosted by the Indian ambassador, B.K. Nehru, and his wife, Fori, for Indira at which Vice President Hubert Humphrey was to be the guest of honour, Lyndon Johnson stayed on tossing glass after glass of bourbon on the rocks while talking to Indira. He readily agreed to stay on for dinner to which he had not been invited. At a reception at the White House, Lyndon Johnson asked Indira to dance with him. She refused on the grounds that it would hurt her image in India. The President understood. He wanted to see that 'no harm comes to the girl'. He sanctioned three million tons of wheat and nine million dollars in aid to India.

The only person on record who made derogatory references to Indira's looks and intelligence (or rather the lack of them) was her aunt, Vijayalakshmi Pandit. Indira never forgave her or her daughters for slighting her. She never forgave anyone who said anything against her.

She was equally touchy about her health. While still a girl she was suspected of having tuberculosis (her mother had died of the disease). She had regular medical check-ups. Most doctors who examined her advised her against having children. 'If it had been up to me, I would have had eleven . . . this diagnosis provoked me, it infuriated me.' It was her husband, Feroze Gandhi, who wanted only two.

Almost as if to prove the doctors wrong, she undertook arduous journeys on horseback, on elephants and on foot, covering vast distances and carrying out punishing schedules of speeches to large audiences across the country. In the elections following her defeat after the Emergency she toured northern India for days, sleeping less than four hours at night. She turned up at a dinner hosted by the German ambassador looking as fresh as the proverbial daisy. When I asked her how she did not feel fagged out, she replied: 'Tiredness is a state of the mind, not of the body.'

There was much speculation about Indira's private life. She admitted to Pupul Jayakar that while she was a student at Santiniketan she'd fallen in love with a German who taught her French. They continued to exchange correspondence till she married Feroze Gandhi. Though advised against marrying a Parsi with no family background, by her father and Mahatma Gandhi (Vijayalakshmi advised her to take him on as a lover rather than as a husband), she stuck to her resolve and married him with their blessings. It was only after his infidelities that the marriage turned sour. He flirted with Indira's cousins, had affairs with Tarakeshwari Sinha, Mehmuna Sultana, Subhadra Joshi and others. Indira temporarily broke up with him but, as often happens, she forgave her husband. Not, however, the women who had associated with him.

It was after the publication of M.O. Mathai's autobiography that some of Indira's affairs came to light. Mathai claimed to have been Indira's lover for twelve years and once made her pregnant. She had to have an abortion. Mathai lost out to Indira's yoga teacher, Dhirendra Brahmachari, and later to Dinesh Singh who was a minister in her cabinet. The historian S. Gopal believes Mathai's relationship with Indira had crossed permissible limits; B.K. Nehru supports him: 'It is more fact than fiction,' he told Katharine Frank. I knew the three men. Mathai was a singularly unattractive man with little to say for himself. But people under the public gaze cannot afford to have liaisons with persons of their choice. The body has its own compulsions and finds outlets that are easily available. Mathai was a live-in secretary-stenographer. Though I regard spilling the beans after enjoying intimacy with a person a most ungentlemanly thing to do, I am willing to believe that for some years Mathai was Indira's lover. Dhirendra Brahmachari was a tall, handsome Bihari who had an hour with Indira behind closed doors every morning. Yoga lessons may have ended up with lessons from the *Kamasutra*. As for Dinesh Singh, it was he who allowed gossip about his relations with the prime minister to spread. At many late-night dinners in the homes of diplomats, he arranged for messages to be sent that Indira would like him to drop in on her on his way home.

None of this tittle-tattle should be allowed to cloud the image of Indira Gandhi as a great leader. She had dictatorial tendencies, indulged in gross favouritism, overlooked corruption and systematically undermined democratic institutions. She wanted to set up dynastic succession. She manipulated and gagged the press. She may not have been averse to having people who knew too much from being bumped off, as Frank seems to suggest in her book. Men like Ram Manohar Lohia who described her as a goongi gudiya or Morarji Desai who called her a chhokree were wide off the mark. Maneka was closer to the real Indira Gandhi in comparing her with the goddess Kali who drank human blood. She was able to get away with what she did because India's poor millions loved her as Amma—Mother.

The Emergency has become an ugly word to be used to malign Indira Gandhi. Frank points out that it was Jayaprakash Narayan's call for 'total revolution', including gheraos of legislative assemblies and the Parliament, that justified the draconian measure. When first imposed, it was generally welcomed. And it was not so much Indira but the people around her who misused its provisions to settle personal scores or enrich themselves. They included her son, Sanjay, his wife, Maneka, and her mother, Amteshwar, family friend Mohammed Yunus, civil servants Krishan Chand (Lt Governor of Delhi), Navin Chawla and a few others. Indira understandably had a say in drawing up the list of people who were to be arrested. The Rajmata of Gwalior and Gayatri Devi of Jaipur were locked up in Tihar jail along with common prostitutes; Amteshwar (described as 'flamboyant, aggressive') and Maneka ('cigarette-smoking . . . loud, boisterous, uninhibited . . . disrespectful of her mother-in-law . . . highly discordant presence' in Indira's 'haven of peace') had their own pet hates they wanted to cut to size; Navin Chawla, according to the Shah Commission, 'not only specified who should be arrested and jailed but also how they should be treated in prison'. His orders included 'the construction of special cells with asbestos roofs to bake' in the summer heat; Mohammed Yunus ordered the information and broadcasting minister to close down the BBC office and arrest its correspondent, Mark Tully, 'pull down his trousers, give him a few lashes and send him to jail'. Indira could not have known that all this was being done in her name. During the Emergency, the reins of power had slipped out of her hands and were grabbed by her son, Sanjay.

There was a strong streak of vengefulness in Indira Gandhi. This came out in all its ugliness in her dealings with her younger daughter-in-law, Maneka. She never liked her or her mother. After Sanjay—whom she both loved and feared—died, she made Maneka unwelcome in her home and showed a marked preference for Sonia. She behaved like any village mother-in-law would.

Another characteristic Indira developed after years of being in power was to snub people who least expected it. At my repeated requests, she agreed to see Kewal Singh who had been her foreign secretary and ambassador in Washington. She berated him till he broke down. She did the same to Jagat Mehta whose posting, as ambassador to Germany, she cancelled after it had been accepted. Her special venom was directed towards her cousin, Nayantara Sahgal. First she superceded Mangat Rai who was living with Nayantara. Then she revoked Sahgal's appointment by Morarji Desai as ambassador to Rome. But in my own way, I admired, loved and feared Indira.

J.R.D. TATA

India owes more to the house of Tata than to any other industrial family for putting it on the path of self-sufficiency in areas vital for its survival in the modern world. They were pioneers in many fields, from the production of steel, hydel power, airlines, automobiles and nuclear research down to the production of cosmetics and tea. And in every undertaking they strove to make their products as good, if not better, than their rivals'. Along with these money-making enterprises, they built hospitals, educational institutions and extended patronage to the arts. More significantly, while other industrial houses were not averse to kowtowing to ministers and civil servants to get their deals through, the Tatas maintained high standards of rectitude (unique to Parsi industrialists and professionals), untainted by personal greed. Till recent years, the Tata board of management was entirely Parsi.

The Tata success story began when Jamshedji Tata (1839–1904) set up a company to mine coal and iron ore in Bihar. In the years to come, it became India's largest steel production centre; the city that grew around it was renamed Jamshedpur. The real diversification and spectacular upsurge in the Tatas' fortunes came during J.R.D.'s fifty-two-year tenure at the helm of its affairs. He took over as chairman at the age of thirty-four and guided its course till he died in 1993.

Jehangir Tata (Jeh to his friends) was born in Paris. His father was Parsi, his mother, French. He spent the better part of his younger days in Paris, and French was his mother tongue. He was sent to a grammar school in England for two years. Being hard-working and studious, he picked up English and began to speak it as fluently as French. He was anxious to join Cambridge but his father summoned him to Bombay to join the family business. He developed a chip on his shoulder for never having gone to university. Bombay was his home for the rest of his life. Though he frequently asserted being an Indian (many Parsis do so grudgingly), neither his biography nor his letters reveal whether or not he could speak Gujarati or any other Indian language.

How much of a Parsi was he? In a letter, J.R.D. wrote: 'I am anything but a good Zoroastrian, at least in the sense of being a practising one.' I'm not sure if he ever went inside an agiary—the Parsi fire temple.

J.R.D. was unabashed about the positive role of capitalism in a developing country. The word had become synonymous with 'bloodsuckers of the poor'. He took up cudgels on its behalf against the half-baked socialism preached by Nehru and JP.

Flying and fast cars were his abiding passions. He was the first Indian to get a flying licence and competed in the Aga Khan Trophy for the fastest flight from London to India. He was beaten to the second place by another Parsi, Aspy Engineer (later Air Chief Marshal of the Indian air force). He knew every new kind of airplane from two-seaters to jumbo jets. It was the same with racing cars, his favourite being a Bugatti.

J.R.D. had a very sharp eye for detail. Every time he travelled on his own Air India planes, he put down his suggestions: why did the coffee and tea taste the same? Why two paper bags of sugar with each cup? Why were the omelettes leathery? When staying in one of the Taj Hotels, he noted that one large double bed disturbed the sleep of elderly couples; telephones in the bedroom and the bathroom should have separate numbers. When sent a sample of Lakmé products, he tried out every item from shaving creams, deodorants and colognes and compared them with the best products abroad. Once visiting Rashtrapati Bhavan, he noticed a gaffe under the portrait of the President. It read

'President swearing at ceremony'. He wrote to Babu Rajendra Prasad informing him of the difference between swearing in and swearing at.

J.R.D. led a full life and departed without any regrets. The last words he spoke were in French: 'I am about to discover a new world. It is going to be very interesting.' Jeh's been gone for many years but his footprints will remain indelibly printed on the sands of time.

On Old Age

Whenever my son, living in Mumbai, was asked why he was going to Delhi, his reply was 'to see my A. Pees'. AP stood for aged parents. Now that he is himself what in modern parlance is described as a senior citizen, and his mother has passed away, he answers the same question, saying 'to see old Pop'.

With the passing of generations, younger people's attitude towards the old has changed. When I was a young man, we used to describe aged people as oldies, or worse sattreah bahattreah (feeble-minded in his seventies). Now persons in their seventies are not considered old. New attitudes and a sizeable vocabulary have been evolved to describe them. For one, their way to show respect to the aged is to keep a respectful distance from them. So we have old people's homes, a good distance from the homes they once lived in and ruled over. There is much to be said in favour of old people's homes. The few that I have visited in England and USA are as luxurious as any five-star hotel; separate cottages with modern amenities like world radio and TV, spacious dining and sitting rooms where you can meet and chat with others in your own age group; light, tasty food and wines, billiard rooms, card tables for bridge, rummy or patience. There are spacious lawns and flower beds. Above all, there are nurses and doctors in attendance round the clock. They cost a packet. Inmates are happy blowing up their life's savings to live out their last days in comfort because they are aware they can't take anything with them when they go. Their offspring don't grudge pitching in because they are relieved of the responsibility of looking after their parents and can get on with their own lives. The notion of a family gathered around the bed of a dying patriarch or matriarch is as dead as a dodo.

However much I approve of old people's homes, I resent being described as a gerry (for geriatric), old boomer, fuddy-duddy, gaffer or old fogey, codger, coot, geezer, etc. Some new coinages like dinosaur, fossil, cotton top, cranky, crumbly are downright offensive. Eighty years ago Chesterton wrote in his essay, 'The Prudery of Slang': 'There was a time when it was customary to call a father a father . . . Now, it appears to be considered a mark of advanced intelligence to call your father a bean or a scream. It is obvious to me that calling the old gentleman "father" is facing the facts of nature. It is also obvious that calling him a "bean" is merely weaving a graceful fairytale to cover the facts of nature.' Call us oldies or what you will, but bear in mind that just as a *saas bhi kabhi bahu thi* (the mother-in-law was once a bride), you too will one day become an old person, and slang words like codger, geezer or fuddy-duddy can be hurtful even to an oldie who is hard of hearing.

I am not quite deaf but getting more hard of hearing by the day. Friends are too polite to draw my attention to my growing infirmity but members of my family are more outspoken. My wife who has been dead for many years, never spared me when I asked her to repeat what she said. Each time said, *'Hain?'* she would snap back: 'Dora! Why don't you have your ears examined?'

Now every time a stranger calls on me, my son, if he is around, tells him or her, 'Speak a little loudly. My Pop is hard of hearing.' And the other day my daughter asked me, 'Aren't you thinking of getting a hearing aid?'

There are pros and cons about hearing aids. I had a Canadian friend, a well-known art critic who had one connected to a battery tucked into his front pocket. I asked him if it was a nuisance. 'No,' he replied firmly. 'I have it switched on when I am out on the road so that I can hear cars hoot to get out of their way.

I also have it on when attending musical concerts. It's only at parties when people begin to bore me that I switch it off and switch on a smile to appear as if I am all ears.'

Two of my friends acquired hearing aids: Prem Kirpal, at ninety-six, got one from Paris at the enormous price of Rs 1.5 lakh. He hardly ever used it. When I asked him why, he replied: 'The battery will run out and I'll have to get another one from Paris.'

Bharat Ram, who was the same age as me, also used a hearing aid but had to cup his ears to catch what anyone was saying. The artist Satish Gujral lost his hearing as a child and was more than able to cope with life: he was able to teach himself to speak in English without being able to hear what he was saying. Then he found a living hearing aid in his comely wife, Kiran, who has taught him to read her lips and hand gestures. He gets over his handicap by doing most of the talking and reducing what he has to hear to the minimum. Some years ago he went to Australia for an ear surgery which would restore his hearing to normal. For some months he kept up the pretence that he could hear sounds he hadn't heard before. Actually the surgery did nothing for him. He is back to his more reliable hearing aid—his wife.

I am not yet a gone case. I can hear people sitting close to me without much difficulty. I have problems hearing people who speak too softly, go on at the speed of machine-gun fire or go on interminably mimi, mim, mimi. Then I assume the mien of the smiling Buddha and occasionally grunt to indicate I am following what is being said. My only fear is that the person might ask me a question. I answer it with a benign smile. I also have problem answering telephone calls. Young people, mainly girls, are awed, as if they were talking to an ogre, and say what they have to at a breathless speed. I have to admonish them, 'Please speak slowly and clearly as I am hard of hearing. It would be better if you spelt out what you have to say on paper. I can see better than I can hear.'

So far I have got away with it. I still enjoy classical music on my satellite radio, follow the news and comments on TV channels. If I am hard of hearing, it's other people's problem, not mine. But use a hearing aid to help them out? No. I often wonder if deaf people are cremated or buried with ear plugs and batteries or sent to the other world as deaf as they were on the day they died.

Sometimes old people in their eighties write to me about the problems of life in its decline. They complain about increasing helplessness, being neglected by their sons, daughters-in-law and grandchildren. Their chief complaint is loneliness: they do not know how to pass their time. Being old, they get little sleep and are up well before dawn. They believe in God, say their prayers, go to temples, gurdwaras and churches or offer namaaz five times a day; and yet time hangs heavy on them. What are they to do?

I am older than most of them. I have old-age problems like rotting teeth having to be replaced by false ones, glasses changed periodically because my vision is getting poorer by the day, having to use hearing aids, carrying a walking stick to prevent myself from falling, taking dozens of pills against fluctuating blood pressure, an enlarged prostate, an irregular heartbeat, etc. But I manage to get at least six hours of sleep at night, despite having to get up twice or thrice to empty my bladder, and another hour in the afternoon. I, too, get up before dawn.

Since I do not believe in God or prayers, my mind turns to more earthly problems. Will my bowels move properly this morning? Should I drink more orange-carrot juice and glasses of water to help me clear my stomach? When I get a good clearing, I am relieved and happy. When I do not, it weighs on my mind. I am edgy and ill-tempered. It affects my work. I do not grumble about being neglected by my children and grandchild. They do their best to look after my needs—see that I eat what I want, take me to doctors, dentists and opticians. They know I prefer to be left alone, so they leave me alone. Time does not hang heavy on me because I always have something to occupy my mind. My days pass as swiftly as a weaver's shuttle.

What advice do I give them? First, reduce your dependence on others to the very minimum and do your best to be as self-sufficient as you can. Fill your time by doing things that occupy your mind and time. Don't waste time on muttering prayers you don't understand but meditate by stilling your mind from wandering. A minute or two will be good enough. If you can't read or watch TV because they strain your eyes, listen to good music on your radio with complete attention. Sit in a park and watch birds, butterflies and insects—not just look at them but watch them closely, try to identify them, read about them and add to your knowledge of nature. Cultivate hobbies like collecting stamps, preserving leaves and flowers, origami—whatever you fancy. Even learn how to knit your own sweaters and socks. Free yourself of the hunger for human company. Befriend dogs, cats, birds—they will respond to your affection more than human beings. Equally important is to cut down on your food intake. Get up from your dining table with hunger unfulfilled: you will then look forward to enjoying your next meal and keep thinking about it. What you eat and drink will taste better. When fully occupied mentally, time will never hang heavy on you. You wake up and before you realize it the day is over and it is time to retire to bed for the night. You will enjoy sound sleep.

Both Zohra Sehgal, who is two years older than me, and her Pakistani sister, Uzra Butt, who is two years my junior, are fitter than I am, both in mind and body. Zohra has a phenomenal memory. She can recite reams of Urdu poetry by the hour without looking at a scrap of paper; I learnt Uzra does much the same in Lahore. The two sisters conceived, concocted and enacted a dialogue between them, *Ek Tthee Nani* (Once There Was a Grandmother), which draws packed houses in India and Pakistan. What is the secret of their physical and mental fitness? From Zohra I gathered she eats very little and lives largely on soups and broths. She spends an hour every morning on the roof strolling about and refreshing her memory of Urdu poetry. She has cut down her social life to the minimum and refuses to give interviews either on the phone or in person unless it is paid for. I chided her when she came to wish me on my ninetieth birthday. I said, 'Zohra, I hear you charge a fee for talking to anyone. Is that true?' She beamed a smile and held out the open palm of her hand, '*Haan*—yes, *lao* fees *do*, pay me at once.'

From Uzra I picked up another clue to longevity. The sisters had been with Prithvi Theatre and then with Uday Shanker's dance troupe doing Bharatanatyam. I once asked Uzra whether she was still dancing. 'There are not many takers for Bharatanatyam in Pakistan. But this time in India I have been learning Odissi—it is less mechanical and more sensuous. I find it more fulfilling.' I was amazed: to learn a new form of dance at the age of eighty-eight is truly defying the passage of the years. Clearly, if you want to prolong your life, look forward to doing something in the tomorrows to come.

It is most important that an old person reconciles himself to the fact that he has become old and does not try to behave like a young man; if he does so, he will only make an ass of himself. It has been truly said: *Jawaanee jaatee rahee/ Aur hamein pataa bhee na chalaa/ Usee ko dhoond rahey hain/ Kamar jhukai hooey* (Youth had fled/ And I did not know about it/I seek for it on the ground/ With my back bent double).

No matter how well a person may look after himself, with age, parts of his body begin to decay. Teeth rot and have to be replaced with dentures. That necessitates radical changes in our diet. No more tough meat or vegetables or fruit that need to be bitten into with sharp teeth. So in every home that has an old man, a parallel menu has to be made to cater to his needs. Eyes go bleary. Lucky is an old man who does not have to wear spectacles and is able to read newspapers or watch television. I still do both but only just.

Hearing becomes defective and one may need a hearing aid. I am sure my hearing is sound but my friends tell me it is not. Memory begins to play tricks. I still pride myself on mine: I can recite passages of poetry by the yard and hardly ever consult the telephone directory to dial a number. But I do forget faces, even those of pretty girls, and have problems recalling names. It does not bother me very much.

What bothers me is having to slow down, and my inability to walk without the help of a walking stick. I recall the days of my youth when I walked from Simla to Narkanda and back non-stop—72 miles. Now I am reduced to doing a few rounds of my little garden and am scared of walking on an uneven path lest I stumble and break one of my bones. That is often the prelude to the end of an old man's life. Old people become slothful, slovenly and lazy. I never suffered from the daily bath fetish. I find rubbing the vital parts of my body with a damp towel as cleansing as immersing myself in a tub or pouring lota-fulls of water on my body. I no longer bother to change for the night and sleep in the same clothes I wear all day long. When I eat, soup, daal and curry drip on my beard and on to my shirt. People around me find it repulsive. I could not care less.

More serious is the problem created by an enlarged prostate gland. The urge to empty one's bladder often does not give one the time to get to a urinal. You wet your trousers or salwar. It is best to pretend you splashed water carelessly. Others know the truth but maintain a polite silence.

With old age, values change. Bowel movements become sluggish. One has to resort to laxatives to ensure proper evacuation. It's odd but an old man's day begins with worrying about his bowels. If he gets a clear evacuation he feels as if he has conquered the fort of Chittorgarh. If he does not, he remains cranky for the rest of the day.

I keep going with the help of a variety of pills, twenty every day. I grumble but I know they keep me alive and kicking.

It is true that a person is himself not aware of the passage of years: he may have turned grey, lost his teeth, become hard of hearing and may barely be able to see, but his vanity prevents him from accepting that he has grown old and senile.

It is other people, mostly children, who rudely remind him that he has aged. Boys and girls who used to call him uncle start addressing him as daadoo or naanoo. The other day a family accosted me in Lodhi park. The mother asked her four-year-old son to touch my feet. The child looked me up and down, shouted 'buddha'—old fellow—and ran away. I was mortified.

I delude myself that I have not really become a buddha. My friends have but I still have a sparkle in my eyes and my heart is as young as it ever was. One of my lady friends, twenty years younger than me, is now a grandmother and has turned grossly fat. I continue to pay her compliments as I did thirty years ago when she was fair and saucy. The truth is encapsulated in another couplet:

Begum, teri husn ke hukkey mein aanch nahin;
Ik ham hee hain
Ki phir bhi gudgudai jaatey hain.
(Begum, there is no fire left
In the hookah of your beauty;
It is only I who still keeps drawing on it.)

You can't do very much about old age. It creeps up on you at a snail's pace to start with, then gathers speed in your middle age, and before you know it, you are an old man or woman. The symptoms appear in different people at different times: hair starts turning grey; some people start greying in their thirties, others in their fifties or sixties; some manage to have black hair into their seventies.

Many dye their hair and beards to appear younger than they are and manage to fool others for some time, but not themselves. There are changes in the body that make you aware of the relentless march of time. Your teeth begin to decay. Every time you visit your dentist, he yanks one out till all are gone and he fits you with dentures that look whiter than the originals.

Once again, the age when people start losing their teeth varies enormously. Some lose them in their forties, others go to their graves or funeral pyres in their eighties or nineties taking all their thirty-two originals with them. The same applies to the eyes and ears; some wear glasses while still at school; others need no visual aid till the end of their days.

Some begin to turn hard of hearing by middle age and need hearing aids; others never have hearing problems.

The most important milestone in people's lives is the state of their libido. Both men and women regard a declining interest in sex as a sure indicator of ageing. With men this is more dramatic than with women, who can enjoy sex long after their menopause. Men continue to fantasize about it all their lives but sometime after they have completed the biblical span of seventy years, they find their bodies unable to fulfil their desire; their minds remain as potent as ever, their organs let them down.

And they have to accept that they are into old age and the fun has gone out of their lives. This is what men need most—as Nazeer Akbara Bedi put it: *Har cheez se hota hai bura burhaapa/ Aashiq ko to Allah na dikhlaaye burhaapa.* (Of all things that happen, the worst is old age/ May Allah never afflict a lover with old age.)

Men never give up the hope of recovering their youth. They try all sorts of elixirs, aphrodisiacs (kushtas) and now Viagra to retain their potency. They may succeed in restoring a little self-confidence and ability to perform. Women find it harder than men to accept old age. They are prone to lying about it and use cosmetics liberally to hide their wrinkles. It takes a brave man to go on paying compliments to an old flame in her older incarnation.

Very reluctantly men give up hope of recovering their youth. The French comedian and singer, Maurice Chevalier, very rightly remarked, 'When you hit seventy, you eat better, you sleep more soundly, you feel more active than when you were thirty. Obviously, it is healthier to have women on your mind than on your knees.'

Chevalier also has the ultimate answer to growing old: 'Old age isn't bad when you consider the alternative.'

Old age need not be an unmitigated curse. It has many advantages. You are freed of ambition to achieve more. 'Of making many books, there is no end and much study is weariness of the flesh,' says the Bible. One can take liberties with young girls because they know and you know it will never go beyond a warm hug. One can get away with bad manners; people forgive you as a cranky, old grey-beard.

In my nineties, I enjoy reading pornography. Old bawdy songs come back to my mind. One favourite used to be a Punjabi doggerel about a white bearded lusty loony. It began with *'toomba vajdaee na, taar bina* (she cannot live without her lover)'. It went on to describe the antics of the buddha baba who was *'vadda bajogee'* (great miracle man, very clever). He made love to a she-camel by climbing a ladder; he spent the night in the brothel and left his companion with a counterfeit four-anna piece (*'chavanni khotee'*). Old age need not be dull or boring.

When I was the editor of *Hindustan Times*, I was usually the first to be in office and the last of the editorial staff to return home, often after midnight. K.K. Birla who owned the paper once asked me, *'Sardar sahib, aap ka* retire *hone ka koi* programme *nahin hai?'* I replied, *'Birlaji,* retire *to main Nigambodh Ghat mein hi hoonga'*—meaning that I would give up work only when I was carried feet first to the cremation ground. I was then in my seventies. Now I am past ninety and am having second thoughts on the subject. I still manage to rise at 4.30 a.m. and work almost non-stop till 7 p.m. Not being religious, I do not waste time on prayer or meditation. My motto still remains 'Work is worship but worship is not work'. I hope I will be able to stick to this motto till the last day of my life.

However, I am coming around to the view that there may be something in the traditional Hindu belief of the four stages of human existence—Brahmacharya (bachelorhood), Grihastha (house-holder), Vaanprastha (retiring to a forest abode) and

Sanyasa (solitude), each of a span of twenty-five years. Guru Nanak described what happens to person who lives into the nineties. In a hymn in Raga Mauha, he wrote (I use G.S. Makin's translation from *The Essence of Sri Guru Granth Sahib*): 'A human being spends the first ten years of his life in childhood, up to 20 years in growing up, at 30 he blossoms into a handsome youth, at 40 he attains full growth: at 50 he starts feeling weak: at 60 he feels old, at 70 he feels the weakening of his senses, at 80 he is not capable of doing any work and at 90 he keeps lying down and does not understand the basic reasons of all the weaknesses.'

Nature has its own calendar of ageing. Human societies in different parts of the world have evolved norms to suit their social structure. By nature's calendar, both males and females may be regarded to be in their infancy till they are old enough to procreate, that is in the case of the female when she begins to menstruate and in that of the male when he is able to fertilize the female. However, human societies prescribe different ages for when they are allowed to do so. So we have legal bars against marriages below certain ages and we provide deterrents against having too many children. The common use of contraceptives makes this possible. The reproductive phase of females comes to an end with menopause, while that of males lasts much longer but with rapidly decreasing capability. Both males and females are at the peak of their physical prowess between the ages of eighteen and thirty-five. Thereafter their bodies begin to decline but their mental faculties remain unimpaired for many more years to come. Nevertheless, man-made rules require them to retire by the time they are sixty. So is human nature in conflict with human rites and laws throughout a person's existence? In addition, medical sciences have made spectacular advances which ensure us much longer lives in good health than our ancestors could have envisaged. Their neatly made-up calendars of the spans and stages of life no longer hold good.

Guru Nanak lived for seventy years (1469–1539). With the kind of medicines and medical expertise available at that time, one can well understand that by fifty, a man started feeling weak; at sixty old, at seventy his senses (sight, hearing, taste, etc.) began to deteriorate, by eighty he was unfit to do any work and at ninety he was largely confined to his charpoy. As one of the Guru's followers, I can cite my own case. I am past ninety. Although my vision is poor, I am hard of hearing and can only hobble around my house, I do not spend most of my time lying in bed. I work much harder than I have ever before. Among my present-day preoccupations is to read the Guru's bani and translate it into English.

As for the Hindu division of life into four periods, I have been in the fourth, i.e. sanyasa, for quite some time. But it has my own definition. It means keeping contact with the outside world to the minimum but enjoying all the creature comforts at home (*ghar hi main udaasa*). I have no intention of entering the actual sanyasa. Where in the jungle will I find a doctor or a dentist when I need one?

In view of advances made in the standards of hygiene and medicine, I think the period of Grihastha should be doubled, as most men are capable of producing their best up to their seventies. For them Vaanprastha should not necessarily mean retiring to an ashram or its modern counterpart, an old people's home, but, while staying with their families, gradually withdraw from decision-making—let their sons and/or daughters take over the family business, give up directorships of companies and being on the governing bodies of clubs, schools, colleges, hospitals, etc. Also, cut down travel and their social life to the necessary minimum. That will give them more time to be with themselves and prepare for the fourth and final stage of their life's journey.

Sanyasa no longer requires them to become a lonely wanderer. I do not recommend spending time in places of worship as that amounts to an admission of inability to be alone. If they need the solace of religion or prayer, let them indulge in them at home. There are other things they could do to distract their minds: work in the garden if they have one, grow potted plants, paint, listen to music and, best of all, immerse themselves in books, all kinds of books, and, if so inclined, write. I am quite happy living in Sanyasa without becoming a sanyasi. I mean to keep reading books, all kinds of books, till my eyes give up on me. And I mean to keep writing till the pen drops out of my hand.

My youngest brother, who among other things owned a restaurant and made it a point to be the last to leave, would often tell me, 'K. Singh, of two things you can never be sure: one, when a person may drop in to have a meal, and two, when death will come to you.'

A vaidji whom I often visited in his shop while taking an after-dinner stroll disagreed. He said death gives you many signals before it finally arrives to take you away. He quoted an anecdote of a wealthy man who became a friend of Yama, the messenger of death. One day he made a request to Yama, 'You and I have been close friends for many years. I ask you for just one favour: please give me timely warning that my time on earth will soon be over so that I can arrange my worldly affairs before I go.' Yama agreed to do so. However, one day the wealthy man suddenly died, leaving his business in a mess. When he met Yama he complained bitterly of having been let down by his friend. 'Not at all,' protested Yama, 'instead of one warning I gave you several. First I made your hair turn grey, then I deprived you of your teeth; then I made you hard of hearing and impaired your vision. Finally I made you feeble of mind. If you still chose to ignore these warning signals, you can only blame yourself.'

It is true that an enfeebled mind is, as it were, the final alarm bell for the start of a long march to the unknown. Other things you may learn to live with, but a mindless existence is like being dead while continuing to breathe. Alec Douglas Home summed it up in a doggerel:

> To my deafness I'm accustomed,
> To my dentures I'm resigned,
> I can manage my bi-focals,
> But oh how I miss my mind.

This view is confirmed by a physiotherapist:

Man is not old when his hair turns grey
Man is not old when his teeth decay,
But man is approaching his long last sleep
When his mind makes appointments
His body cannot keep.

The trouble with us humans is that we begin to think of death only in our old age. In our young years time hangs heavy and we delude ourselves into believing it will go on for ever and ever.

Time picks up speed as we grow old:

When as a child I laughed and wept
Time crept.
When as a youth I dreamt and talked
Time walked.
When I became a full-grown man
Time ran.
And later as older I grew
Time flew.
Soon shall I find when travelling on
Time gone.
Will Christ have saved my soul by then?
Amen!

MULK RAJ ANAND

Mulk Raj Anand was one of the first three Indian writers of fiction in English to be published in England. It is common knowledge that both Mulk's and R.K. Narayan's first novels were turned down by a number of English publishers till they found sugar daddies whom they could persuade to risk their money on them. And so, Graham Greene became a sponsor for R.K. Narayan; Mulk had the Bloomsbury group which included T.S. Eliot to back him. Only Raja Rao's *Kanthapura* made it without any sifarish. Needless to say, all three were lionized by their countrymen.

Mulk's chief patrons were socialists and communists. There were many English men and women who suffered from a sense of guilt over what the British Raj had done to India. He was well aware of what India's rich and powerful had done to the poor and powerless and the humiliations lower castes had suffered at the hands of the privileged higher castes. They became the themes of many of his novels and short stories. He became the chief spokesman for progressive writers who wrote to serve social purposes and did not bother so much about style and turn of phrase. Mulk's writing became progressively propagandist.

Mulk returned to India after the publication of his first two novels—*Untouchable* and *Coolie*. He was accorded a warm welcome by literary groups across the country. The reception he got at Lahore was tepid. A literary circle comprising some judges of the high court, a couple of ICS officers, professors of English literature and lawyers invited him for tea. They had read his novels and felt they could write as well as he did. Mulk sensed the condescending attitude but kept his cool till someone blurted out: 'We can write as well as you, but who will publish us?' Then, Mulk exploded, 'First write, then talk,' and walked away in a huff.

He was right. Many in that circle wrote. Not one was able to break the apartheid of the publishing houses. There were hardly any Indian commercial publishers worth going to. Most of these aspiring writers published their books at their own cost.

Though born in Peshawar (in 1905), there was nothing Pathan-like about Mulk. He was short, with fuzzy hair and, like the son of a Punjabi bania, dressed in khadi kurta pyjamas. He had a strange way of speaking: a lot of lisping and sentences ending in squeaks. But he loved holding forth, was warm and friendly. He liked living well and enjoyed the company of women. After his marriage to his English wife broke up, he had a Sri Lankan mistress, followed by a Parsi one. He lived in a ground-floor flat on Cuffe Parade, Bombay, facing the sea. I called on him one morning and saw him at work. He was perched on a high chair specially designed for him with his feet resting on the rung below. He was bending over a writing pad.

Mulk wrote quite a few novels and short stories. His characters were caricatures of stereotypes: rajas were rich and stupid, Brahmins, wily; banias, mean; women, wanton; Mussalmans, bullies; Sikhs, dim-witted. He was the first to break the taboos against the use of dirty language. In England, no one quite knew what these words meant; in India they were, and are, the common currency of abuse (if you were to take the frequency of use rather factually, this would have to be one hotbed of incest). He was right in doing so, otherwise spicy dialogue would lose its pungent flavour.

Mulk had a setback in his later years. He was commissioned by *Evergreen Review* of New York to do an article on the erotic in Indian art. It was very well received till the magazine was issued a legal notice alleging that it was a copy of an article translated from German into English.

Mulk's explanation was naïve beyond belief. Dosu Karaka, editor of the weekly *Current*, who hated the communists' guts, had the news splashed in big headlines—'Commie Author Caught Plagiarising'. It took some months of retirement to his villa in Lonavala for Mulk to bounce back.

But bounce back the man did, and resumed pontificating to audiences across the country. He never took notice of the topic under discussion nor the time set for speakers. He would go on and on about how his father used to beat his mother. He ignored the chairperson's bell and taps on the back. He had his say and never ever repented it.

Even as a young man he took himself seriously. He sought to cultivate the lions of English literature in the 1930s before he got down to writing his first novel. He had that valuable passport to the world of intelligentsia, a ticket to the British Museum library. Since the museum was next door to Bloomsbury, where many celebrated authors lived, he was soon able to acquire visas to their homes and was invited to sherry parties, to have tea and crumpets in elegant homes. Among others with whom he discussed the problems of writing fiction or philosophic theses were E.M. Forster, T.S. Eliot, Aldous Huxley, Leonard and Virginia Woolf, Clive Bell, Eric Gill, Laurence Binyon, Bonamy Dobree, Herbert Read and C.E.M. Joad. Evidently, he recorded his conversations in detail in his diary because it was almost a half a century later that they were put in print.

Young Mulk, when he arrived in London, had positive views of his own on literature, sculpture and painting. He also had a chip on his shoulder about the British Raj in India. He had been jailed and whipped by a policeman for taking part in an anti-government agitation. At the same time, he was inspired by Allama Iqbal's poetry and the philosophy of Khudi (belief in the supremacy of the will). In London, he wanted to write about Iqbal, but his professor turned down the project. He discussed it with Aldous Huxley. 'Can one introduce a personal diary into a novel?' asked Mulk. 'Why not?' asked Huxley in return. The follow-up question was somewhat esoteric. 'You mean integrates, consantia, and claritas in the *Portrait*' (referring to James Joyce's *The Portrait of an Artist as a Young Man*). Huxley's reply was more lucid: 'The professor forgets that novels are not written on university campuses for students to write theses on. They are written from non-scholastic compulsions. A novel is glorified gossip. Not a lexicon. It is a free form, rather loose, miscellaneous and digs down and reveals things like Freud is talking about. And each character needs a particular kind of form. Hardy's peasants are laborious and slow in speech, Hemingway's Americans talk in brief staccato as the new young talk like machines.'

Once Mulk had been invited for tea by Eliot in his office. This is how the conversation went:

'A piece of cake, Mr _____?'

'Anand,' Mulk added.

'Oh, like the Scotch Anand.'

'No, it's a derivaton from Ananda, one of the names of the Hindu supreme God, meaning bliss. My full name is Mulk Raj Anand, which means "king of the country of happiness"—and I try to look it.'

Friends and admirers of Mulk Raj Anand noticed how Chacha Mulk mellowed with age and how the once acerbic-tongued critic had only the kindest things to say about everyone in the last decade of his life. A great one for dropping names, he once did not spare anyone. But in his saintlier anecdotage, his compassion turned him into a crashing bore.

KAMLA PATEL

Few of the present generation would be familiar with the name Mridula Sarabhai. And even fewer would have heard of the name Kamla Patel. Both were undoubtedly the heroines of independent India. Apart from being Gujaratis, they had little in common in terms of their backgrounds. Mridula Sarabhai (1911–74) was the eldest of the eight children of Seth Ambalal Sarabhai, a textile magnate from Ahmedabad who was among the top ten richest men of the country. They were Shwetambar Jains. Better known among the siblings was Mridula's younger brother, Vikram, who rose to eminence as a nuclear and space scientist. Mridula was involved in the freedom movement before she was asked to take over operations to rescue women abducted during the Partition riots in Pakistan and India. Later she espoused the cause of Sheikh Abdullah who had been imprisoned by the Nehru government. In 1958, she too was arrested and put in Tihar jail for a year. She developed cancer and was packed off to Ahmedabad and kept under house arrest. She succumbed to the disease in 1972.

Kamla Patel (1912–92) came from a middle-class family. She became a disciple of Gandhi and spent many years in the Sabarmati ashram where Mridula was a frequent visitor. That's where they met. The one thing the two women shared with passion was veneration for Gandhi and what he stood for. The most important lesson they learnt from him was that once you are convinced your cause is just, fight for it without fear of consequences: fear is cowardly, fear is sinful.

Mridula was a born leader. Being the eldest, her siblings looked up to her. She grew up knowing how to organize and give orders. Everyone in the family called her 'Boss'. Bossy she was—with no small talk or banter. She cut her hair short, wore no cosmetics or jewellery. When she joined the freedom movement, she took to wearing Punjabi style salwar-kameezes. After Independence and the Partition of the country, she realized there was more work to do and moved to Delhi. Gossipmongers said she had developed a Nehru fixation. The most important work on hand was the rehabilitation of the millions of Hindu and Sikh refugees forced to flee from western Pakistan. And the most humanitarian task requiring immediate action was rescuing the women abducted on either side of the border and restoring them to their families. In a speech delivered on 7 December 1947, Gandhiji brought up the matter in his usual matter-of-fact manner of speaking. He said it was reported at a joint Indo–Pak meeting held in Lahore that the number of kidnapped women was 12,000 for Muslims abducted on this side and over twice that number of Hindus and Sikhs abducted in Pakistan. His figures were undoubtedly underestimates. But how were these women to be located and taken out of the clutches of their abductors and given the freedom to choose their destinies? On the Indian side, Mridula Sarabhai was chosen to lead the operations. In her turn, she chose Kamla Patel to be her principal aide and posted her at Lahore.

The atmosphere on either side of the border was full of hate and distrust. Though Muslims had asked for the division of the country, they felt more aggrieved than non-Muslims. Their hatred was further inflamed by the ongoing war in Kashmir. The Pakistan government and army continued to let in frontier tribesmen to infiltrate Kashmir, which they did in the thousands, pillaging, looting, raping women—including nuns—as they advanced towards Srinagar. Then the Indian air force and army pounced on them and drove them back with great slaughter. What the Pakistani authorities believed would fall into their hands like a ripe apple turned out to be a scorpion. They had more reason to hate India. Soon after came the annexation of Hyderabad.

Indians called it 'police action'; Pakistan saw it as yet another example of Hindu perfidy to extinguish a Muslim dynasty. How could they trust any Indian?

The most tragic part of the operation to rescue the abducted women was the way Punjabis looked down upon them as cattle or household chattel to be looted, sexually abused, shared with friends, sold or discarded. Police, civilian authorities and the general public connived with the abductors to frustrate the efforts of the do-gooders who came to rescue them. Everyone lied, everyone believed that murdering innocent people in cold blood and raping their women were acts of heroism: indeed human beings had become a sub-human species worse than beasts.

Kamla Patel put down her experiences of shuttling between Lahore, Amritsar and Jalandhar, going into remote Pakistani villages looking for lost women, and the walls of resistance she had to break through. Wherever she went, there was grave danger to her life. There were cases where underage Muslim girls had willingly eloped with Hindu boys, and Hindu girls who had run off with their Muslim lovers: such liaisons were not acceptable to their parents. The most heart-rending were the cases of women with babies still in their wombs or those whose children were born out of wedlock. Who did these women and their children belong to? Hindus, Sikhs or Muslims? To India or to Pakistan?

Kamla Patel's experiences were first published in Gujarati under the title *Mool Sotan Ukhdelan* and was received well enough to be translated and published in English to reach wider audiences. Mridula's younger sister, Gira Sarabhai, made funds available from the family's charitable trust to make this possible. Unfortunately, like Gandhiji's speeches which were short on oratory but came from the heart, Kamla Patel's text has no literary flourishes but also was from her heart. Despite being cliché-ridden, choppy and repetitive, it is worth reading because it reminds us of the darkest period of our recent history. It is a timely reminder that we have yet to purge ourselves of communal venom, which was evident in the anti-Muslim riots in the home state of Mridula Sarabhai and Kamla Patel.

MOTHER TERESA: THE GREATEST INDIAN

I have a few bones to pick with the editor and the organizers of this poll for the greatest Indian. You have chosen names from politics, industry, social service and sports. Why did you leave out films? Though Sachin Tendulkar is the greatest cricketer India has produced in recent years, Bollywood has produced persons of equal stature like Amitabh Bachchan.

And what exactly did you have in mind when you asked readers to cast their votes to choose the greatest? How does greatness differ from excellence in one's profession? We have produced musicians and artists and dancers who have achieved the highest degrees of perfection in their fields and at least three have been awarded Bharat Ratnas. Why were they left out of the reckoning?

Having got that off my chest let me come to the results of the poll. I had anticipated that Pandit Nehru would emerge as the outright winner with Sardar Patel, Jayaprakash Narayan and Indira Gandhi following close behind. I thought Dr Ambedkar and the industrialists would be somewhere in the middle and Mother Teresa at the bottom. I am glad I have been proved wrong.

First, Jawaharlal Nehru (1889–1964). He was the prince charming of Indian politics. The only son of a rich father and educated at Harrow and Cambridge. Gandhi paid him fulsome compliments: 'He is as pure as crystal, he is truthful beyond suspicion. The nation is safe in his hands.' With that sort of unqualified support from the Father of the Nation, none of his rivals for power—Jinnah, Patel, Subhas Bose and Jayaprakash Narayan—had much chance of toppling him. He was also sophisticated, unencumbered by religious prejudices and forward-looking. He answered Allama Iqbal's requirements of a Meer-e-Kaarvaan—leader of the caravan: '*Nigaah buland, sukhan dilnawaz, jaan pur soz/Yahee hain rakht-e-safar Meer-e-Kaarvaan ke liye* (Lofty vision, winning speech and a warm personality/These are all the baggage a leader of the caravan needs on his journey).'

Nehru was a visionary, he found the right words to use for historic events. Nothing could be better-worded than his 'tryst with destiny' speech and 'the light has gone out of our eyes' on the assassination of Bapu. Those who had the privilege of being close to him felt the warmth of his personality. What added to his aura were the eleven years he spent in jail during the freedom movement, dreaming dreams of a great future for his country and putting them down on paper in felicitous prose. Three times he was elected president of the Indian National Congress, including the most crucial year when the British handed over power to the Indians and he automatically became India's first prime minister.

Nehru was not above political chicanery. Having accepted the Cabinet Mission plan to hand over power to a united India, he reneged on his undertaking when he realized it might end up with M.A. Jinnah becoming prime minister. He was party to the division of the country into India and Pakistan. As a socialist, he was strongly opposed to any kind of collaboration with the axis powers during the Second World War. But he did not say a word against Netaji Subhas Bose (missing from the list of greats) or the INA. When he was sure his arch rival, Netaji, was dead, he took up the cause of the INA prisoners with great enthusiasm and rode the crest of its popularity to keep himself hero number one of the nation.

Nehru was prime minister for seventeen years till the day he died in 1964. He could be described as Plato's ideal of a Philosopher King. He did his best to convert his belief of a socialist democracy into reality. He bulldozed traditionalists into giving Hindu women equal rights to property, monogamous marriage and divorce. He put India on the world map by getting the less powerful nations to stay aloof in the conflict between superpowers.

He had his blind spots too. He refused to believe that our exploding population needed to be contained. He refused to see the gathering strength of Muslim separatism which led to the formation of Pakistan. He failed to come to terms with Pakistan and was chiefly responsible for the mess we made in Jammu and Kashmir. He was given to nepotism and favouritism. The prime example was when he forced his friend, Krishna Menon, on the nation, first as high commissioner in England, then as his principal adviser on foreign affairs and, finally, as defence minister. Menon was allergic to the US. Nehru shared this allergy. Throughout Congress rule, India kept a cool distance from the US and paid a heavy price for its anti-Americanism. It was Menon's mishandling of our relations with China that led to a short war against our neighbour. Our ill-equipped troops suffered an ignominious defeat at the hands of the Chinese in October 1962. Nehru died disillusioned and broken in spirit.

Many people are of the opinion that Vallabhbhai Patel (1875–1950) would have made a better prime minister than Nehru. Nehru had his head in the clouds, Patel had his feet firmly on the ground. Nehru was a city-bred aesthete who liked the good things of life including the company of women, beautiful and not so beautiful. Nehru assiduously played the role of a prince charming, ever smiling, full of fun and laughter. Patel was born in a village and was of peasant stock. There were no women in Patel's life, save his daughter who looked after him after he lost his wife. He was a dour, unsmiling man who inspired awe rather than affection. He did not have a high opinion of Nehru but grudgingly accepted Gandhi's decision that Nehru should head independent India's first government with Patel as deputy prime minister.

Sardar Patel's place in history is assured by the way he coerced 562 princely states to join the Indian Union. Most of them sensed the way the wind was blowing and readily signed the instruments of accession relinquishing their ruling powers in exchange for privy purses. Three—Hyderabad, Junagadh and Kashmir—held back. The Nawab of Junagadh opted for Pakistan. Indian troops moved in and annexed the state. The Nawab fled to Pakistan. The Nizam of Hyderabad, encouraged by Pakistan, opted for an independent state of his own. In a short and swift move euphemistically described as a 'police action', the Nizam's troops and a rabble styled as the Razakars were routed and Hyderabad state integrated with India. Kashmir proved more intractable. The maharaja tried to play for time with both India and Pakistan till Pathan tribesmen, aided by Pakistani troops, overran large parts of the state and came within a few miles of Srinagar. The maharaja quickly signed the accession with India and fled. Indian troops were flown into Srinagar in the nick of time to drive back the invading tribesmen. When India clearly had the upper hand in Kashmir, Nehru agreed to refer the matter to the UN where it stays till this day. Patel was against the move but gave in reluctantly. In hindsight, Indians believe Patel was right, Nehru wrong. There was a calculated propaganda to portray Sardar Patel as a communalist with an anti-Muslim bias—most of it by Nehru's supporters who included Krishna Menon and a Bombay tabloid. There was not an iota of truth behind the charge. The Sardar was as committed to secularism as the Pandit.

I am not surprised to see Indira Gandhi ranked fourth; she could well have been lower. She squandered the goodwill she earned in her early years in power by acts of political foolhardiness. When Indira (1917–84) was born, her grandfather, Motilal Nehru, predicted, 'She may prove better than a thousand sons.' Although she went to Santiniketan, Badminton (a famous girls' school in England) and Oxford, Indira passed no examination. Despite coming into a political legacy, she had no political principles save that of a survivor, i.e., trust no one. Her father put the levers of power in her hands. In 1955, she was made a member of the Congress Working Committee, in 1959 its president and became prime minister on the death of Lal Bahadur Shastri in 1966. She made a poor start and was dubbed 'goongi gudiya'. She soon asserted herself as a woman with a will of her own and an uncanny sense of timing to strike when the iron was hot. But for a couple of years out of power, she remained prime minister till the day she was assassinated.

During Indira's tenure as PM, India made rapid strides in scientific research: the Green Revolution, exploration of the ocean bed, setting up a research station in the Antarctic and exploding a nuclear device. She could not take credit for them but could take credit for the way she cut Pakistan into two in 1971. She was lauded as the Empress of India, equated with the country itself ('India is Indira, Indira is India'). Power went to her head. One after another she destroyed the institutions of democracy by giving preference to her loyalists in the legislature, judiciary and bureaucracy. When she felt threatened, she imposed an emergency rule, depriving citizens of their democratic rights and jailing political opponents. And after she was returned to power for a second term, she blatantly imposed a Nehru–Gandhi dynastic rule. This explains why her public image fell from that of a goddess to a petty, vengeful woman.

Dr Bhimrao Ambedkar (1891–1956) was to India's Harijans what Gandhi was to other Indians. Gandhi fought for Indian independence; Ambedkar for the freedom and dignity of the untouchables. The two men did not see eye to eye on many national issues and Ambedkar sympathized with Jinnah in his attempt to free Muslims from Hindu domination. I am not surprised his name appears seventh on the list. And that, I suspect, is because of the major role he played in drawing up our Constitution and later as law minister in Nehru's cabinet.

The people who make a country prosperous are not politicians who make all the noise and take the credit for all the achievements but farmers, entrepreneurs and scientists, who produce wealth and open up new vistas for employment. They shun publicity and work quietly. At the top of the country's list of entrepreneurs is the house of Tata. The Tatas have been at the number one position for four generations. Their founder, Jamshedji Tata, was the pioneer of the textile and steel industry. His grandson, J.R.D. Tata (1904–93), carried the legacy forward by putting India on the air map of the world. Both our domestic and international airlines owe their existence to him. The house of Tata is into chemicals, textiles, fertilizers, hydel power, automobiles, rail engines, tea and publishing. What distinguishes them from other big industrial houses is that they plough back most of their income into charities, scholarships, scientific and medical research and cultural organizations. None of their charities are linked to their community, the Parsis. They pay their employees handsomely and workers' strikes are unknown. Above all, they maintain high ethical standards (as does the other big Parsi enterprise, Godrej) and never descend to bribing politicians for favours.

I think Dhirubhai Ambani was put on the list because he started as a poorly-paid school teacher and made a vast fortune. And died relatively recently. I do not know much about him. But I did know Jayaprakash Narayan (1902–79) and spent some days in his farmhouse-cum-ashram in Bihar. I found him more loveable than inspiring. He wasted a lot of time commiserating with people in distress and had little left to deal with major issues or to organize parties to oppose the government. He did become the nation's conscience keeper and was the moving spirit behind the opposition to Mrs Gandhi's dictatorial rule. He was imprisoned for five months during the Emergency till his health became precarious and he had to be set free. He died a broken man. Instead of calling him 'Lok Nayak' (leader of the people), we should rename him 'Lok Priya' (beloved of the people).

Atal Behari Vajpayee (b. 1924) landing at the bottom of the list needs analysing. I would have placed him much higher as he is able, warm-hearted, without communal prejudices, and is the greatest orator in Hindi that I have heard. I suspect the voters are not against Vajpayee but against L.K. Advani and other Hindu kattarvadis (bigots) who matter because Vajpayee matters.

It is evident that the people of India are totally disenchanted with politics and their political leaders. The general feeling is *'sab chor hain'*. That explains the vote in favour of Mother Teresa who had nothing to do with any politician nor was unduly concerned working in a Calcutta ruled over by godless communists. They loved and respected her as much as the bhadralok and the filthy rich. But to regard the votes in favour of Mother Teresa (1910–97) simply as a negative reaction to politicians and capitalists would be a grave error. I spent four days with her in Calcutta in the early 'seventies. At the time little was known about her outside Bengal and there was a lot of prejudice against Christian missionaries whipped up by right-wing Hindu organizations. I spent many hours at her centre, Nirmal Hriday, and an afternoon at the house of the dying in Kalighat and some orphan homes set up by her Missionaries of Charity. I saw the affection people had for her. Once on our way back to Nirmal Hriday, we had to abandon our taxi and walk because the road was blocked by the massive funeral procession of a communist leader. I saw men and women carrying red flags step out of the procession and touch her feet. Again when we boarded a train, passengers wrangled with each other to buy her ticket. The conductor refused to take their money and paid for her ticket himself. Since Christmas was approaching, she went to call on the manager of the biggest biscuit manufacturing company in the city. He pleaded that business was bad. She asked him to let her have broken biscuits. When we returned to our taxi, it was laden with crates of good biscuits. I accompanied her to the home of the dying to see if she performed any miracles. There were over ninety old men and women lying alongside, gasping for breath. One died in the hour that I was there. She went from bed to bed putting her hand on the dying people's foreheads. They clutched her hands and cried for help. All she said in reply was *'Bhagwan aachhen'*—there is God. They were strangely comforted.

Mother Teresa was without any charisma and as plain a woman as I have ever seen. She told me she read nothing besides the Bible nor had been influenced by anyone save Jesus Christ. Goodness oozed out of her and was very infectious. People opened up their purses and gave her all they had. They gave up their jobs to work for her. In 1979 when she was given the Nobel Prize for Peace everyone agreed that no one deserved it more than her. Among my most valued possessions is a letter from her which says, 'I am told you do not believe in God. I send you God's blessings.' I have it framed by my desk.

NAZRUL ISLAM

Every time I go to Calcutta and take the broad two-way highway from the airport to the city and back, I promise myself I will find out more about Nazrul Islam after whom it is named.

I know he was a very popular writer of songs, a revolutionary—the first Indian poet to be jailed by the British for writing a poem demanding complete independence—and that a stroke deprived him of his voice and impaired his mind. After the establishment of Bangladesh, he was taken to Dhaka where he died in 1976.

I read a few of Nazrul's poems translated into English: patriotic poems and those on love. I found the first exhortative, the second maudlin in the Urdu tradition of the eternal, unrequited love of the bulbul for the rose. Translated poetry can never do justice to the original. The Bangladeshi poet, Shamsul Haque, put it very neatly: 'It is like kissing a girl's photograph instead of her lips.'

Nazrul was born on 25 May 1899, at Churulia (in Burdwan district), the fifth child of Fakir Ahmed, the imam of a mosque. All his older brothers had died in infancy. For some reason Nazrul's nickname as a child was 'Dukhoo Mian'.

The family adopted the honourific 'kazi' from an ancestor who had been appointed judge by a Mogul king. The nickname Dukhoo was prophetic since dukh remained his life-long companion and he embraced sorrow as something of his own.

Nazrul lost his father when he was only nine. Within a year of his father's death his mother took on a second husband, leaving Nazrul alone to fend for himself. He never forgave his mother for deserting him and refused to see her throughout his life.

Dukhoo Mian was not interested in looking after the dargah or in leading prayers as an imam. He was a born poet. He also had a passion for playing the flute. He took on menial jobs to fill his belly and spent most of his time composing folk songs and dramas and enacting them in villages.

Within a few years he became a household name in the Bengal countryside. While his contemporaries like Rabindranath Tagore and Sarat Chandra Chatterjee wrote for the educated, elite bhadralok, Nazrul addressed himself to the tillers of the soil, the fishermen and workers in factories and offices.

Nazrul never made much money. He worked as a domestic servant and a baker's assistant. For a while he joined the army: he believed every freedom fighter must know how to wield arms. Although he held Mahatma Gandhi in great respect, he did not subscribe to non-violence.

It was during his army service that his first short story—*Awara Kee Kahani* (The Life of a Vagabond)—appeared in print in 1919. It was followed by other stories and songs.

Vagabondage was in Nazrul's blood. After having agreed to marry Syeda Khatoon, he fled the scene of the nikah without consummating the marriage. Poor Syeda Khatoon waited for Nazrul for fifteen years before she took on a second husband. In 1924, he became acquainted with the Sen Gupta family and married Indrakumar's widowed aunt and Girivala Devi's daughter, Pramila. She bore him two children, both of whom died in infancy. Their names were Krishna Mohammed and Arindam Khalid. Pramila died in 1962.

Nazrul's fame as a writer, poet and journalist spread in Bengal. His articles appeared in *Navyug*, *Dhoomketu* and *Langal*. His best known poem is entitled 'Vidrohi'. In *Dhoomketu* he spelt out his views, 'First and foremost complete independence for India—to achieve this aim we have to have a revolution to change the existing order of government and social norms.'

Nazrul Islam attended sessions of the Indian National Congress where national leaders including Gandhi and Jawaharlal Nehru heard him recite his fiery poems. He spent a year in jail but his spirit remained undaunted. Gurudev Tagore aptly summed up Nazrul's poetry in a sentence: 'He used a sword to shave his beard.'

Nazrul was not a Marxist but a socialist; he was not an agnostic but respected all religions. He stood for complete equality for women. He wrote: 'O women, tear away your veil, break the chains that bind you! Throw away your burqa, throw away all the ornaments that enslave you.'

He conducted many programmes for All India Radio. On 10 July 1942, while presenting a children's programme from Calcutta station, he suffered a stroke which deprived him of the power of speech.

For the remaining thirty-four years of his life, Nazrul could only write out what he had to say. Since he had strongly opposed Pakistan, there was no question of his moving to East Pakistan when Bengal was partitioned in August 1947.

It was after Bangladesh was liberated, at the specific request of its first prime minister, Mujibur Rahman, that Nazrul Islam shifted from Calcutta to Dhaka. He was a very sick man: he had lost his voice, his mind had also suffered deterioration. On 29 August 1976, he died in a Dhaka hospital, acclaimed both in Bangladesh and West Bengal and immortalized by having Calcutta's main highway named after him.

ON KALAM ON THE EVE OF BECOMING PRESIDENT

Having seen and heard him on TV and read his short book, one cannot but conclude that the next President of India is not going to be like any one of his predecessors. Nor indeed like the President of any other country, least of all that of the largest democracy in the world. He is not impressive to look at; with his tousled, untidy hair and buck teeth he looks more like a character from a comic strip than the head of a state. Though his speeches do not rise to heights of oratory, they do manage—like Mahatma Gandhi's mumblings—to get to the hearts of the common people. His own achievements inspire respect and hope: if the son of a poor boatman from Rameswaram can make it to the palatial residence of the President atop Raisina Hill, why not I? That, in short, is the message that comes through *Ignited Minds*.

Did Kalam have a role model? When asked by a child who his favourite character in the Mahabharata was, Kalam replied without hesitation, Vidura. It may be recalled that Vidura was the son of a low-caste handmaiden. Kalam was impressed by him because he 'showed grit against the wrongdoings of authority and had the courage to differ when everyone else chose to surrender before the tyranny of adharma'. He was also the wisest of the brothers. Kalam must be fully aware that he belongs to a discriminated-against minority and owes his selection as a candidate for the presidency of our republic largely to the covering up of the sins of adharma committed by the members of the ruling coalition in Gujarat. He will have plenty of opportunities to bring people who pursue the path of evil in the name of dharma back on the right track in a secular democracy.

Kalam is a dreamer of great dreams, not for himself but his country. Unlike most of his countrymen who boast of their achievements, he is refreshingly free of vainglory. He plays down all he has done by way of scientific research in missile and nuclear technology. He gives credit to the team he has worked with and pays homage to Indians who have achieved spectacular success in mathematics, medicine and other sciences. All of them were dreamers who, against great odds, translated their dreams into reality. He exhorts the young of India to be inspired by their examples. No matter how wild and unpractical your dreams may appear at first sight, persist in giving them practical shape. If you think the waters of the oceanic Brahmaputra should be brought to green the arid and sandy wastes of Rajasthan or slake the thirst of Tamilians, get down to laying canals across the length and breadth of India. Nothing ventured, nothing gained is his motto.

He suggests a list of his priorities: increase agricultural production to keep ahead of the increasing population, make electric power available in every village, provide education and healthcare to everyone (it will automatically bring down the rate of increase in population), take information of the latest technologies down to the masses and make the country powerful in nuclear, space and defence technologies. He is convinced that this can be achieved in the next eighteen years, by 2020, if we have the will and determination to do so.

Kalam is not blind to our failures. He lists them with equal candour: 'Lament, my friend, at the passing away of a generation of politicians with a voice, vision and reach that went far beyond our borders. Lament at our State-sponsored, abnormal and paranoid fixation with a particular country that has blinded us to the rest of the world, including the third world, which we used to head not so long ago. And weep softly at what we have reduced ourselves to in the comity of nations. For a large country with a billion people, a country with a thriving industry and a large pool of scientific talent, a country, moreover, that is a nuclear power, India does not count for as much as it should. In terms of our influence in world affairs, probably no other country is so far below its potential as we are.'

Kalam, however, is convinced that 'purity' is possible even in politics. 'I believe if the nation forms a second vision today,' he writes, 'leaders of a stature to suit our ambition will appear once again, in all walks of life, including politics.'

Ignited Minds will fire the minds of the young to whom it is primarily addressed. However, one hopes that like Atal Bihari Vajpayee who mercifully stopped writing poetry after he became prime minister, Kalam too will stop his little attempts at versification after he takes over as President of India.

THE SIKHS: POETS OF ENTERPRISE

On 13 April 1999, the Khalsa was 300 years old and Sikhism, from which it emerged, over 500 years old. Sikhism was, and is, a pacifist creed started by Guru Nanak (1469–1539) and developed by four succeeding gurus whose writings were compiled in an anthology, the Adi Granth, by the fifth, Guru Arjan, around 1600 AD. The Adi Granth comprises over 6,000 hymns composed by five gurus (mainly those of the compiler Guru Arjan) and includes compositions of Hindu and Muslim saints as well as some bards. In the final version, made by Guru Gobind Singh, he inserted hymns composed by his father, Guru Tegh Bahadur. Guru Gobind compiled an anthology of his own, the Dasam Granth. While the Adi (first) Granth is essentially a distillation of the Vedanta in Punjabi, the Dasam (tenth) is a compilation of tales of valour of Hindu goddesses, some composed by the Guru himself, others by the bards of his court. It is not accorded the same status as the Adi Granth. Thus we have two parallel scriptures, one extolling the virtues of peaceful submission, the other of combating oppression with force. The martyrdom of two gurus changed the course of Sikh history. Guru Arjan succumbed to torture in Lahore jail in 1606; his son, and the sixth guru, Har Gobind, took up arms. Tegh Bahadur was executed in Delhi in 1675; his son Gobind Rai (later Singh) converted a sizeable chunk of hitherto peace-loving Sikhs into the militant fraternity called the Khalsa or the pure.

As a consequence of these historic changes, we have several brands of Sikhs. There are Hindus who believe in Sikhism, visit gurudwaras, have a Granth Sahib in their homes and perform rituals according to Sikh rites. A large section of them are from Sindh, mainly Amils. Then there are Sahajdharis (slow adopters) who don't wear the external forms of the Khalsa viz., unshorn hair and beard. The majority of Sikhs are Khalsa who undergo baptism (pahul), take vows to observe the five Ks—kesh, kangha, kaccha, kada and kirpan—and add the suffix Singh, and if female, Kaur, to their names. Those Khalsa who cut off their hair and shave their beards are regarded as patits (renegades) but still see themselves as Sikhs. The matter becomes more complex as while all the above categories of Sikhs revere only ten gurus and the Granth Sahib as their living embodiment, there are two sects—Nirankaris and Namdharis—who have living gurus but nevertheless describe themselves as Sikhs.

The transition from one Sikh sect to the other, indeed from Hinduism to Sikhism, is without many hassles. Intermarriage is not uncommon. The relationship between Hindus and Sikhs has always been *roti-beti ka rishta* (breaking bread in common and giving daughters in marriage), or *nauh-maas da rishta* (as the fingernail is to the flesh). In this situation, the Khalsa find themselves losing ground, as an increasing number of their youth cut their hair and shave their beards to become no different from Hindus believing in Sikhism, while the number of Hindus accepting baptism to become Khalsa is becoming rarer.

When the Khalsa was in the ascendant politically, their numbers rose steadily. After they lost their kingdom in 1849, their population began to decline. Fortunately for them, the British came to their aid by giving them preferential treatment in services like the army and the police, separate electorates and reserved seats in elected bodies like municipalities, legislatures, the central assembly. With Independence such privileges were abolished and the economic benefits that came with being Khalsa disappeared.

In growing numbers, young Sikhs began to abandon the external symbols of the Khalsa. This was more noticeable among

Sikhs settled in foreign countries. Wherever they were in large numbers and could form compact social groups—as in some East African countries and Singapore—social pressures kept the younger generation from reneging on their ancestral faith; where they were scattered in small numbers as in England, Canada and the US, a second generation emigrant conforming to Khalsa traditions became a rarity. The same phenomenon is visible among the educated elite who live in Indian cities and are exposed to western influences. Young Sikh boys question the necessity of keeping long hair and growing beards to be religious. The only rational answer is that it gives them a sense of belonging to the Khalsa Panth. Many don't find that convincing enough and become like Hindus performing Sikh rituals and prayer. The real danger to the Khalsa has always been, as it is today, the absorptive capacity of Hinduism. An English scholar correctly described it as the boa constrictor of the Indian jungles: it can swallow religions which come in contact with it, with a special taste for its own offspring.

The real challenge facing the Khalsa Panth is to find ways and means to arrest, possibly reverse, the process of disintegration. Perhaps the most important issue to be considered by the scholars of Sikh theology will be to convince people that there is a continuous and unbroken line between the teachings of Guru Nanak and the first five gurus enshrined in the Adi Granth and the militant tradition begun by the sixth guru and brought to culmination by the tenth and last guru, Gobind Singh, with the establishment of the Khalsa Panth.

The roots of Sikhism lie deep in the Bhakti form of Hinduism. Guru Nanak picked what he felt were its salient features: belief in one God who is undefinable, unborn, immortal, omniscient, all-pervading and the epitome of Truth; belief in the institution of the guru as the guide in matters spiritual; unity of mankind without distinction of caste; rejection of idol worship and meaningless ritual; sanctity of the sangat (congregation) which was expected to break bread together at the *guru ka langar*; the gentle way of sahaj to approach God while fulfilling domestic obligations; hymn singing (kirtan); emphasis on work as a moral obligation. A slogan ascribed to Guru Nanak is *'kirt karo, vand chhako, naam japo'* (work, share what you earn, take the name of the Lord). There's little doubt that Nanak felt he had a new message that needed to be conveyed after him, as he nominated his closest disciple, Angad, to be his successor in preference to his two sons. Angad, likewise, nominated his disciple, Amar Das, to succeed him. Thereafter, the guruship remained among the members of the same family, the Sodhis.

The compilation of the Adi Granth around 1604 AD was a landmark in the evolution of Sikhism. Though an eclectic work with compositions of Hindu and Muslim saints, it echoes the Vedanta through most of its nearly 6,000 hymns. There is a new breed of Sikh scholars who bend backwards to prove Sikhism has taken little or nothing from Hinduism. All they need to be told is that of the 15,028 names of God that appear in the Adi Granth, Hari occurs over 8,000 times, Ram 2,533 times, followed by Prabhu, Gopal Govind, Parbrahm and other Hindu nomenclature for the Divine. The purely Sikh coinage 'Wahe Guru' appears only sixteen times.

There can be little doubt that the martyrdom of Guru Arjan in 1606 resulted in a radical change in the community's outlook. Though its creed remained wedded to the Adi Granth, it was ready to defend itself by the use of arms. Guru Arjan's son, the sixth guru, Har Gobind, raised a cavalry of horsemen. He built the Akal Takht facing the Harmandir as the seat of temporal power and came to be designated Miri Piri da Malik (the Lord of Temporal and Spiritual Power). For some years he was imprisoned in Gwalior fort. The final transition came after the execution of the ninth guru, Tegh Bahadur, in 1675. His son, Guru Gobind, justified the transition in a letter, Zafarnamah, said to have been addressed to Emperor Aurangzeb: 'When all other means have failed it is righteous to draw the sword'. Guru Gobind's concept of God underwent a martial metamorphosis. In his Akal Ustat (Praise of the Timeless God) he wrote:

Eternal God, thou art our shield,
The dagger, knife, the sword we wield.
To us Protector there is given
The timeless, deathless Lord of Heaven;
To us All-steel's unvanquished might,
To us All-time's resistless flight;
But chiefly Thou, Protector brave
All-steel, wilt Thine own servant save
(Translated by M.A. Macauliffe)

In his ode to Goddess Chandi, Guru Gobind asked Lord Shiva to grant him the most fitting end to a warrior's life:

O Lord, these boons of Thee I ask,
Let me never shun a righteous task,
Let me be fearless when I go to battle,
Give me faith that victory will be mine,
Give me power to sing Thy praise,
And when comes the time to end my life,
Let me fall in mighty strife.

Though not very successful in the campaigns he fought, he fired his followers with martial fervour. 'I will teach the sparrow to hunt the hawk, one man to fight a lakh and twenty-five thousand (sava lakh).' He made the downtrodden feel they were God's chosen people—*Wahe Guru ji da khalsa*—and would be ever victorious—*Wahe Guru ji di fateh*.

The guru succeeded in creating a new breed of intrepid warriors imbued with a do-or-die spirit. Within a few years of his death, his disciple, Banda Bairagi, overran the region around Sirhind and laid waste large domains of the Mogul kingdom. Even after the capture and execution of hundreds of Banda's followers, bands of Sikh horsemen harried Nadir Shah's forces and forced his successor, Ahmed Shah Abdali, who blew up the Harmandir twice, to retreat. When the Sikhs became rulers of the Punjab, Maharaja Ranjit Singh realized the value of having troops of Nihangs whom he threw into battles against Ghazis waging jehad against him. The determination to never give in came to be deeply rooted in the Sikh psyche; even in adversity they were exhorted to remain in buoyant spirits—*charhdi kala*. With it came the conviction that destiny was in their hands. At the end of each congregational prayer, comes the chant '*Raj Karega Khalsa*' (the Khalsa will rule). No one will be able to resist them. Those who confront them will be routed. Those who seek their protection will be saved.

The Green Revolution in the production of wheat and rice was largely the achievement of the Sikh farmers. Its epicentre was the Punjab Agricultural University at Ludhiana set up in 1962. Within a few years the production of crops per acre was doubled, then trebled. Simultaneous with the Green Revolution came the opening up of the Middle East and Western countries to emigrants. Since the turn of the century, small Sikh communities had existed in Canada, the US, England, Australia and countries on the East African coast. Taking advantage of their status as citizens of the Commonwealth, thousands of Sikhs who emigrated to the UK, Canada and Australia acquired British citizenship. Others, who could, went to the United States. Many found employment in the Arab countries of the Gulf and the Middle East. The remittances they sent home helped their families wipe out old debts, buy more land and build new houses. The well-to-do Sikh farmer never had it as good as he did in the 'sixties and 'seventies.

The halcyon years of the Green Revolution and foreign remittances did not last long. After the orgy of prosperity came the hangover of overindulgence. Young Sikhs graduating from schools and colleges found there was not enough for them to do on the land; they couldn't go abroad because of the restrictions placed on emigrants by foreign countries and there was hardly any industry in Punjab that could absorb them. As the number of landless increased, so did the numbers of uneducated unemployed. They were willing to lend their ears to Marxists as well as to preachers of religious fundamentalism. The latter proved to be more persuasive.

The Sikh religious revival coincided with the Green Revolution. The man who started it was Giani Zail Singh. His motives were entirely political, viz., to get the better of the Akalis who had monopolized the propagation of Sikhism. Zail Singh, the chief minister of Punjab for five years, 1972–77, utilized every opportunity to give a Sikh orientation to the government: official functions began with an ardas; kirtan darbars were organized on a provincial scale; the new university set up in Amritsar was named after Guru Nanak; a new township was named after one of Guru Gobind's sons. The most ludicrous was his discovery of horses said to be the descendants of the stallion ridden by Guru Gobind. They were led down a 400 km road, renamed Guru Gobind Singh Marg, running from Anandpur to Patiala—villagers reverentially collected their droppings to take home. It was Zail Singh, more than anyone else, who brought forward the rustic preacher, Jarnail Singh Bhindranwale, who had earned a name for himself for bringing back into the Khalsa fold thousands of young Sikhs who had strayed from the path of orthodoxy. He exhorted Sikhs to become shastradhari (bearers of arms), added firearms (revolvers and rifles) to the kirpan and replaced horses by motorcycles. He was no orator but his uncouth village vocabulary was full of disparaging references to Hindus as *dhotian vale, topian vale*; he referred to Mrs Gandhi as *Panditan di dhee*—daughter of a Brahmin. He acquired the charisma of an acerbic-tongued saint-warrior. The special target of his ire were the Sant Nirankaris who recognized a living guru, an anathema to orthodox Sikhs. Bhindranwale's followers (he was not among them) clashed with the Nirankaris on 13 April 1978, Baisakhi day—seventeen lost their lives. Two years later (24 April 1980), Baba Gurbachan Singh, the head of the Nirankari sect, and his bodyguard were gunned down in Delhi. Bhai Ranjit Singh was convicted of the crime and sentenced to fourteen years' imprisonment. While in jail, he was nominated jathedar of the Akal Takht by Gurcharan Singh Tohra, the president of the Shiromani Gurdwara Parbandhak Committee (SGPC).

Bhindranwale's followers spread terror in the state by killing eminent Hindus like Lala Jagat Narain, founder-owner of the Hind Samachar group of newspapers (his son, Ramesh Chandra, too, was killed later). Thereafter, hardly a day went by when gangs owing allegiance to Bhindranwale did not kill between ten to twenty Hindus and Sikhs opposed to his ideology. When Bhindranwale was arrested from his Chowk Mehta residence, it was at a date and time of his own choosing (Zail Singh was then the Union home minister and enjoyed the support of Mrs Gandhi's son, Sanjay). When he was released, he felt he would be safer in the Golden Temple complex than in Chowk Mehta. He took up residence in the Akal Takht and began to fortify it.

Killings, bank robberies, extortions, hijacking of planes continued apace. Bhindranwale discovered the easiest way of preventing the absorption of the Khalsa into Hinduism was to create a gulf between Sikhs and Hindus. For a while he succeeded in splitting the two communities: Punjabi Hindus who were alienated from their Sikh brethren answered abuse with abuse and the desecration of Hindu temples with the desecration of gurudwaras. Attempts to resolve disputes with the government failed and Mrs Gandhi decided to settle Bhindranwale's hash once and for all. She persuaded Zail Singh, who had by then become President of the Republic, to put Punjab under military rule. Then without informing him, she ordered the army to storm the Golden Temple. She chose to do so on 5 June 1984, the anniversary of the martyrdom of the founder of the temple, Guru Arjan, when thousands of pilgrims were present. In the action that took two nights and two days, there were heavy casualties on both sides; hundreds of innocent worshippers were killed in the crossfire, the Akal Takht was wrecked, the entrance to the central shrine damaged and the shrine itself pocked with bullet marks. Amongst the dead was Bhindranwale. Operation Bluestar, as it was called, shocked the entire community, including a substantial number of those who strongly disapproved of Bhindranwale. Army operations to wipe out Bhindranwale's supporters in the state, though ruthless, did not produce results. The Khalsa do not have a spirit of forgiveness. On 31 October 1984, two of Mrs Gandhi's Sikh bodyguards killed her in her garden. The ruling coterie decided 'to teach the Sikhs a lesson'. In many towns and cities of northern India, scores of gurudwaras and Sikh properties were destroyed and thousands of Sikhs burnt alive by frenzied mobs instigated by members of the Congress. The police looked on as bemused spectators. Far from being suppressed, Sikh terrorism picked up and over a dozen gangs—some trained and armed by Pakistan—spread terror in the state. It took the government over a year to realize that strong-arm tactics wouldn't work with the Sikhs. Dialogue was reopened with Akali leaders. By then Punjabis had had their fill of violence by the terrorists and the Punjab police and were longing for peace. On 24 July 1985, a comprehensive pact covering all points of dispute was signed by Sant Longowal, representing the Akalis, and Prime Minister Rajiv Gandhi. After ten years of violence, in which over 10,000 lives were lost, peace was finally restored to the state. The elections that followed gave the Akalis a decisive victory.

It took another decade for the alienated community to regain its self-esteem and resume its leading role in nation-building. Sikhs have enormous resilience and self-confidence born of the conviction that anything others do, they can do better. They are about the only religious community who make jokes on themselves and laugh at jokes made at their expense. A good instance of this is the one that made the rounds during the pogrom of Sikhs following Mrs Gandhi's assassination: one of her assassins, Beant Singh, gunned down after the crime, went to Bhindranwale in paradise to receive blessings for what he'd done. Bhindranwale said: 'Son, you have done well; ask for any reward and it will be yours.' Beant Singh replied: 'Santji, I am now out of a job, give me something to do.' Bhindranwale assured him, 'Name it and it's yours.'

'Santji, the only job I know is of protecting people. Employ me as your personal bodyguard.' Bhindranwale paused and replied:

'Son, ask for anything else because I can't take the risk of having you as my personal guard.'

The Khalsa are outgoing, loud and obstreperous. They were among the first Indians to seek their fortunes abroad—not as bonded labour but as farmers and entrepreneurs. They prospered wherever they settled, on the west coast of Canada and in the US as lumbermen and farmers, in East Africa as industrialists and tradesmen, in Arab countries as building contractors, in Malaysia and Singapore as shopkeepers, in north-eastern Australia as growers of bananas and avocado pears, in New Zealand as cattle breeders. In every country in the world, a few Sikh families will be found. The story goes that when the first American astronauts landed on the moon they ran into a sardarji taking his family for a stroll. The Americans, more than surprised, asked: 'When on earth did you get here?' The sardarji replied: 'Oh, we came here soon after the Partition.'

After the Partition, Sikh refugees from Pakistan spread to all corners of India, another migration began to foreign countries. Go to Indira Gandhi International Airport at any time, you'll find that almost half the Indian passengers leaving the country are Sikhs. In India, besides farming in Haryana, the Ganganagar district of Rajasthan and the Terai region, they went into the road transport business in a big way and virtually monopolized the manufacture of motor spare parts. A few families prospered in industry: Ranbaxy in pharmaceuticals, Raunaq Singh in the manufacture of pipes and tyres, the Inder Singhs and the Sahus of Mumbai in steel, the Majethias in sugar. Though their proportion in the defence services has declined sharply since Independence, they're still well represented in the upper echelons. They have regained their pre-eminent position in politics, not only in Punjab but at the Centre. They gave India one of its most distinguished prime ministers, Manmohan Singh, the brightest of civil servants in Montek Singh Ahluwalia and election commissioner M.S. Gill. It is hard to believe that Sikhs form less than 2 per cent of the population of India. In a country ridden with beggars, it's rare to see a Sikh stretch out his hand for alms. This is not short of a miracle. The miracle was performed by Guru Gobind Singh 300 years ago on 13 April 1699 AD.

Mahatma Gandhi

I can't think of another person in the history of the world about whom more is known and written than Mahatma Gandhi: the entire corpus of Gandhiana would fill several libraries. Besides his autobiography, written early in life, he wrote extensively for the journals he edited, gave long interviews to mediapersons, carried on correspondence with hundreds—almost all of this has been meticulously collected and published. Many distinguished writers wrote his biographies, psychologists like Erik Erikson and Sudhir Kakar published analyses of his relationships with different women. A year or so ago, his grandson, Rajmohan Gandhi, published what appeared to be the definitive version of his grandsire's life (*Mohandas—A True Story of a Man, His People and an Empire*). One would have thought all that could be said about the Mahatma had been said. That is not so. Soon after, another grandson, Rajmohan's younger brother, Gopalkrishna, came out with a massive 863-page tome on the same subject. The first question that comes to mind is: does it fill any gaps left by the others? On going through the text, my answer is a categorical yes. Primarily for the reason that, in a strange way, it brings the Mahatma alive and clears many misconceptions about him.

The Gandhis were grocers who became dewans of different Kathiawar states. They were orthodox Hindu banias influenced by Jainism: strictly vegetarian, teetotallers and observing the rigid code of conduct of a middle-class Hindu joint family. Mercifully, the family was free of anti-Muslim prejudices. This was young Mohandas's make-up when he left for England to study law.

He made feeble attempts to turn himself into a brown sahib but instead became a vigorous propagator of vegetarianism and abstinence from liquor. When he returned home, his first clients were Muslims. One of them took him to South Africa. A majority of the members of the Natal Indian Congress set up by M.K. Gandhi, attorney, were Muslims. It is not surprising that he had a soft corner for the community.

Gandhi evolved his values of life and code of conduct in South Africa. He realized that the most potent weapon to use against an enemy stronger than yourself was passive resistance based on the conviction that truth was on your side; thus was born the concept of satyagraha—truth force. It was to be wielded without any ill-will, but with the conviction that the opposition would come to see your point of view and lay down arms. However, in order to make satyagraha a potent force, one had to shed fear and, if necessary, suffer humiliation and physical violence. Gandhi was often beaten up and put in jail. There were attempts made on his life and more than once he came close to being killed. He never flinched and soon the White rulers, both British and Dutch, came to respect him. He was able to talk to generals, Governors, Viceroys and kings on the level. Even so, when wars broke out, as they did with the Boers and the Zulu revolt, he raised corps of volunteers to tender medical aid to the injured. It was this kind of conduct that gave him the image of a saint.

In the ashrams he set up in South Africa, he laid down strict rules of conduct: early morning prayers, cleaning your mess yourself, growing vegetables, cooking, making your own garments and shoes. Consumption of liquor and tobacco was forbidden; sex tolerated only among married couples. The slightest deviation from the norm was punished by Gandhi undertaking a fast for penance for what he regarded as sins. It earned him the image of a crackpot. He admitted it himself. 'Some look upon me as a fool, a crank, or a faddist, wherever I go I am sought out by fools, cranks and faddists,' he wrote. One can't be blamed for drawing that conclusion. He gave up drinking cow's or buffalo's milk because they were subjected to phooka (whatever that means). But goat's milk was okay. His secretary made sure the goat in question was of good character and looked into its eyes for signs of randiness. Once when goat's milk was unavailable, he made do with goat-milk butter. And promptly went down with diarrhoea. Alcohol was to him sheer poison. Once Nehru, who was sick in Poona jail, refused to take brandy because Bapu disapproved of it. So brandy was injected into him by the prison doctor. Gandhi assured him he had done no wrong. He wrote: 'You cannot be blamed for the doctor having given you an injection of brandy. You did not drink it for pleasure. Moreover, an injection of brandy is not as objectionable as a vaccine.'

His formula was simple: whatever gave pleasure to the senses was perforce sinful. There was an element of a sadistic killjoy in him. In a way he became the chief spokesman of the SPTD (the Society for the Promotion of a Tasteless Diet). Boil vegetables if you must, but don't add salt, spices, chilli, garlic or pickles to it. They are tamasic—of the lowest grade. To make sure, he examined the stools of people to see if they had shat out undigested food. The last meal he took before he was assassinated was raw carrots. He laughingly described it as cattle fodder.

More bizarre were his relations with his wife and sons. He treated them very shabbily. Once he threw his wife, Kasturba, out of his house. After having expended his lust on her when she was young, he took a vow of celibacy without consulting her. He had himself massaged by female disciples. To ensure that he had got the better of his libido he had young women sleep beside him on the floor: Kasturba was no longer a temptation to be resisted. He would never have tolerated her having masseurs or young men sleep beside her to test her virtue. He was never close to any one of his four sons. It is easy to understand why Harilal took to hard drinking and converted to Islam. He wanted to attract his father's attention by spiting him.

Despite being aware of his fads, by the time Gandhi returned to India to lead the freedom movement, he was acclaimed by people as their messiah. Why? Because what people know of the world's great teachers is largely based on myth, legend and make-believe. They could raise the dead, walk on water, fly in the air and perform other miracles. Artists painted their portraits without having a clue what they looked like. They put halos around their heads to give them an aura of divinity. About Gandhi people knew everything and did not think he needed a halo around his head to put himself beyond their reach. They knew he never told a lie, never flinched in the face of danger or against threats of violence. He rose to supreme heights when India won its battle for freedom. While others were preparing to celebrate, Gandhi went to places hit by communal violence—Calcutta, Bihar, Noakhali and Delhi. He fasted and prayed for peace to return. Where the police and the army had failed, he succeeded. In Delhi, he held prayer meetings in a Dalit temple and insisted that passages from the Quran be read. Angry Hindus stopped him thrice from doing so: the fourth time they relented. When mobs of infuriated Hindu and Sikh refugees from Pakistan destroyed a part of the mausoleum of Bakhtiar Kaki in Mehrauli, he went there to pray for forgiveness. When anti-Pakistani feelings were at a fever pitch and the Indian government refused to honour its pledge to pay Pakistan Rs 55 crore, he went on a fast and forced the government to abide by its word. He knew he was asking for trouble but did not give it a second thought. A calumny was spread about his having agreed to the partition of India on communal lines. He told his secretary Pyarelal: 'Today I find myself alone. Even the Sardar (Patel) and Jawaharlal think that my reading of the situation is wrong and peace is sure to return if the Partition is agreed upon . . . I shall perhaps not be alive to witness it, but should the evil I apprehend overtake India and her independence be imperilled, let it not be said that Gandhi was a party to India's vivisection.' He was pretty certain he would not be allowed to live. In a prayer meeting on 16 June 1947, he said, 'I shall consider myself brave if I am killed and if I still pray to God for my assassin.' As he had anticipated, the assassin finally got him on 30 January 1948. He went with the name of Rama on his lips—a glorious end to a glorious life.

Of one thing I am pretty certain: if the Mahatma were to visit Calcutta today, he would not be staying with his grandson at the Raj Bhavan despite the exemplary service he has rendered to him.

ON THE '84 RIOTS

There are two anniversaries so deeply etched in my mind that every year when they come around I recollect with pain what happened on those days. One is 31 October 1984, when Mrs Gandhi was gunned down by her two Sikh security guards. The other is the following day, when the 'aftermath' consummated itself: frenzied Hindu mobs, driven by hate and revenge, killed nearly 10,000 innocent Sikhs across north India all the way down to Karnataka. In 1989, Mrs Gandhi's assassin, Satwant Singh, and Kehar Singh, a conspirator, paid the penalty for their crime by being hanged to death in Tihar jail. Twenty-four years later, the killers of 10,000 Sikhs remain unpunished. The conclusion is clear: in secular India there is one law for the Hindu majority, another for Muslims, Christians and Sikhs who are in minority.

31 October 1984: The sequence of events remains as vivid as ever. Around 11 a.m., I heard of Mrs Gandhi being shot in her house and taken to hospital. By the afternoon, I heard on the BBC that she was dead. For a couple of hours, life in Delhi came to a standstill. Then hell broke loose—mobs yelling *'khoon ka badla khoon se lenge'* (we'll avenge blood with blood) roamed the streets. Ordinary Sikhs going about their life were waylaid and roughed up. In the evening, I saw a cloud of black smoke billowing up from Connaught Circus: Sikh-owned shops had been set on fire. An hour later, mobs were smashing taxis owned by Sikhs right opposite my apartment. Sikh-owned shops in Khan Market were being looted. Over 100 policemen armed with lathis who lined the road did nothing. At midnight, truckloads of men

armed with cans of petrol attacked the gurudwara behind my back garden, beat up the granthi and set fire to the shrine. I was bewildered and did not know what to do. Early next morning, I rang up President Zail Singh. He would not come on the phone. His secretary told me that the President advised me to move into the home of a Hindu friend till the trouble was over. The newly-appointed prime minister, Rajiv Gandhi, was busy receiving guests arriving for his mother's funeral; Home Minister Narasimha Rao did not budge from his office; the Lt Governor of Delhi had no orders to put down the rioters. Seventy-two gurudwaras were torched and thousands of Sikh houses looted. Over the next few days, TV and radio sets were available for less than half their price.

Around mid-morning, a Swedish diplomat came and took my wife and me to his home in the diplomatic enclave. My aged mother had been taken by Romesh Thapar to his home. Our family lawyer, Anant Bir Singh, who lived close to my mother, had his long hair cut and beard shaved to avoid being recognized as a Sikh. I watched Mrs Gandhi's cremation on TV in the home of my Swedish protector. I felt like a Jew must have in Nazi Germany. I was a refugee in my own homeland because I was a Sikh.

What I found most distressing was the attitude of many of my Hindu friends. Only two couples made it a point to call on me after I returned home. They were Sri S. Mulgaonkar and his wife, and Arun Shourie and his wife, Anita. As for the others, the less said the better. Girilal Jain, editor of the *Times of India*, rationalized the violence: the Hindu cup of patience, he wrote, had become full to the brim. N.C. Menon, who succeeded me as the editor of *Hindustan Times*, wrote of how Sikhs had 'clawed their way to prosperity' and well nigh had it coming to them. Some spread gossip of how Sikhs had poisoned Delhi's drinking water, how they had attacked trains and slaughtered Hindu passengers. At the Gymkhana Club where I played tennis every morning, one man said I had no right to complain after what the Sikhs had done to the Hindus in Punjab. At a party, another gloated, '*Khoob mazaa chakhaya*—we gave them a taste of their own medicine.' Word had gone around: 'Teach the Sikhs a lesson'.

Did the Sikhs deserve to be taught a lesson? I pondered over the matter for many days and many hours and reluctantly admitted that Hindus had some justification for their anger against Sikhs. The starting point was the emergence of Jarnail Singh Bhindranwale as a leader. He used vituperative language against the Hindus. He exhorted every Sikh to kill thirty-two Hindus to solve the Hindu–Sikh problem. Anyone who opposed him was put on his hit list and some eliminated. His hoodlums murdered Lala Jagat Narain, the founder of the Hind Samachar group of papers. They killed hawkers who sold their papers. The list of Bhindranwale's victims, which included both Hindus and Sikhs, was a long one. More depressing to me was that no one spoke out openly against him. He had a wily patron in Giani Zail Singh who had him released when he was charged as an accomplice in the murder of Jagat Narain. Akali leaders supported him. Some like Badal and Barnala, who used to tie their beards to their chins, let them down in deference to his wishes. So did many Sikh civil servants. They lauded him as the saviour of the Khalsa Panth and called him Sant. I am proud to say I was the only one who wrote against him and attacked him as a hate-monger. I was on his hit list and continued to be so on that of his followers—for fifteen long years—and was given police protection which I never asked for.

Bhindranwale, with the tacit connivance of Akali leaders like Gurcharan Singh Tohra, turned the Golden Temple into an armed fortress of Sikh defiance. He provided the Indian government the excuse to send the army into the temple complex. I warned the government in Parliament, and through my articles, against using the army to get hold of Bhindranwale and his followers as the consequences would be grave. And so they were. Operation Bluestar was a blunder of Himalayan proportions. Bhindranwale was killed but hailed as a martyr. Over 5,000 men and women lost their lives in the exchange of fire. The Akal Takht was wrecked.

Symbolic protests did not take long coming. I was a part of it; I surrendered the Padma Bhushan awarded to me. Among the people who condemned my action was Vinod Mehta, then the editor of the *Observer*. He wrote that when it came to choosing between being an Indian and a Sikh, I had chosen to be a Sikh. I stopped contributing to his paper. I had never believed that I had to be one or the other. I was both an Indian and a Sikh and proud of being so. I might well have asked Mehta in return, 'Are you a Hindu or an Indian?' Hindus do not have to prove their nationality; only Muslims, Christians and Sikhs are required to give evidence of their patriotism.

Anti-Sikh violence gave a boost to the demand for a separate Sikh state and Khalistan-inspired terrorism in Punjab and abroad. Amongst the worst was the blowing up of Air India's Kanishka (23 June 1985), which killed all its 329 passengers and crew, including over thirty Sikhs. Sant Harchand Singh Longowal, who signed the Rajiv–Longowal accord (24 July 1985), was murdered while praying in a gurudwara just three weeks later. In August 1986, General A.S. Vaidya, who was the chief of staff when Operation Bluestar took place, was gunned down in Pune. The killings went on unabated for almost ten years. Terrorists ran a parallel government in districts adjoining Pakistan, which also provided them arms training and escape routes. It is estimated that in those ten years over 25,000 were killed. Midway, the Golden Temple had again become a sanctuary for criminals. This time the Punjab police led by K.P.S. Gill was able to get the better of them with the loss of only two lives in what came to be known as Operation Black Thunder (12–18 May 1988). The terrorist movement petered out as the terrorists turned gangsters and took to extortion and robbery. The peasantry turned its back on them. About the last action of the Khalistani terrorists was the murder of Chief Minister Beant Singh, who was blown up along with twelve others by a suicide bomber on 31 August 1995, in Chandigarh.

It is not surprising that with this legacy of ill-will and bloodshed a sense of alienation grew among the Sikhs. It was reinforced by the reluctance of successive governments at the Centre to bring to book the perpetrators of the anti-Sikh pogrom of 31 October and 1 November 1984. A growing number of non-Sikhs have also come to the conclusion that grave injustice has been done to the Sikhs. Several non-official commissions of inquiry—including one headed by retired Supreme Court chief justice S.M. Sikri, comprising retired ambassadors and senior civil servants—have categorically named the guilty. However, all that the government has done is to appoint one commission of inquiry after another to look into charges of minor relevance to the issue without taking any action. The Nanavati Commission has been at it for quite some time: I rendered evidence before it in 2002. It has asked for a further extension of time, which has been granted till the end of 2005. The only word I can think of using for such official procrastination is 'disgraceful'.

I have to concede that the attitude of the BJP government, led by Atal Bihari Vajpayee and L.K. Advani, towards the Sikhs has been more positive than that of the Congress, many of whose leaders were involved in the 1984 anti-Sikh violence. Some of it may be due to its alliance with the principal Sikh political party, the Akalis, led by Prakash Singh Badal. It also gives them a valid excuse to criticize the Congress leadership. Nevertheless, I welcomed the Congress party's return to power in the Centre because it also promises a fairer deal to other minorities like the Muslims and Christians. And I make no secret of my rejoicing over the choice of Manmohan Singh, the first Sikh to become prime minister of India, and he in his turn selecting another Sikh, Montek Singh Ahluwalia, to head the Planning Commission.

The dark months of alienation are over; the new dawn promises blue skies and sunshine for the minorities with only one black cloud remaining to be blown away—a fair deal to the families of the victims of the anti-Sikh violence of 1984. It was the most horrendous crime committed on a mass scale since we became an independent nation. Its perpetrators must be punished because crimes unpunished generate more criminals.

AMRITA PRITAM: AN UNSTAMPED TICKET

Amrita was a very beautiful girl, the daughter of a widower who was a pracharak from Gujranwala, now in Pakistan. She was brought up as an orthodox Sikh and moved with her father to Lahore where, at the age of fifteen or sixteen, she started writing poetry. It was syrupy stuff about Sikh gurus and Sikhism. It earned her instant acclaim from the orthodox. She also became the toast of the Punjabi literary circles, largely because of her stunning good looks. I was one of the many who bought her first collection. Among her many admirers was the then upcoming poet Mohan Singh Mahir, who claimed to be closer to her than anyone else. Most of it was fantasy and unknown to her.

Because of her acclaim in literary circles and, of course, her good looks, a leading hosiery merchant of Lahore's Anarkali Bazaar arranged a marriage between his son, Pritam Singh, and her. Amrita became Amrita Pritam. They had a son. After the Partition, they came to Delhi where Pritam Singh tried his hand at business, but failed. Amrita got a job with All India Radio. In Delhi, she made a decision to wipe out her past. She divorced her husband, but got custody of her son. She cut her hair and became a heavy smoker. She composed a dirge addressed to Waris Shah, the author of the tragic Punjabi love saga *Heer Ranjha*. Those few lines she composed made her immortal, both in India and Pakistan.

Aj aakhan Waris Shah noon,
Kithon kabraan vichon bol,

Te aj kitab-e-Ishq da koi agla varka phol!
Ik roi si dhee Punjab di,
Toon likh likh maare vaen
Aj lakkhan dheeyan rondiyan,
Tainu Waris Shah noon kehan
Utth dardmandan dia dardeya,
Utth tak apna Punjab
Aj bele laashaan bichhiyaan,
Te lahu di bhari Chenab

A rough translation of the last four lines would be:

Oh, comforter of the sorrowing
Rise from your grave and see your Punjab
The fields are strewn with corpses
And blood flows in the Chenab

Amrita was a woman of modest education and she wrote only in Punjabi. She could barely read any other language and was therefore unsophisticated in her writing. She was besotted with Bollywood. For her, the ultimate in success was to have some of her novels and short stories filmed. Her first novel to be translated from Punjabi into English was *Pinjar* (*The Skeleton*). I did the translation, purely out of love for her. I gave her all the royalties on one condition: to repay me with a candid account of her love life. She did so over many sessions. The only passion she admitted to was for the film lyricist Sahir Ludhianvi whom she had never met. But she had corresponded with him. I was disappointed. 'All this could be written on a postage stamp,' I told her. So when she wrote her autobiography, she called it *Raseedi Ticket* (*Postage Stamp*). She eventually met Ludhianvi here in Delhi. He was afraid of flying, so he took the train from Bombay. They met at Claridges, ready to consummate their great love affair. Nothing happened. Ludhianvi was a very heavy drinker.

She used to drop in frequently when I lived in my father's house at 1, Janpath. I think she was impressed like many others by the large house and garden. She reminded me a lot of Kamala Das who also visited me in my father's house a couple of times.

The two women had a lot in common. I interviewed both of them on different occasions. Each time I asked them a simple question, they would raise their voices and disappear into the clouds. They were both incapable of giving a simple answer to a simple question.

Amrita's real love affair was with Imroze (despite his name he was not a Muslim but a clean-shaven Sikh). There was total devotion on his part and this she accepted as her due. He was a reasonably good artist and painted her eyes, which were her most attractive feature, on the door and walls of her bedroom. He designed her book jackets. He was her lover, handyman and nurse, all in one. I still have his drawing of Waris Shah which they gave me.

Amrita was a taker, not a giver. She was unwilling to acknowledge what other people had done for her. Even when *Pinjar* was eventually made into a film, she did not once acknowledge that it was I who had translated it into English.

Amrita started a monthly magazine called *Nagmani*, named after the mythical gem in the head of the serpent. It largely consisted of her own writings. She persuaded her friends to subscribe to the magazine for life. I was also one of them.

My first disappointment came when she won the Sahitya Akademi award for Punjabi literature. She was a member of the selection panel and had cast the deciding vote in her own favour.

She wrote more than a dozen novels and many collections of short stories and poetry. I translated many of her poems when she won the Jnanpeeth award. Her novels and stories are contrived and no character comes alive. They are mainly about misunderstood and misused women who frequently break into tears. She couldn't have made a living by her writing because there are few readers in Punjabi. She published her books first in Hindi and later in Punjabi. She also made a tidy fortune in awards. After winning the Jnanpeeth prize money, the Delhi government gave her a few lakhs and the Punjab government gave her another ten or eleven lakhs. Money was never a problem for her.

Amrita got into trouble many times because of her writing. Once she was summoned by a court in Amritsar for something offensive she'd written about Sikhism. I not only wrote in her defence but agreed to appear in court with her. The case was withdrawn. Then, the Hindi writer Krishna Sobti took her to court for breach of copyright. Sobti had written her autobiography under the title *Zindagi Nama* (Life Story). Amrita later wrote about the life of some nondescript revolutionary under the same title. I again appeared in court in her defence, saying that there could be no copyright on a title like Zindagi Nama. I collected over a dozen books with the same title from the Iranian embassy because 'zindagi nama' is a Persian phrase. I also submitted my two volumes of Sikh history to the court to prove that Guru Gobind Singh's life story by one his disciples was also called *Zindagi Nama*.

This earned me the ire of Krishna Sobti. She exploded in rage in the high court after the hearing, shouting: 'Your Honour, don't believe a word of what he said. He belongs to the same mafia of rich writers.'

I think the most moving part of Amrita's life were her later years. She was stricken with illness and couldn't move. It was Imroze who looked after her with a devotion I've never heard of: changing her clothes, feeding her and keeping her clean.

All the praise that is now being lavished on her is mainly from people who have not read her. I feel that Amrita's only claim to immortality are those ten lines of lament to Waris Shah. Those haunting lines will remain long after the rest of her writing is forgotten.

Kasauli: My Mini Baikunth

I plan my summers to conform to nature's calendar. I stay in Delhi in July and August, go up to Kasauli in early September when the mountains are well-washed and green, and the hillsides flecked with wild flowers.

By the last week of August the monsoon is usually beating a retreat. So this year I left Delhi on 1 September, relying on the weather keeping its time-schedule, prepared to spend the month of September in my earthly paradise. It would not be as warm as Delhi and not too cold for comfort. Delhi was denuded of flowers, Kasauli's hills would still have its monsoon blossoms, chiefly the spectacular cactus, yucca gloriosa, with dozens of bell-shaped, ivory-pale white flowers suspended from one green stem and wild dahlias of various colours blazing away on the hill slopes.

But even before the Shatabdi Express had passed Sonepat (25 miles down the route), it began to rain and continued to pour all the way to Chandigarh. It seemed the rain had just been woken up after sleeping through June, July and most of August till alarm bells sounded, warning of a drought. Then it opened up its much delayed bags full of bountiful waters to make amends for its tardiness. The Sidhus, Poonam and Karanjit, were to drive us (my daughter, Mala, was with me) to Kasauli to spend the afternoon and evening with us. The downpour washed out their plans. Poonam had brought food and drink meant for four. My daughter and I ate it for four days.

We were not the only people to be fooled by the weather. There was heavy uphill traffic on the Chandigarh–Simla road, right into the heart of Kasauli. So instead of sitting out in the garden under the shade of the toon, and gazing into the blue heavens, I spent the first few days indoors by the fireside, wrapped up in a shawl, wishing I was back in Delhi.

It takes a day or two to get used to the solitude and all-pervading silence of the mountains. It takes an afternoon or two for the locals to know you are back so that they can drop in for some gup-shup. As for the total absence of the sounds of traffic and loudspeakers, I can only describe it as deafening except for the sound of the wind sloughing through the pine trees. Besides, the occasional plane going overhead, the siren from the Solan brewery and the peal of bells from Christ Church are all that I hear in the day. At this time of the year birds seldom sing. Their period of courtship is long over, the eggs have hatched and the parent birds are busy feeding their hungry chicks.

Being locked up indoors all day and all night can be boring beyond endurance. I want company, not necessarily human company because humans are demanding and talk too much. I found exactly what I was looking for—Billoo.

Two monsoons ago, when there was a short break in the downpour, I was sitting in my garden. I saw a tiny pup, black-and-white, fluffy and of no pedigree, stumbling along and shivering in the cold. I picked it up and cuddled it in my shawl. It looked up with its shiny black eyes to ask who I was. I rubbed its ears gently. It licked my hand to say thank you, made sweet moaning sounds, stopped shivering and fell asleep. There are few experiences more gratifying than to have a young thing fall asleep in one's arms.

Then its mother came along and I put it down on the ground. She scolded her pup for allowing strangers to take liberties with it and led it back home. I found out that the bitch belonged to the caretaker of the bungalow just below mine. It didn't take much for me to persuade them to give me the puppy as soon as it was weaned. The little one had been promised to my housekeeper, Prem Kumar. A month or so later, when it had been weaned, it was formally handed over. The puppy was a male; I named him Billoo. He spent an hour every evening in my lap nibbling at my cardigan buttons, pawing my hands and nipping my fingers with its pin-sharp teeth. I looked forward to its evening visits. He was a good listener and never talked back.

When I returned to Raj Villa the following summer, Billoo had grown to his full height. He did not recognize me. I had to bribe him with buttered toast and biscuits while having my afternoon tea. He had a nose for meat. Any evening he smelt chicken or mutton, he sat under the dining table waiting for his share.

Billoo was full of zest for life. Every evening his friends from the neighbouring bungalows assembled in my garden, waging mock battles. At times Billoo's mother also joined them. But Billoo proved to be a poor watchdog. When rhesus monkeys invaded my garden, he barked at them from a safe distance. When I egged him on, he made a brave show of attacking them but as soon as a big one turned to fight him, he ran back for protection. Now when monkeys come, he pretends not to see them. As for strangers, all he does is to bark to tell me: 'You have visitors.' As soon as they shake my hand, he wags his tail in welcome.

This time when I alighted from my car, Billoo was at the doorstep waiting for me. He licked my hands, jumped up on my legs and made me feel welcome. The third day, when Billoo was out for a morning stroll on the Upper Mall, he ran into a car. He howled in pain as he lay on the road. Prem's sister-in-law, Bhagwanti, and her son ran up to see what had happened. The car driver was good enough to take all of them to the vet. Mercifully, he had broken no bones.

He was brought home. He could not stand up and wailed in pain. It seemed as if the lights of Raj Villa had been switched off. For a day Billoo lay on the floor whining. The next day, he tried to drag himself down to the hill where his mother lived.

He did not get far and howled for help. Bhagwanti took him in her arms and brought him back. His mother had heard him cry. She came trotting up to see him. Now she comes every morning and evening to be with her son. Billoo is on the mend. He is still unable to walk properly but manages to wobble up to my bedroom window and make his presence felt. It won't be long before he is able to join me for breakfast, tea and supper. The lights of Raj Villa have been switched on again.

My housekeeper in Kasauli kept two dogs to keep uninvited visitors and monkeys at bay, Neelo and Joojoo. Neither could claim any pedigree and both had been picked out of litters of bitches living in the vicinity. Both were ill-tempered but their barks were stronger than their bites. Their ill-temper was more in evidence when I happened to be in Kasauli.

As is common with most dogs, they sense who is the master of the house, and attach themselves to him rather than to those who feed them. No sooner had I arrived than the two would vie with each other to claim closeness to me. Neelo being the younger and the tougher of the two would sit by my chair and snarl at Joojoo if he came anywhere near me. But Joojoo found ways to get around his rival. Neelo did not like to go for a stroll in the evening and would wait for me at the gate. I did not like Joojoo coming with me because he was prone to pick up quarrels with any dog we met during our walks. While going through the small stretch of the bazaar, Joojoo would fight with half-a-dozen dogs belonging to shopkeepers. However, over the years, I got used to the temperaments of the two dogs and stopped fussing over them.

This went on for fourteen years. Both Neelo and Joojoo aged but not very gracefully. White hair sprouted round their mouths, they became slower in their movements. I noticed the signs of ageing in the two dogs but refused to admit to myself that I, too, had aged and was now reluctant to step out of the house. When I last came to Kasauli in June, Neeloo was missing. My servant told me that the dog catchers employed by the cantonment board had fed him poison because he wore no collar. Joojoo, who had spent his lifetime quarrelling with Neeloo, looked older than ever before. His skin sagged over his bones, his genitals hung like a dilapidated sack under his belly, his legs trembled as he walked and his eyes looked bleary and unseeing. He would join me at tea time to beg for a biscuit or two because he could not chew anything harder.

One morning he came and sat by my side while I was having my morning tea. When I got up, he stood up on his trembling legs and looked pleadingly at me. I spoke to him gently: 'Joojoo *tu buddha ho gaya.* Joojoo *main bhi buddha ho gayaa.'* (Joojoo, you have grown old, so have I.) He looked at me with uncomprehending eyes and slowly went away. An hour later one of the boys living in the house came and told me: 'Joojoo *mar gaya.'* (Joojoo is dead.) I saw him lying by the club house. The cantonment board took his body away in a cart. So ended our fifteen-year-long friendship.

My constant companions, ever since I have been coming to Kasauli, are a family of spiders. They live apart in three bathrooms. I have no phobia of spiders. So I never disturb them. But I am curious to know why they stay in dark, smelly bathrooms and what they live on. They do not spin webs to catch flies or other insects; in any case there aren't any to catch. They hardly ever move from their chosen spots on the wall; and when they do, they only scamper along to some place where they cannot be seen. However, one evening I spotted one along the seat of my WC. I didn't want to chance being bitten on my bum: some spiders are known to be venomous. I brushed it aside with a newspaper before I lowered my bare bottom on the seat.

My curiosity was aroused. Back in my study, I consulted my book on insects. Lo and behold, it said spiders are not insects at all but only insect-like. Insects have three parts—head, thorax and abdomen; spiders have only two—four pairs of legs and no antennae. 'Okay,' I said to them, 'you are no miserable insects, but belong to the species arachnida, but what on earth do you live on? Where and how do you breed? Do you have predators that live off you?' One day I hope to solve the mystery of the webless spider and the vagaries of the monsoon. I must also find out why Kasauli has no fireflies (jugnu) but lots of glow-worms.

After two days of absolute solitude with no one to talk to besides the caretaker's mongrel, I begin to miss human voices and welcomed a visitor or two. I had two in succession, neither of whom I had seen before. I was lucky both times. The first was Nagina Singh of the *Indian Express*, Chandigarh edition. A comely, elegantly dressed young lass with a diamond sparkling in her nose pin. And all of nineteen. A no-nonsense young lady who came armed with a photographer. It was a business-like interview about the changes I had seen in Kasauli over the eighty years I have been coming here. The interview over, she shut her notebook and departed. The other was Baljit Virk, a teacher at Pinegrove School not far from Kasauli. I expected a middle-aged, blue-stockinged, bespectacled person with a schoolmarmish manner. In walked a statuesque beauty wreathed in smiles. She was an ex-air hostess, tired of seeing the world and being a glorified waitress. She decided to stay grounded and teach English (she had an MA in literature) and sociology. She wanted me to see the manuscript of the second novel she had written. 'Just read a page or two and tell me if it is any good.' I kept the manuscript: 'I will read all of it. Give me a week and then collect it.' I did not want to miss the opportunity of another tête-à-tête with the air hostess turned pedagogue. I was surprised with the theme of her novel, *Jockstrapped*. It was based on a young dipsomaniac who drinks at all hours, gets into scraps, smashes cars, has affairs with women and does not have to work for a living. I could not understand why Baljit chose to write about a good-for-nothing, foul-mouthed character, when she herself is a strait-laced teetotaller of the type in whose mouth butter would not melt. I'll find out the truth on her next visit.

At tea time, a strapping sardar and his comely sardarni joined me. 'How did you come by a name like Likhari?' I asked him. 'One of my ancestors was a master calligrapher who wrote with his nail. So we came to be known by that name,' he replied. His wife said, 'He also has a beautiful handwriting. I preserve his letters.'

'They must be love letters,' I suggested. 'Yes,' she replied with a blush. 'From when he was courting me.'

I asked them another question that Ghalib might well have asked visitors calling on him. 'Are you drinking people?' Both nodded their heads indicating yes.

Among the visitors who descended on me in my hide-out in Kasauli was Rajni Walia who came all the way from Simla to spend a couple of hours with me. Rajni was colourful in every sense of the word. She was decked up like a filmstar ready to face the cameras: heavily made-up, a dupatta with the colours of the rainbow and a paisley-shaped bindi more colourful than any I had seen. She carried a handbag studded with stones and marbles of many hues.

'Where on earth did you get that?' I asked.

'Baghdad,' she replied. 'My dad was an adviser to the Iraqi government for some years, I spent quite some time with him and did a lot of shopping.'

'And what do you do?' I questioned her.

'I am the associate professor of English literature at the government college, Simla,' she replied.

'Why Simla? Why not Chandigarh or Delhi?'

'My husband is in the Himachal Pradesh forest services. Simla is his base.'

'Can you tell me the name of the tree under which we are sitting?' I asked her because I was still uncertain of its identity.

'Toon.'

'And that big one facing us?' I saw a lot of langurs on it eating its leaves.

She took one glance and replied, 'Himachalis call it Khirik. My husband will give you its Latin name. I have picked up information about trees because I often go out with him on tours into the hinterland.'

'Where else have you been?'

'Just about everywhere,' she replied and fished out a book from her handbag. 'I did this in Australia. It was written under the guidance of David Parker, professor of English at the Australian National University, Canberra.'

Rajni Walia has written the book *Women and Self: Fiction of Jean Rhys, Barbara Pym & Anita Brookner*. I had not read anything by these ladies; nor, I suspect, have many Indians. The one thing that they share (according to Rajni) is their disappointment in love and marriage: something most women in love, married or single, experience in their lives.

Rajni has an MA, an MPhil and a PhD from Punjab University, and is a first class first throughout. She is currently writing about contemporary Indo–American women's fiction. Appearances are deceptive. This lady, whom I took as a light-weight because of the care she had taken in decking up, is quite a scholar. Long after she left, the fragrance of the perfume she wore lingered in the pine-scented air of my little garden.

For reasons unknown to me, many of the younger generation look upon me as a man-eating ogre, a cannibal sardarji. They come to see me in droves but keep at a safe distance as they do when seeing a tiger in a zoo. It takes me quite a while to convince them that I will not bite them and am as harmless as a teddy bear. Then they relax and say what they want to in rapid machine gun fire speed till they have run out of breath. One such couple who paid me a visit in Kasauli will stay in my mind a long time.

I was sitting in the garden under the shade of the massive toon tree, reading the morning papers. I heard the sound of footsteps at some distance from me. I looked up. It was a couple, a strapping young sardar in his fifties and a buxom, cuddlesome lass in her thirties. 'Can we disturb you for a moment?' asked the man. 'Come,' I replied, 'I am only whiling away my time doing a crossword puzzle.' They approached me gingerly, took their seats and introduced themselves: 'I am Major Joginder Singh Aulakh, the security officer of Punjabi University, Patiala,' said he. 'And I am his wife, Ravinder Pal Kaur Bajwa,' she said. Then began a rapid fire of questions from him interspersed with him taking my snapshots with a camera. All I was able to gather in the interludes allowed to me was that the Major had fought in two wars against Pakistan and was proud of his record. He had also taken part in Operation Bluestar under the command of Generals Sunderji and Brar, was witness to the destruction of the Akal Takht and had seen the bodies of Bhindranwale and General Shabeg Singh. He did not want to talk or even think about it. The episode had left deep scars on his psyche. He was an unhappy widower till he ran into Ravi Bajwa, equally unhappy because of her broken marriage and her two children in the custody of their father. They had a whirlwind romance: met one day, and got married the next, ignoring the twenty years' difference in their ages. They looked happy. I asked them to join me for a drink the next evening before they returned to Patiala.

They were much more relaxed the next day. Though the question-and-answer session was resumed, it was not as hectic as the day before. Ravi gave me a shawl to put over my knees and proceeded to scribble something on a greeting card her husband had given me. After they left, I read what she had written in Gurmukhi: a poem entitled 'China Dupatta' (white headcover). A rough translation would read as follows:

I am not a widow
Nor living in matrimonial bliss;
Nevertheless I drape myself in spotless white
White is a combination of many colours in display
White also combines other colours
As well as colours that lead one astray,
White is like milk

White the colour of purity
Bright as sunshine
And quiet as silence.
(Many things colourful white can hide)
I wear white because now I am a bride.

A welcome addition to Kasauli's landscape are refugees from Tibet. There are only about a dozen families who have opened up small kiosks made of gunny sacks, tarpaulin and wooden planks along the most frequented stretch of road extending from Jakki Mull's building housing the main provision store, run by Guptaji, a tailor and photographer, to Kalyan Hotel with its statue of a black cocker spaniel and a liquor vend.

They sell woollen goods like sweaters, scarves and gloves. Tibetan refugees, wherever they are, manage to live amicably with the locals. They are courteous, ever-smiling and law-abiding. In the very short season extending from April till the end of October, they manage to sell enough to make both ends meet. Then they go down to the industrial township of Parvanoo for the winter. The cantonment executive board used to charge them Rs 10 per month per stall. The rental rates were raised to Rs 70 per month. They paid that as well as other taxes.

The board allowed vegetable and fruit sellers to set up stalls as well. The board has now served them notices to shut shop so that it can build permanent shops. There is nothing wrong with that provided those hapless victims of persecution are assured that they will get the first option to resume their trade where they were and the kiosks not auctioned to the highest bidders.

There is a lot of pressure from local shopkeepers who have a lot more money to take over the site. This would be unethical and unfair. The Tibetan refugees are our guests till as long as they can return to their homeland. And Kasauli will not be the same without their winsome smiles.

As often in the past, on most days that I was in Kasauli, it rained intermittently every day and night. But the morning I left, the sky was an azure blue and the hills looked rain-washed and bright green. I had to wear my sweater, dressing gown and a shawl against the cold. Half an hour down the hill, it became warm enough to shed the woollen garments.

An hour later we were caught in traffic jams at Parvanoo, Kalka and Pinjore. For many years I have been hearing of plans to build a bypass which would skirt around these growing towns but so far even blueprints have not been prepared. The chief ministers of the states concerned are taken up with more important matters like staying in power. By the time I got off at the Kalka railway station, I was sweating and trying to cool off under the hot breeze churned downwards by ceiling fans.

I had an uneasy feeling that I was being given a final farewell. In Kasauli, munshi Mohan Lal, our local millionaire who comes to me at least once every few weeks for my kadam bosi (feet kissing), came twice—the second time to invite me to a reception for his son-in-law who had been elevated to the rank of a brigadier in Lucknow.

At Kalka station there was quite a turn out of celebrities to shake hands with me: A.S. Deepak, Poonam (the editor of *Preet Lari*) and her husband, Gaur, and the pretty Nagina. Cold drinks were served all around.

I was escorted to my seat on the Shatabdi Express where Kaushik, conductor-cum-man of letters, took charge of me. They may have wanted to bid me a final farewell, but I had no intention of allowing them to do so. Come next spring, I will be back in the Shivaliks.

NIRALA: POET, LOVER AND MADMAN

Even those who don't read Hindi know the poet Nirala (rare) as a highly eccentric character, a moonh phat (face-spitter) who took on Bapu Gandhi and Jawaharlal Nehru, had a crush on Vijaylakshmi Pandit (it was never reciprocated) and went crackers in the last years of his life. Now, for the first time, I have been able to read his work translated in English—*A Season on the Earth: Selected poems of Nirala*. It has been translated by David Rubin, once professor of Hindi at Columbia University. I have come to the conclusion that besides being a crackpot, Nirala was a great poet, and Rubin is a great translator.

Suryakant Tripathi was born in 1896 in the village Mahishadal (district Midnapur, West Bengal), in a family of Kanyakubja Brahmins who had migrated from Kanauj (Uttar Pradesh). He spoke both Hindi and Bengali fluently. He took on the poetic pseudonym Nirala in 1923. He lost his mother when he was only two years old. Nirala married Manohradevi (then eleven) from Kanauj. He failed in his matriculation examination and was thrown out of his home by his father. He lived for many years with his wife's parents, and a son and a daughter were born to him. Despite early setbacks, Nirala made his name as a poet.

He went to Calcutta to edit a magazine for the Ramakrishna Mission and then another journal, *Matvala*. He then moved to Lucknow where he lived for twelve years and saw the publication of his collection of poems, *Anamika*. He came to be known as the 'Tagore of Hindi'. Gandhiji made the mistake of asking his hosts at a meeting of Hindi littérateurs in Indore in 1936: 'Where is the Tagore of Hindi?' Sometime later, Gandhi happened to be in Lucknow. When Nirala went to see him, Gandhi's secretaries stopped him saying he was seeing some important politicians. Nirala snapped back: 'I am an even more important poet.'

Another time he cornered Pandit Nehru in a rail compartment and demanded to know why he had failed to pay tribute to Munshi Prem Chand on his death. In his later years Nirala began to have illusions of grandeur. He claimed to be a wealthy man, attached university degrees to his name and talked of his dialogues with Queen Victoria. He coined his own obituary a long time before he died. When visitors came to call on him, he would tell them, 'Nirala doesn't live here. The man you are looking for died long ago.' He died in a mental home in 1961.

Nirala was a poet of rare sensibility towards nature and feminine beauty. In an early composition he describes a young girl:

She sat on a rock,
Her blue skirt gently fluttering—thus,
Uninhibited, the evening breeze
Held some silent conversation with the lovely girl
And smiled.
Her curling hair,
Black and luxuriant,
Blue, loose and fragrant over her pale face,
Tumbled over her breasts,
Teased her affectionately.
From the open sky
The chill spray scattered,
Exhilarating,
On her shapely limbs.

In an earlier poem composed in 1916, which roused some controversy, he compared the blossoming of a jasmine bud to that of a young girl being embraced by her lover:

On a vine in the deserted wood
She slept, blissful in dreams of love,

Pure tender slender girl—
The juhi bud—
Eyes closed, languorous in the folded leaf.
A spring night. Her lover,
Tormented by separation in a distant land,
Was that wind they call
The southern sandal-mountain breeze.
He recalled their sweet reunions,
The midnight drenched in moonlight,
The lovely trembling body of the girl.
And then? That wind
Crossed over grove lake river mountain wood
And vine-entangled jungles
To reach where he could dally with the
budding flower.
She slept—
For, tell me, how could she suspect
That her lover was at her side?
The hero kissed her cheek,
And she swayed, shivering from it,
But even now she did not waken
Nor ask forgiveness for her fault.
The long curved sleepy eyes stayed shut
As though she swooned,
Intoxicated from the wine of youthful
longings—who can say? Ruthless, her lover,
Of a sudden cruel,
Struck that tender body hard,
Slapped her pale full cheeks.
The girl started up,
Stared all about her, astonished,
And found her darling by her bed.
She smiled, gratified in her desire,
And blossomed in her lover's arms.

ON KISSING

Some years ago I took the liberty of greeting the then Pakistani high commissioner Ashraf Jehangir Qazi's daughter with a kiss. She was around sixteen; I, nearing ninety. Her grandfather and granduncle were in college with me in England. A photograph of my embracing the teenager appeared in the *Indian Express* and was picked up by some Pakistani papers. It created a furore in Pakistan. Qazi was summoned to Islamabad to explain his daughter's conduct. He did so to their satisfaction. They felt pretty foolish about it. There were two postscripts to the event.

A few days later a Pakistani family, including their young daughters, came to call on me. As I opened the door to welcome them, the father said to me, 'First give my daughters a kiss, then we will come in.' And before the Qazis left India for USA, they came to say goodbye to me. This time it was their daughter who took the initiative, put her arms round my neck and kissed me on both my bearded cheeks. I often wonder what would have happened if instead of Qazi's little girl, I had taken the same liberty with her grandaunt, Pyari Begam, who was a great beauty and was in my age group. Perhaps it would have led to a war between the Baluchis and the Sikhs. It was truly said by Don Marquis: 'Mayhem, death and arson have followed many a thoughtless kiss not sanctioned by a person.'

There are a number of ways of kissing: an avuncular on the forehead, the fraternal on both cheeks, the more intricate on the lips, or side of the neck. The choice largely depends on the female recipient because males are over-eager to convert the gesture into an intimate relationship. It is said high-heeled shoes were specially invented for short women who were tired of being kissed on their foreheads. An honest kiss demands the meeting of the lips. Even with this there are countless ways of expressing the range of emotions.

Vatsayan made a list of over sixty ways in his sex classic *Kamasutra*. In the matter of kissing no one needs a textbook to guide him or her. They know all there is to know from the day they were born. Nor do they have to wait for astral signs to tell them of auspicious days to go ahead. There is an old English saying: 'Kissing is not in season when the gorse is not in bloom.' Gorse is in full blossom right through the year. It grows in profusion in the Shivaliks: it is a foot-high bush with tiny pink flowers.

One does not have to define a kiss. Henry Gibbons made a silly attempt which robbed it of all the joy it yields, to wit: 'The anatomised juxtaposition of two orbicularis oris muscles in a state of contraction.' Nonsense. The poet Robert Herrick was much closer to the mark when he wrote: 'What is a kiss? Why kiss, as some approve; they pave sweet cement, glue and lime of love.'

Kisses can be lethal as well as life-giving. There was the Kiss of Judas which betrayed Jesus Christ and led to his crucifixion. It was the kiss of death. There is also the prolonged kiss of resuscitation to save the life of a drowned person. There is the kiss that reveals a past relationship. There is a kiss which means nothing but the meeting of lips as an old Italian proverb says: 'A kiss on the lip does not always touch the heart.' It is the kind of kiss that film actors plant on each other under the glare of lights in front of cameras with dozens of people watching them. These are fake emotions that don't exist. Meanwhile, I find solace in an old Spanish saying: 'A kiss without a moustache is like an egg without salt.' I have plenty of moustache.

ON THE NANAVATI REPORT

I have only two words for Justice G.T. Nanavati's inquiry report on the butchery of Sikhs: utter garbage. I have the report in hand, all 349 pages, plus the Action Taken Report presented by Prime Minister Manmohan Singh's government in Parliament on 8 August 2005. I thought it would take a whole day or two to go through it. It took only a couple of hours because it is largely based on what transpired in zones of the different police stations and long lists of names which meant nothing to me. There are broad hints about the involvement of Congress leaders like H.K.L. Bhagat, Jagdish Tytler, Dharam Dass Shastri and Sajjan Kumar. Nanavati gives them the benefit of the doubt and suggests yet another inquiry commission to look into the charges against them. Yet another commission? For God's sake, is he serious? To say the least, I was deeply disappointed with the whole thing. But the game of shirking responsibility was to attain higher levels!

First, the government took its own sweet time to put the report on the table of the House, waiting till the last day allotted to it for doing so. Union Home Minister Shivraj Patil had assured the House when the report had been submitted to him six months ago that the government had nothing to hide. However, he hid it till he could hide it no more. That shows the government's mala fide intent in the whole business. Even the Action Taken Report makes for sorry reading. Most of it is aimed at the policemen who are now retired from service and hence no longer liable for disciplinary action. Any wonder why, despite monetary compensation, the sense of outrage among the families of the victims has not diminished with the passage of the years?

On 31 October 1984 northern India witnessed a bloodbath the likes of which the country had not experienced since Independence nor after. In Delhi, over 3,000 Sikhs were murdered, their wives and daughters gangraped, their properties looted, seventy-two gurudwaras burnt down. The all-India total of casualties was close to 10,000, the loss of property over thousands of crores. Indira Gandhi's assassination, by her two Sikh bodyguards, triggered off the holocaust. As the news of her death spread, rampaging mobs of Hindus armed with cans of petrol, matchboxes and lathis set upon Sikhs they met on the roads—easily identifiable because of their distinct appearance—and set them on fire. Sikh-owned shops and homes were attacked and looted. Most of this mayhem and murder took place in Congress-ruled states. The police was instructed not to intervene. It was only then that people realized how much ill-will Sikhs had earned because of the hate-filled utterances of Bhindranwale against Hindus and the years of killings carried out by his hoodlums in Punjab. No Sikh leader, neither Congress nor Akali, had raised his voice in protest. Consequently, when Mrs Gandhi ordered the army to enter the Golden Temple to get Bhindranwale dead or alive, no Hindu condemned the action as unwarranted. Sikhs were deeply hurt by Operation Bluestar and ultimately two of them decided to murder Mrs Gandhi. What followed was largely condoned by Hindus and the Hindu-owned media. There were few people left to share their pain. It must be acknowledged that some leaders of the Sangh Parivar and the RSS, including A.B. Vajpayee, went out of their way to help the Sikhs. So did men like Ram Jethmalani, Soli Sorabjee and a few others.

It was evident that the Central government had abdicated its authority. President Giani Zail Singh, who returned from a foreign tour, called in at the All India Institute of Medical Sciences and after paying homage to Mrs Gandhi's body returned to Rashtrapati Bhavan. His car was stoned on the way. Thereafter, he refused to entertain phone calls. When a group led by I.K. Gujral and General J.S. Arora and Patwant Singh muscled their way into Rashtrapati Bhavan, he assured them he was doing everything he could. He had done the same kind of thing earlier: Operation Bluestar took place without his knowledge. He learnt about it from the media. Then he made noises in strict privacy but did not resign. Nor did he resign when fellow Sikhs were being butchered. He brought the prestige of the President of the Republic to an all-time low.

Rajiv Gandhi, who flew in from Calcutta with his cousin and confidant, Arun Nehru, was quickly sworn in as prime minister by Zail Singh without consulting other ministers or chief ministers of states. Rajiv was busy receiving foreign dignitaries coming to attend his mother's funeral. Days later, in his first public speech, he exonerated the murderers: 'When a big tree falls, the earth beneath it is bound to shake.' He meant to take no action in the matter and retained men named as leaders of mobs in his cabinet. Home Minister Narasimha Rao did not stir out of his house. When a few eminent Sikhs approached him, he listened to them in studied silence. He remained, as he always was, the paradigm of masterly inactivity. With the three men at the top refusing to do their duty, little could be expected from the Lt Governor of Delhi or the police commissioner. Section 144 of the IPC, forbidding gatherings of more than five people, was not promulgated or enforced; no curfew was imposed, no shoot-at-sight order given. A unit of the army was brought in from Meerut but when it was discovered that they were Sikhs, they were ordered to stay in the cantonment and not meddle with the civic unrest. The only term I could think of using for the way the authorities carried out their duties is 'downright disgusting'. It was like spitting in the face of all democratic institutions.

However, there were citizens' organizations that refused to allow a crime of this magnitude to go uninvestigated and unpunished. Leading them were Dr Rajni Kothari and Justice (retd) V.M. Tarkunde. Kothari's report, 'Who Are the Guilty', named men like H.K.L. Bhagat, Jagdish Tytler, Sajjan Kumar, Dharam Dass Shastri—all MPs and leaders of the Delhi municipality and leaders of goonda gangs. None of those named took these men or organizations to court for criminal libel. When Jagdish Tytler claimed that none of the commissions of inquiry implicated him in the anti-Sikh violence, he was lying. Only sarkari commissions let him off the hook.

More important than Kothari's and Tarkunde's findings were those of the non-official commission of inquiry set up under retired chief justice of the Supreme Court, S.M. Sikri. Comprising retired ambassadors, Governors and senior civil servants (none of them a Sikh), the commission castigated the government in no uncertain terms. The government could not ignore its verdict. Ultimately, Rajiv Gandhi took the Sikh problem in his own hands. He appointed Arjun Singh, the Governor of Punjab, to make contact with the Akali leaders who were in jail. They were released in small batches to create a favourable atmosphere. Secret negotiations with Sant Harchand Singh Longowal were started. Zail Singh, Buta Singh and others were kept in the dark. On 24 July 1985, the Rajiv–Longowal Accord was signed. Amongst other items, it provided for an inquiry commission into the incidents of violence of November 1984. Justice Ranganath Mishra of the Supreme Court was appointed as a one-man commission. 'Operation Whitewash' had begun. Before Mishra was half-way through, the panel of lawyers representing the victims of the holocaust led by Soli Sorabjee expressed its lack of confidence in the learned judge's impartiality and withdrew from the commission. Mishra went ahead and submitted his findings to the government. As expected, he held the Lt Governor and the police commissioner of Delhi guilty of dereliction of duty. It must have occurred to him that neither of the two could have acted the way they did without the instructions of higher-ups, like the prime minister or someone acting on his behalf or the home minister. I doubt if Mishra can look at his own face in a mirror.

I don't think Rajiv Gandhi was himself a party to the anti-Sikh pogrom. If he was guilty of anything, it was allowing it to go on for two days and nights till his mother's funeral was over. Behind it all was his eminence grise who sent out the message: 'Teach the Sikhs a lesson'. No commission of inquiry, official or unofficial, has looked into the role of this sinister character, although he is still very much alive and around in Delhi's political circuit. Nor, unfortunately, can I look into it at this stage.

After the Mishra Commission, nine others were instituted by the government. Their terms of reference were restricted. Nothing much came out of their findings as most of them focussed on the shortcomings of the Delhi police in handling the crisis. Resentment against the government continued to simmer. Ultimately, in May 2000, the government set up yet another commission of inquiry under Justice G.T. Nanavati. He was to submit his report in six months. At the leisurely pace at which he heard evidence tendered, it took him five years to do so. I did not expect very much from him. But H.S. Phoolka, who had taken charge of presenting victims' grievances, persuaded me to file an affidavit and appear before him. I did so, but the way the inquiry commission functioned didn't inspire much confidence. It was less like a court dealing with criminal charges and more like a tea party with lawyers on both sides exchanging pleasantries. I told the commission what I had seen with my own eyes taking place around where I live: the burning of Sikh-owned taxi cabs and the desecration of a gurudwara behind my flat, the looting of Sikh-owned shops in Khan Market—all in full view of dozens of policemen armed with lathis lined along the road but doing nothing. I also told him of my futile attempts to get President Zail Singh on the phone.

There is no doubt about it: the November 1984 anti-Sikh violence will remain a blot on the face of our country for times to come. No one will take the findings of these sarkari commissions of inquiry seriously. It will be left to historians to chronicle events that led to this tragedy and the miscarriage of justice that followed.

A few salutary lessons that the experience has taught us should be kept in mind by our leaders. The most important is to understand that unpunished crimes breed criminals. Another equally important thing to bear in mind is that the state must never abdicate its monopoly of punishing criminals; if it overlooks its duty or delays dispensing justice beyond limits of endurance, it encourages aggrieved parties to take the law in their own hands and settle scores with those who wronged them. If we do not learn these lessons now, we will have more holocausts in the years to come.

ON NAMES

People's names can produce a lot of bawdy humour, particularly when translated into other languages. When I was a student in England, I had two pretty girls in my class: one was named Yvonne Bych. Despite her admonishing classmates that the name was pronounced 'Bikh', everyone called her Yvonne Bitch. The second girl was Laura O'Gilvy. Laura is a pretty common girl's name in England but it took me months of close friendship to tell her what it meant in Hindustani.

Once on a visit to Sweden, I was introduced to a Professor Lund who was due to go on a lecture tour of India. Lund is also a common name in Scandinavia. After a few drinks I confided in him that when being introduced to Indian audiences he should be prepared for a few sniggers. He took it very calmly and replied: 'That is very interesting. I was in a similar predicament when a lady professor from your country came here to deliver some lectures and I had to introduce her. Her name was Miss Das. In Swedish, the word "doss" means shit.'

I have quite a collection of Indian names which sound very odd to my ears. Some years ago, I exchanged correspondence with a gentleman whose name was Mr Chootiah. Every Christmas when I go for a short vacation at Bogmalo beach in Goa I pass a clinic with the name printed in bold letters, Doctor Chodankar. It is just as well the doctor practises among the Konkanese and not in northern India. The same goes for many Tamilian friends whose names are based on the lingam: Shivalingam, Mahalingam, Bhootalingam, etc.

168

Sikh names do not provide the same kind of fun. Most of them are of Hindu origin with the appendage Singh (lion) or in the case of females, Kaur (lioness or princess). A few like Nawab, Iqbal, Mubarak, Gulzar are Muslim. They also borrowed some from the British: Angrez (English), Jarnail (General), Kaptaan (Captain) and Major. Sikh aristocracy, which employed English nannies, accepted nicknames given by them: boys got names like Cecil, Robin, Dicky, Richard and the like. Girls were named Jewel, Ruby, Diamond, Dolly, etc. About the oddest Sikh name I have come across is But Shikan (Idol-breaker) Singh. He is a member of the Foreign Service. Another combination of the first name, the surname and assumed pseudonym which sounded strange was that of the eminent scholar, Rajya Sabha member and Governor of Goa, Dr Gopal Singh Dardi, which meant Protector of Cows and Lion Who Feels Others' Pain.

Some names are more popular than others, creating confusion when they occur in the same family. In my extended clan we had three Kartar Singhs. Pseudonyms were attached to their names to distinguish them from each other. The one who wore glasses became Kartar Singh Ainkee; the one who was potbellied became Kartar Singh Dhiddal; the third who stammered became Kartar Singh Thuthal. All three gracefully accepted these appendages.

Sikhs claim they abolished caste distinctions and use a single surname, Singh. Now that caste has raised its ugly head, many have re-attached caste names like Randhawa, Brar, Gill, Sandhu, Sidhu (all Jat agriculturist tribes), Ahluwalia, Sethi, Narula, Chhatwal, Malhotra, Joshi, Raina (all Khatri Arora or Brahmin). Some have got around the problem by attaching names of their villages or towns: Longowal, Badal, Barnala, Ramoowaliah.

Names are more important than people realize. At my naming ceremony, as the Granth Sahib was opened, the letter that appeared at the top of the page was 'kh'. My grandmother to whom I was devoted gave me the name Khushal. I hated it because of its abbreviation 'Shalee' by which everyone called me. At school, boys tortured me by chanting a doggerel: *'Shalee*

Shoolie, Bagh dee Moolee (This shalee or shoolee is the radish of some garden).' I got rid of Khushal and changed it to Khushwant to rhyme with my elder brother's name, Bhagwant. According to a dictionary of names it means full of happiness. Come to think of it, I might well have stuck to being Khushal Singh. As they say what difference do names make?

Natha Singh, Prem Singh
One and the same thing.

GHALIB

The biggest name in Persian and Urdu literature produced in the Indian subcontinent is that of Mirza Asadullah Khan Ghalib (1797–1869). And the most revered interpreter of Ghalib's life and works is the professor emeritus at London's School of Oriental and African Studies, Ralph Russell. He already has half a dozen books on Ghalib to his credit; *The Oxford India Ghalib: Life, Letters and Ghazals* is a compendium which includes all that is known about Ghalib's life from his own pen, the letters he wrote and received from his friends and admirers, observations made by eminent men of letters like the poet Altaf Husain Hali, translations of select poems in Persian and Urdu. This is the last word on Ghalib in every sense of the word.

Ghalib was born in Agra on 27 December 1797. His father and forefathers were Seljuk Turk soldiers of fortune who sought employment in the armies of princes. They regarded themselves as members of the aristocracy. His father married into a distinguished and prosperous Agra family but died when Ghalib was just five. Ghalib spent most of his childhood in his maternal grandparents' home and received an education in Persian, Arabic, Urdu, logic and philosophy. He started writing in Urdu at a very young age and in Persian when he was eleven.

Ghalib was thirteen when he married Umrao Begum, aged twelve, who was distantly related to the ruling family of Loharu. At his wedding, his eyes fell upon a dancing girl and he fell in love with her. While he gave his wife several children (all of whom died young), he continued patronizing dancing girls and prostitutes.

It is believed that he converted to the Shia faith in order to have a mutaa (time-bound) marriage with a courtesan.

In his youth, Ghalib was evidently well-provided for by grants from his mother's and his wife's family. He lived in style with a retinue of servants, rode on a palanquin or a horse and demanded the respect due to him. He was a tall, handsome man who loved women, wine and gambling. Ghalib was nineteen when he migrated to Delhi to seek the patronage of Emperor Bahadur Shah Zafar, himself a poet of some calibre, the umrah (nobility) who frequented the palace, the British in Calcutta and Queen Victoria in London. Poets could not survive on poetry and felt rulers owed it to them to keep them in comfort. In a letter to the Queen, Ghalib wrote that the kings of Persia 'would fill a poet's mouth with pearls, or weigh them in gold, grant them villages in fief or open the doors of their treasuries to . . . him'. It is ironic that the man who enriched Persian and Urdu literature remained a beggar all his life.

Ghalib was a non-conformist and a bon viveur. Though he revered Allah and the Prophet, he never said his five daily prayers, never fasted during Ramzan, nor went on a pilgrimage to Mecca. He patronized houses of pleasure, consorted with courtesans and was inordinately fond of liquor. He preferred French wines or rum. He also liked Scotch, which he took with scented water every evening while he composed poetry. When someone warned him that the prayers of persons who drank wine were never granted, he said: 'My friend, if a man has wine, what else does he need to pray for?'

When a Hindu friend brought him a bottle, Ghalib thanked him in verse:

Long had I wandered door to door,
Seeking a flask of wine or two—no more,
Mahesh Das brought me that immortal draught
Sikander spent his days in seeking for.

Hali mentions a dialogue with the king, who was very particular about fasting during Ramzan. The king asked Ghalib: 'Mirza, how many days' fast did you keep?' Ghalib replied, 'My lord and my guide, I failed to keep one.' He made his name as a man of ready wit who answered awkward questions with a touch of humour.

After the 1857 mutiny had been put down and the British had driven all Muslims out of Delhi, Ghalib, who had no sympathy for the mutiny and had stayed inside his home while it lasted, was summoned by a Colonel Burn and asked, 'You a Muslim?' Ghalib said, 'Half. I don't eat pork, but I drink wine.'

Next to alcohol, Ghalib loved mangoes. During the season he'd eat up to a dozen every day. Hali recounts an incident when the poet was strolling with the emperor in the palace orchard and kept staring at the mango trees laden with fruit. The king asked, 'Mirza, what are you looking at so attentively?' Ghalib said, 'My lord and my guide, some ancient poet has written: "Upon the top of every fruit is written, clearly and legibly, this is the property of A, the son of B, the son of C". And I am looking to see whether any of these bears my name and those of my father and grandfather.' The king had a basketful of his finest mangoes sent to him the same day.

As Ghalib's fame spread as a poet of unusual talent, he was much sought after by the literati as well as the kothawalis. He lived beyond his means. And when his grants dried up, Ghalib was in dire straits and fell heavily in debt. He was also a gambler and once spent three months in jail on charges of gambling. About himself he wrote: 'Fame and wealth are alien to me. I am myself the worst enemy of my good name. I am friends with all kinds of riff-raff and hand-in-glove with all sorts of rabble. My feet are used to loafing about aimlessly and my tongue has the habit of talking nonsense. I am the ally of a cruel fate in my own misfortunes and a prompter of my enemy. My rushing about has raised the dust in the mosque as well as the idol house and has made the Sufi's cloister and the tavern fall on each other.'

Throughout his life, Ghalib lived a hand-to-mouth existence, ever short of cash, ever living on credit.

It's strange that Ghalib initially thought that deep emotions could not be expressed in Urdu and preferred to pen them in Persian instead. Fortunately, he changed his mind in time and left a veritable treasure-house of gems. The poems lose much of their lustre in translation. The meaning comes across but the music of the words is lost. The best one can do is to read the original and then Russell's translation.

Ghalib loved India and its changing seasons:

> But in India even in autumn there is spring! And greenery, as if in Holi, douses the city with colour. In the winter months the north is snow-bound. And in this realm, roses blossom! To console the gardener, mourning at the departure of lilies, immediately blossom the roses of a hundred petals! Here sugarcane stands row upon row to block the way for anything withered and dropping.

It appears that Ghalib loved just about every place he visited. When almost reduced to begging, he betook himself to Calcutta to plead with the English rulers to restore the pension due to him. It was a tedious journey on palanquin, horseback and boat with long stops in different cities that fell on his route.

He was particularly enamoured with Benares and its beautiful women. He wrote: 'What to say of Benares! Where else would you come across such a city: I happened to visit it in the evening of my youth. Had I been young at that time, I would have settled down there and would never have left it.'

And again:

> Glory to the land which bestows peace upon souls;
> The heart is purified here of all filth.
> And no wonder—in the air of this city
> The perishable body itself is like pure air.
> But what especially raises one's spirit is the
> Contemplation of feminine beauty.
> Even if you have no understanding of beauty, come
> And look at the local fair ones, born of parts;

Be absorbed in the contemplation of incorporeal souls.
Can clay mixed with water glitter like this?

Ghalib had great admiration for the English race, its inventiveness, discipline and its fair, white, uninhibited women.

On arrival in the capital, he composed a rubai in praise of Bengal:

Every tune of life has its melody,
Every corner of the world has its own ambience.
They have as if removed fetters from my soul,
Wonderful are the water and air of Bengal.

He was ecstatic about everything he saw in Calcutta:

My friend, when you referred to Calcutta,
You shot an arrow right into my heart, alas, alas!
That rain-fed, succulent greenery, oh God
And those graceful, well-dressed fair ones, alas, alas!
Their glances try one's patience, God save them
From the evil eye!
Those fresh and sweet fruits, wah, wah,
And those pure and tasty wines, alas, alas!

Ghalib's last years were less stressed as he received monetary assistance from friends and from the nawab of Rampur. However, his health began to deteriorate. He had a premonition of death:

You wrote all over the pages of life and all came to an end;
You had no equal in poetry and all came to an end;
In old age wine was your consolation, Ghalib,
But you were deprived of it also, and all came to an end.

Ghalib tried to forecast the year of his demise but went woefully wrong in his guess. He was closer to the truth, though, when he wrote:

Life gallops on at a reckless pace,
I know not where it will stop,
The reins are not in my hands,
My feet not in the stirrups.

Ghalib died on 15 February 1869. Exactly a year later to the day died his wife, Umrao Begum.

Bathing Is Good for Your Soul

At different times in history, different people have had different notions on the importance of bathing. Indians must be the only people who made a daily bath an essential part of religious ritual. After clearing one's bowels, the next thing one has to do is to take a bath. No bath, no breakfast. No bath, no entering a temple or a gurudwara. Sikh practice puts a bath (ishnaan) on par with prayer (naam) and charity (daan). Bathing in rivers, notably the Ganges, washes away sins. Likewise, Sikh ritual prescribes a bath in the sarovar (sacred tank) alongside the gurudwara as a spiritual cleanser. The most important sarovar is the one in the middle of which stands Harimandir, the Golden Temple. The tank was dug by the fourth guru, Ramdas. The incantation that goes with the holy dip is: *Guru Ramdas sarovar haatey, Sab utrey paap kamaatey* (Bathe in the holy tank of Guru Ramdas, And all the sins you have committed will be washed away).

I have accumulated a lot of sins but have not yet washed them off in any sacred tank or holy river. I also discovered from experience that a hot bath during the winter months often gave me a cold and I could clean myself just as well by rubbing my body with a damp towel. My college years in England changed my attitude towards bathing. Like other Indians, I believed that wallowing in a long bathtub in your own body dirt was unwholesome. After some months I came to the conclusion that an English bath was far more cleansing than pouring water over oneself with a lota. So during winter, I bathed only twice a week. And was none the dirtier for it.

During my stint in Paris, I discovered that most French homes did not have a bathroom. Instead, they used a contraption called a bidet on which they sat astride as on a horse and turned on a tap which shot a shower of warm water on their bottoms and genitals. This, when repeated after soaping their private parts, did quite a thorough job. They sponged their armpits and liberally sprinkled them with talcum powder. A proper body wash was a weekend ritual performed in a public bath. On most Saturdays, girls from the office where I worked spent an hour or more in these public baths and were ready for a prolonged weekend with their boyfriends. When I rented a house in a suburb of Paris, I had to have a bathroom installed.

Europeans have an interesting history of bathing. Long before they turned Christian, Scandinavians and Germans bathed naked in lakes and rivers during the summer months, and in public baths during the winter. With the advent of Christianity, nakedness came to be associated with vulgarity, lascivious thoughts and, therefore, became sinful. St Agnes never took a bath; St Margaret never washed herself. Pope Clement issued an edict forbidding bathing or even wetting one's face on Sundays. Between the sixteenth and eighteenth centuries, the practice of bathing in rivers was frowned upon. In 1736, in Baden, Germany, the authorities issued a warning to students against 'the vulgar, dangerous and shocking practice of bathing'.

Slowly, very slowly, this prejudice against nudity and bathing abated. Nudist clubs sprang up. Sunbathing in the nude became fashionable. Today, at any seaside in Europe, Canada, Australia or New Zealand, you will see men, women and children strolling along beaches, naked as on the day they were born. And bathing together in the nude does not shock anyone except those who still regard nudity as a sin. Having a bath everyday has become a common practice.

I am reminded of an exchange of words in the British House of Commons in the early years of the Second World War. A labour minister in charge of power was pleading that a lot of coal could be saved if it was not used to heat water for bathing and that a bath a week was good enough. Winston Churchill stood up and remarked, 'No wonder the Labour Party is in such bad odour.'

L.K. ADVANI

L.K. Advani redrew the political and communal map of India. Whether it was for the good of the country will be a matter of debate for years to come. His recently published memoir, *My Country, My Life* is a massive tome running up to nearly a thousand pages. I thought it best to read his views on matters which were of vital interest to me and so decided to consult the index and see if it had something to say about me. I do not have an ego problem, it is just that for a brief period I played a role in promoting his career. Advani writes: 'Khushwant Singh became a good acquaintance of mine after the Emergency. I admired his writing and substantial scholarship on many subjects. He in turn admired our party for its work in fighting the carnage in Delhi in 1984, in the aftermath of Indira Gandhi's assassination. However, our relationship soured after the Ayodhya movement when he became quite critical of me.'

It is a fair assessment but something is missing. After the 1984 pogrom of the Sikhs when Advani stood for election to the Lok Sabha, I signed his nomination paper. The Sikhs were determined not to vote for the Congress because its leaders and cadres were involved in the killings and yet they were not sure of the BJP. They were undoubtedly influenced by the publicity given to my signing Advani's papers. Advani won and came to thank me.

I visited Advani's home a few times. I was charmed by the congenial atmosphere. The family watched Hindi films, welcomed anyone who dropped in. I felt comfortable. I also admired him. There was not a breath of scandal about money, nepotism or extra-marital affairs about him. He was a puritan: he neither drank, nor smoked nor womanized. He was clear-headed and modest. My disenchantment began after he launched his rath yatra from Somnath to Ayodhya. I turned critical. Advani was the chief guest at a public meeting that I was presiding. He was then home minister and arrived with a retinue of Black Cat commandos. I said to his face, 'Mr Advani, you sowed the dragon seeds of hatred in this country . . .' And much else. In his address, he said he would answer my charges at a more appropriate time. I hoped to find them in his autobiography; they are not there.

I turned the pages to see what he had to say about Mahatma Gandhi who remains the national touchstone to test political and moral decisions. He tells us that the RSS held Gandhi in high esteem and he, in turn, praised its military discipline. When Advani heard that cadres of the RSS were also involved in communal riots and that they took on Muslim hoodlums in street battles that erupted periodically, he went to the sarsanghchalak. The latter explained, 'If we object to the conduct of some Muslims in our society, it is not because they follow Islam but rather because of their lack of loyalty to India. The partition of India has proven us right. Therefore to call the RSS anti-secular is to show one's ignorance of what secularism stands for and what the RSS stands for.' Advani adds: 'This was my first lesson in secularism. I was twenty-one then.'

Advani did not pursue the matter further. He might well have asked: 'If the RSS is secular, how many Muslims and Christians does it have on its rolls?' Advani was fourteen years old when he enrolled himself as a worker for the RSS in Karachi. His views on secularism are naïve beyond belief. He tries to equate Gandhi's concept of Rama rajya in which all religions will be treated with equal respect—*sarva dharma samabhava*—with the RSS concept of Hindutva, 'a noble concept', according to him. The RSS was suspect in the assassination of Mahatma Gandhi. His assassin had been a member of the organization. Advani tells us that on Gandhi's murder the RSS was ordered to observe thirteen days of mourning. The gesture did not help: the RSS was declared illegal and many of its leaders put behind bars.

The one event that pitchforked Advani to the centre stage and reshaped India's politics was his yatra from Somnath to Ayodhya leading to the destruction of the Babri Masjid on 6 December 1992. He, more than anyone else, sensed that Islamophobia was deeply ingrained in the minds of millions of Hindus and it only needed a spark to set it ablaze. The choice of Somnath as a starting point and Ayodhya as the terminal was well-calculated. Mahmud Ghazni had destroyed the temple at Somnath; Ayodhya was believed to be the birthplace of Sri Rama (the year of his birth is unknown). It was bruited about that a temple to mark the birthsite had stood there till Babar destroyed it and built a mosque over the ruins. This is disputed by historians and the matter was being pursued in law courts. Advani ignored legal niceties and arrived with great fanfare at the site. Since he was determined to build a new Rama temple at the same spot, the fate of the mosque was sealed. What happened there on that fateful day was seen on TV by millions of people around the globe.

In his book, Advani claims that breaking the mosque was not on his agenda and that he actually sent Murli Manohar Joshi and Uma Bharati to plead with the people breaking it to desist. If that is so, why were the two seen embracing each other and rejoicing when the nefarious task was completed? We don't have to wait for the verdict of the Liberhan Commission to tell us what happened: we saw it with our own eyes. The destroyers were Shiv Sainiks and members of the RSS and they boasted about what they had done. Advani records the jubilation that followed at the site and along his triumphal return to Delhi. The repercussions were felt all over the world: Hindu and Sikh temples were targeted by irate Muslims from Bangladesh to the UK. Relations between Hindus and Muslims have never been the same in India. There were communal confrontations in different parts of the country: the serial blasts in Mumbai, the attack on the Sabarmati Express in Godhra and the massacre of innocent Muslims in Gujarat can all be traced back to the fall of the Babri Masjid. However, the BJP reaped a rich electoral harvest, won many of the elections that followed, and eventually installed Atal Bihari Vajpayee as prime minister and L.K. Advani as his deputy. He is now their candidate for the top job and asserts that he will not allow the Babri Masjid to be rebuilt.

The one time Advani faltered in his steps was during his visit to Karachi when he praised Jinnah's speech to the Pakistan Constituent Assembly on 11 August 1947 as 'a classic exposition of a secular state'. It might well have been so but it was delivered at a time when millions of Hindus and Sikhs were being driven out of Pakistan with slaughter and an equal number of Muslims driven out of India. It was the bloodiest exchange of populations in which over a million died and over 10 million were uprooted. Advani's eulogy must have pleased the Pakistanis; it was badly received in India, particularly by his RSS and BJP colleagues. He was severely censured and asked to step down from the leadership of the party. It seemed as if his political career was at an end. But he bounced back and within a year was again on the centre stage.

What now stands between Advani and his ambition to become prime minister is the Sonia Gandhi–Manmohan Singh partnership. Advani is doing his worst by trying to create a rift between them. He continues to harp on the issues of her Italian birth, her tardiness in taking Indian citizenship and her being close to a fellow Italian, the scamster Octavio Quattrocchi. He has described Manmohan Singh as a nikamma (useless) prime minister because the seat of power is not 7, Race Course Road, where he lives, but 10, Janpath, where Sonia and her family reside. So far his attempts to create a divide between the two have flopped. Sonia has proved an astute politician who has so far not made a single wrong move. Likewise, Manmohan Singh has played his role as a nominee prime minister with skill. He has many more plus points to his credit than any of his predecessors. The partnership has worked well with Sonia looking after political matters and Manmohan the administrative. The country has prospered.

Advani has quite a lot to say about Narendra Modi, the chief minister of Gujarat, in his book. He exonerates him from the charge of allowing the massacre of innocent Muslims to occur following the attack on the Sabarmati Express at Godhra. It is a symbiotic relationship: Modi helps Advani win elections from Gandhinagar in Gujarat; Advani stands by Modi whenever his conduct comes under question from the higher echelons of the BJP.

The importance of Advani's memoirs is not in their literary quality but in the possibility of the author becoming India's man of destiny. Either we remain a secular state envisaged by Gandhi and Nehru or we succumb to Advani's interpretation of it and become the Hindu Secular Socialist Republic of Bharatvarsha. Perish the thought.

Mrinalini Sarabhai

Among the many duties I had to perform as the public relations officer of the Indian high commission in London following Independence was to ensure adequate media coverage for visiting Indian artistes. Of them, the most daunting was to rouse interest for classical Indian dance. Few in England were aware that such a thing existed. For most of them, Indian dancers were nautch girls gyrating to the jingle of ankle bells. The only one who had established himself as a class dancer was Ram Gopal. He had a sizeable following in England's gay circles. Then came Uday Shankar, his wife, Amala Nandi, and their troupe, partly sponsored by our government. There were not many willing to buy tickets to see something they knew nothing about. We had to persuade the staff of India House to bring their families to fill at least half the hall.

With Mrinalini Sarabhai it was slightly different. She came from the well-known Swaminathan family of Madras and her mother was a member of Parliament. Her husband, Vikram, was on the make as a space and nuclear research scientist; he was also a Sarabhai from Ahmedabad, one of the ten richest industrial families of the country. Wherever Mrinal went, the red carpet was laid out with embassy receptions for her Darpana troupe. The only thing we failed to galvanize was an audience. We were in luck if the halls were half-full. Indian ballet got very perfunctory notices in the English press. Whatever appeared was faithfully wired back to India where it made the front pages.

Mrinal's autobiography claims that 'she is single-handedly responsible for taking classical Indian dance beyond the shores of India and making Bharatanatyam a dance form that is revered and respected throughout the world'. The statement has to be digested with a large dose of salt. She was by no means the first nor was she single-handed. There were a few before her and many contemporaries who excelled her, including, later, her own daughter, Mallika, who outshone her in looks, as a dancer and as an honest raconteur of her life.

Mrinalini's autobiography makes tedious reading. It is a succession of events, including trivia like lost and found baggage on her trips abroad, important people like Presidents, prime ministers, godmen, faith healers, miracle men and men of eminence whom she met, which makes it read like a catalogue in the diary of a name-dropper. Even when she digresses into matrimonial differences and family squabbles after her husband's death, she conceals more than she reveals. While Mrinal was preoccupied in conquering the world with her dancing, her husband found a more fetching and understanding companion in the sociologist Kamla Chowdhry who had taken up a job in one of the institutions set up by the Sarabhais. It came as a shattering blow to Mrinal's amour propre. In her account of her relationship with Vikram, Kamla makes it quite clear that it was more than platonic. And remained so till the end of his life. Kamla still organizes an annual Vikram Sarabhai Memorial Lecture in Delhi.

After the deaths of the founding father of the Sarabhai enterprises, Seth Ambalal, and his eldest son, Suhrid, the entire burden of managing the industrial empire, which included Calico Mills and Sarabhai Chemicals, fell on the eldest remaining son, Gautam. The rest of the clan was busy doing their own thing and treated the family fortune as theirs for the asking without contributing to its management or looking after any part of the business. All of them had spacious bungalows separated by ancient tree-lined avenues overrun with peacocks in an area called The

Retreat. Whenever they were in Ahmedabad, they stayed in their bungalows and indulged in their favourite hobbies. One ran a school, another set up a botanical garden with all the flora and fauna of Gujarat, one reared pheasants, another reared snakes. Everyone had a consuming passion of his or her own. The business of earning money was left to Gautam who, with his youngest sister, Gira, as his companion, did the best he could. He put an end to the practice of non-working members of the family withdrawing money at will. But by then it was too late to salvage the Sarabhai enterprises.

RANJIT SINGH

Maharaja Ranjit Singh was undoubtedly the greatest son of the Punjab, but he was not a handsome, anaemic, saintly character. He was an ugly, small man who loved the good things in life: liquor, good-looking men and women around him. He loved horses and leading his troops in battle. To wit Rudyard Kipling:

Four things greater than all things are
Women and horses and power and War.

While still a boy, Ranjit got smallpox, which blinded him in one eye and left his face dotted. Emily Eden, who was with her brother, the Governor-General, Lord Auckland, when they called on the maharaja, described him as 'exactly like an old mouse, with grey whiskers, one eye and a grey beard.' A legend claims that his favourite Muslim mistress, Bibi Mohran, in whose name he had a coin struck, once asked him where he was when God was distributing good looks. He replied, 'When you were asking for a comely appearance, I asked Him for power.' Before meeting him, the Governor-General asked the maharaja's chief minister, Fakir Azizuddin, what his master looked like. Fakir Azizuddin gave him a diplomatic answer: 'His face has so much jalaal (dazzle) that I have never dared to look at him.'

Emily Eden wrote about Ranjit Singh's partiality for strong liquor. Dr Martin Honigberger, who prepared gunpowder for the maharaja's artillery, also prepared brandy for the royal table. At the state banquet, Emily took care to sit on the blind-eye side of the maharaja, who poured the drinks himself in the gold goblets of the guests seated on either side of him. Every time he turned to talk to the Governor-General, Emily quietly emptied her goblet on the carpet. Ranjit filled it over and over again and then turned to one of his courtiers and said in Punjabi: '*Mem taan khoob peendee hai* (this white woman can hold her drink).' Once he asked a Frenchman whether it was better for the health to drink after a meal as some doctors advised or before the meal as others said. The Frenchman replied that drinking, both before and after meals, was good for one's health. The maharaja roared with happy laughter.

One aspect of Ranjit Singh's character which made him unique among the Indian rulers was that he was totally free of religious prejudice. Though slaughter of kine was forbidden and many of his Hindu and European officers did not cut their hair and beards to please him, he did not impose his views on anyone. His council of ministers was dominated by the three Fakir brothers; it included Dogras and, of course, Sardars, Sandhawalias, Majithas, Attariwalas and others. Likewise, his army, trained by European officers, comprised all communities. The cavalry was largely Sikh, the artillery, commanded by General Elahi Bakhsh, largely Muslim, and the infantry, a mix of Dogras, Gorkhas, Sikhs and Muslim Najibs. His commanders on the battlefield were men like Diwan Mohkam Chand and his son, Diwan Chand, Hari Singh Nalwa and Prince Sher Singh. In short, it was a composite Punjabi fighting force that created history by reversing the tide of conquests back to the homelands of the traditional invaders—the Pathans and the Afghans.

Nothing proves Ranjit's credentials more than when it came to determining the future of the diamond, Kohinoor. Instead of leaving it to one of his sons or donating it to the Harimandir, which he had renovated in marble and gold leaf, he wished it to be given to the temple of Jagannath in Puri.

It is ironic that it was the Akali Dal–BJP government of Punjab, led by Prakash Singh Badal, which took the lead in organizing the celebrations of the second centenary of his coronation some years ago. Ranjit Singh had little respect for the akalis of his time: *'Kuj faham wa kotch andesh* (of crooked minds and short-sightedness).'

SHEILA DHAR: LOVE FOOD, WILL SING

The day Sheila Dhar died in July 2001 was the day we lost the only person who could explain the intricacies of Hindustani classical music in simple words to the uninitiated. Her going was a grievous loss to those who enjoyed listening to Indian classical music but could not tell one raga from another, why they were meant to be sung at dawn, afternoon or after sunset, what dhrupad, dadra, khayal, thumri meant, the depiction of ragas and raginis in Ragamala paintings or what the gharanas (households)—Gwalior, Agra, Kirana, Jaipur–Atrauli and Patiala—had to do in rendering them. Sheila could tell you all about them.

Sheila was a stickler for pakka raga without frills or compromises. She once walked out of a concert by Mehdi Hassan, whom I regarded as the greatest ghazal singer, with lofty disdain exclaiming, 'He is a crooner.' Classical Hindustani music in its pristine form was her passion. Her mission in life was to propagate it among the masses. She took me to her ustad, Pandit Pran Nath, a couple of times. I sat through their joint singing sessions without comprehending any of the subtleties of notes. They disputed between themselves. Though she remained as friendly as ever before, she gave me up as a lost case as far as music was concerned.

In *Raga 'n Josh: Stories from a Musical Life*, Dhar made out a laboured case pointing out the similarities between good eating and good music. Pakka gaana she assures us is derived from pakaana (cooking). Just as a tasty dish gives mazaa—enjoyment—so does a well-rendered raga. It is chancy: at times neither the food nor the raga comes out just right. As the proverb goes: *Raga, rasoi, pagree, kabhi kabhi ban jaye* (melody, food and the turban do not always come out right). Dhar continues: 'I have not encountered one [ustad] to whom cooking and serving of food was not extremely important. When Zia Moinuddin Dagar went to stay with an ardent American disciple, the first thing he did was to take charge of the kitchen and start operations on lamb korma so that it could be ready by the time the first day's music session ended. Pandit Pran Nath used to say that real music was only for those who could replicate the aroma of kebabs in every note. Bade Ghulam Ali Khan once announced to an inadequate host that he could hardly be expected to produce his kind of music if he was given ghaas phoos (grass) to eat. *Aaye khaana to aaye gaana*—if you have food, you will have singing.' Dhar names other great ustads like Faiyaz Ahmed Khan and Munawar Ali Khan who swore by gourmet food as they swore by their music. Ustadinis were not far behind. Siddheshwari Devi was 'an inspired cook'. Begum Akhtar relished kakori kebabs. Writes Dhar: 'I have heard it said many times by ustads, *ek hi baat hai*—it is the same thing.'

Dhar's missionary zeal to convert people to appreciating pakka raga was shared by her friend, Nalin, who lived in New York. He would assemble his American friends, including his blonde sweetheart, Beatrice, and subject them to hours of classical ragas played over his hi-fi stereo. His friends slowly dropped out of his circle and Beatrice ditched him.

G.D. BIRLA

If a list of the builders of modern India were to be drawn up, the Birlas would undoubtedly be on top. There is, of course, the house of Tata but they kept themselves aloof from politics, politicians and the media. The Birlas, on the other hand, took a keen interest in political affairs, financed political parties and politicians and published newspapers. As a result, they were always in the public eye. They were also the biggest builders of temples in modern times, earning respect in every Hindu house.

The most famous among the Birlas was Ghanshyam Das (1894–1983). The Birlas are Marwaris from Pilani and belong to the Maheswari subcaste. Strict vegetarians and teetotallers, they venerate the cow and conform to Vaishnavite rituals. They marry within their subcaste: a breach of this tradition can invite ostracism. For years they regarded the crossing of the seas as sinful and had to undergo ritual cleansing before being readmitted. They prospered as small-time traders in Pilani till they found greener pastures in the metros, mainly Bombay and Calcutta. Wherever they went, they carried their family traditions with them and remained a close-knit community. They earned goodwill where they settled by generous donations to charitable institutions.

By the time G.D. was brought to Calcutta in the 1890s, the family was well-set on the road to opulence: his father, Baldev Das, had acquired the honorific of raja. They made their home in the Marwari mohalla of Bara Bazaar. Fortunes were built on trading in opium, import of cloth and jute. For a while, G.D. was sent to Bombay where he picked up English and read the classics. He followed the strict regimen of his childhood, rising well before dawn and spending at least two hours before sunrise in prayer and physical exercise. (He even toyed with the idea of becoming a professional wrestler.) Back in Calcutta, he joined the Bengali terrorists. He was named among those wanted in the Rodda conspiracy case to smuggle arms and went underground for three months.

There was an upward swing in the Birlas' fortunes in 1911. Besides opium and silver, they made a killing supplying jute bags and uniforms to the army when World War I broke out. They went into the textile industry in a big way setting up mills across the country. They also acquired two English newspapers, the *New Empire* and *Bengalee*. G.D. also became the chief spokesman of the Marwari community in the European-dominated Chambers of Commerce and the Bengal assembly. He was always involved in politics. His instinctive bias was towards right-wing Hindu nationalism and he generously gave money to Pandit Madan Mohan Malviya and the Benares Hindu University. He was also taken up with Lala Lajpat Rai—he gave him money for personal expenses—and his Servants of India society. Ultimately Birla turned to Mahatma Gandhi, extended him hospitality in the Birla houses in Calcutta, Bombay and Delhi, and bailed out the Congress when it was in dire need of funds. It was no coincidence that the Mahatma was staying at Birla House in Delhi when his assassins got him. The Birlas donated the house to the nation.

G.D. was never one to take the steering wheel but was content to remain a backseat driver. But with the Mahatma's death, he lost this privileged position. For a while, Pandit Nehru heeded his advice. Birla approved of the first five-year plan setting out the roles of the public and private sectors in nation building. As Nehru decided to keep his distance from big business houses and put his idea of socialism in practice, the Birlas receded into the background. Birla disapproved of the second five-year plan and the influence of P.C. Mahalanobis in decision-making. Birla tried to reestablish contact with the government when Indira

Gandhi became prime minister. But she inherited her father's distrust of industrialists. 'Our private enterprise is more private than enterprising,' she scoffed. She returned a gift he had sent on Rajiv's marriage. But she accepted his money. Likewise, Morarji Desai disdained associating with him but had no compunction taking money from him. G.D. abandoned his attempts to influence the government and contented himself with his business enterprises and his extended family. His health also began to fail. He died in London on 11 June 1983 and according to his wishes was cremated there. His sons brought his ashes to India to be immersed in the Ganga.

GENERAL DYER

Believe it or not, the real saga of the Dyer family began about 200 feet below the bungalow in which I spend my summer months. Their connection with India can be traced back to the 1820s with the East India Company. Reginald's father, Edward, came to India sometime around 1850 and stayed with his elder brother, John, who was a practising barrister in Mussoorie. He wanted to find out what he could do to make a living and John advised him to set up a brewery as there was a great demand for beer among the British, and English beer, coming via the Cape of Good Hope, was expensive. Edward returned to England for two years to learn the art of making beer and brought the latest machinery with him when he returned. He bought over a dilapidated brewery in Kasauli, renovated it and started making beer. It was an instant success. He expanded his operations and set up a larger brewery in Solan, about 20 miles uphill on the Kasauli–Simla Road, then took over the management of the Meakins brewery in Murree (where Reginald was born in October 1864), and opened yet another one in Lucknow. The family lived in Kasauli for a few years before moving to Simla, which had become the summer capital of the Central and the Punjab governments as well as the headquarters of the British Indian army. In Simla, where all the action was, Edward Dyer bought a large house and an estate, and a house from which the Punjab plains were visible. Dyers' was the richest English family in town. By then, Dyer–Meakin beer had flooded the Indian market.

Reginald was the sixth of Edward and Mary Dyer's nine children. From their ayahs and servants the children learnt to speak Hindustani. The boys went to Bishop Cotton School. Reginald was there for six years before he and his brother were sent off to a non-district school in Ireland. They did not see their parents for twelve years. Reginald was an average student, good at mathematics and doing things with his hands. He was also a good boxer. At nineteen, he got admission to Sandhurst and then joined the British Indian army. He saw action in Burma before he was posted to Jhansi. There, much against the wishes of his parents, he married Annie Oomanny, the daughter of the commanding officer. She bore him a daughter and two sons. It was a close-knit happy family.

Reginald saw more action in World War I, extending from Hong Kong in the Far East to the NWFP and East Persia. He won acclaim as a fearless officer who led his men from the front. What made Reginald Dyer the butcher he turned out to be? We can only guess. There was the rigid caste structure of British Indian society. Despite their wealth, the Dyers were looked down upon as parvenus by Britishers in the army and the civil services: they were boxwallahs and not pucca. Reginald inherited that chip on his shoulder. As a schoolboy, he stuttered badly and was mimicked mercilessly for it by his schoolmates. He also shared the prejudices of Whites against coloured races. In Burma, for every White soldier killed by a sniper, they destroyed the sniper's entire village, killing everyone, including women and children. Coloured races were to him, as Kipling put it, 'lesser breeds without the law'. They deserved to be treated as naughty children and pinched on their bare bottoms if they behaved badly. It was with this kind of mindset that Colonel Reginald Dyer found himself posted in Jalandhar as a brigadier-general, with Amritsar in his military jurisdiction, when political agitation rose to a fever pitch in the first few days of April 1919.

On 10 April 1919, Dr Saifuddin Kitchlew and Dr Satyapal were arrested and deported to Dharamsala. The city went up in flames. Railway yards, banks and post offices were looted and burnt, English managers of banks lynched, an English nurse badly roughed up. Civil authorities and the police were unable to restore law and order. Without so much as a by your leave, Reginald Dyer came over from Jalandhar and put the city under military rule. All processions and meetings were banned. When he heard that a large crowd upwards of 20,000 people had assembled at Jallianwala Bagh—a seven-acre plot enclosed on all sides by high walls with only one narrow entrance—he marched his troops to the site. Then, without warning the assemblage to disperse, he ordered his men to open fire. The firing continued for fifteen minutes, killing between 350 and 500 men, women and children. By then it was evening and a curfew had been imposed on the city. He left the dead with the dying and the grievously wounded where they were lying and drove back to his office-cum-bungalow in Rambagh. In those fifteen minutes he had wiped out all the goodwill the British had earned in modernizing India, setting up telegraph lines, telephones, railway tracks, roads, law and order and introducing democratic institutions.

Did Reginald Dyer have any sense of guilt for what he had done? Quite clearly not. He had men flogged in public and made them crawl on their bellies down the lane where the English nurse had been assaulted. He was convinced he had saved the Punjab and India for the British Empire. In this, he also had the backing of the Lieutenant Governor of the Punjab, Sir Michael O'Dwyer (who was later assassinated in London by Udham Singh).

He successfully exploited the Sikhs by bestowing favours on them and keeping them aloof from the the Hindus and Muslims. He visited the Golden Temple and was given a saropa by the sarbrah, Aroor Singh, in the presence of Sundar Singh Majitha. He was offered conversion to Sikhism without having to grow his hair and beard or quit smoking. He politely declined the offer. Both Aroor Singh and Sundar Singh Majitha had knighthood conferred on them.

The realization of the enormity of the crime he had committed came only when the formation of the Indian National Conference Committee of Enquiry was followed by the British setting up an enquiry commission of their own under Lord Hunter. It had three Indian members and Reginald Dyer was put through a gruelling cross-examination which lasted the whole day, leaving him exhausted and in low spirits. Worse was to follow in the debates in both houses of the British Parliament. Among his severest critics was Winston Churchill, then a Liberal Party cabinet minister in Lloyd George's government. He described Dyer's action as 'an extraordinary event, a monstrous event, an event which stands in sinister isolation'. A shocked Dyer and his tearful wife left the House in a state of deep depression.

Reginald Dyer had supporters both in India and in England. The *English Morning Post* started a fund for him. So did British-owned papers in India: the *Statesman*, the *Pioneer* and the *Civil and Military Gazette, Rangoon Times* and the *Madras Mail*. Contributions poured in, till the total was close to £30,000. In addition, he was even presented a Sword of Honour for saving India for the British Empire. Remorse, if any, came to him after he suffered a stroke. He survived it to live another five years, being pushed around in a wheelchair, keeping awake all day and night, reading. Before his end came on Saturday, 23 July 1927, he told his daughter-in-law, 'I don't want to get better. So many people who knew the conditions of Amritsar say I did right . . . but so many say I did wrong. I only want to die and know from my Maker whether I did right or wrong.'

FIRAQ GORAKHPURI

There is a gross misconception that Urdu is the language of
Muslims. There were, and are today, many good poets of Urdu
who are Hindus. The greatest amongst them was Raghupat Sahai,
better known as Firaq Gorakhpuri. He was a Kayastha from
Gorakhpur, Uttar Pradesh. Besides being a good poet, he had
a good academic record and qualified for the civil services. He
resigned to join the freedom movement and spent some months
in jail with Jawaharlal Nehru.

For four years he was the undersecretary of the Congress. He
topped in the MA examinations, taught English at Allahabad
University before retiring as reader in 1958. In 1961, he won the
Sahitya Akademi award, two years later the Soviet Land Nehru
award and in 1970 the Jnanpeeth award. He wrote in Hindi, Urdu
and English but opted for Urdu as the better medium to put across
his ideas. He soon came to be sought after for mushairas. His
closest rival and friend was an equally good poet—the Muslim,
Josh Malihabadi.

Besides the love of poetry, they shared much in common. Both
were patriotic, loved the good things in life, were connoisseurs of
liquor and women. Many bawdy stories were told about them.
Both thought immensely of their looks and talents and boasted
about their prowess as poets and lovers. Firaq had a disastrous
marriage and wrote a lot of nasty things about the woman who
bore him two children. (Their daughter died young, their son
commited suicide.)

Firaq admitted that often it took him weeks to perfect a couple of lines of poetry. He was one Urdu poet who, instead of turning to Arabic and Persian vocabulary and imagery, as most poets of the language did, injected a lot of Hindi words in his poems. Instead of using Laila Majnu, the bulbul, the rose, the moth and flame as symbols of eternal love, he turned to Radha and Krishna. He also used a lot of the imagery from Keats, Shelley, Wordsworth and Tennyson in his compositions. Firaq's ideal of a female companion was:

Moan aur behen bhi, aur chehetee bhi
Ghar ki rani bhi aur jeewan sathi
Phir bhi voh kamini sarasar devi
Aur seyj par voh beswa ki petlee.
(Mother, sister and a daughter I adore
Queen of my home, life companion and more
Also much desired as a goddess as well
But when in bed, a voluptuous whore.)

When Malihabadi decided to migrate to Pakistan because he could not find suitable husbands for his daughters in India, Firaq was deprived of a friend and a rival with whom he could cross swords. When he heard of Malihabadi's death he is supposed to have said, 'Once again the fellow has beaten me to it.' He died a few days later.

ON GREAT TALKERS

Great talkers are drawn to me like iron filings to a magnet. I am a patient listener but after an exposure or two, I do my best to dislodge them without hurting their feelings; most crashing bores are also well-meaning, good people. The other day, having nothing better to do, I made a list of those who came into my life and what made them go on talking by the hour.

The first man, on the top of my list, was Danial Latifi. A great gentleman and a great bore—that is how I thought of Danial. Good people tend to be somewhat tiresome and Danial was goodness personified. He never lied, or ever said a hurtful thing about anyone. We became friends in Lahore. He was the son of Sir Alma Latifi, ICS, one of a distinguished clan comprising the Tyabjis, Futtehallys and Salim Ali. He was a graduate from Oxford University and a barrister-at-law. Everyone expected him to start practice at the high court and end up as a judge. Instead, he joined the Communist Party of India and was in the bad books of the police and the Criminal Investigation Department.

One night he was caught pasting subversive posters on the city walls. He spent a while in jail. After his release he shifted to the party headquarters. He lived on daal and roti. He was always lean and fragile; he became leaner and frailer; his long nose appeared longer—he had a vulpine profile. I persuaded him to move in with me. I had reason to regret my offer of hospitality.

Every evening, as I sat down to enjoy my whisky, Danial, who was a teetotaller, would start an endless monologue on Marxism, class struggle, imperialism, et al. It ruined the taste of my good

Scotch. One day when my cook and I were away, my mother turned up unexpectedly. She took Danial to be my servant, reprimanded him for sitting on the sofa and ordered him to get her luggage from the tonga and bring it up. He did so without a word. When my mother discovered who he was, she was most embarrassed. He often teased her about it.

One point in favour of endless talkers is they do not interrupt their monologue by asking questions: the listener need not listen provided he or she keeps his or her eyes fixed on the monologist. Once some friends dropped in after dinner. Both of them were a little drunk. I introduced them to Danial and decided to take a stroll. When I returned Danial was propounding the theory of class struggle: both my friends were fast asleep.

It was in my flat that he met Sarah Itiyarah, a Syrian Christian teacher in Kinnaird College for Women and as ardent a communist as he. They fell in love and got married. Danial would often smile but rarely laugh. Sarah did neither. They were admirably suited to each other. The only thing they had in common was a passion for Marxism. They had no children.

Danial and Sarah did not live together very much. So when she died, he was not shattered. He was not designed for domesticity. So I was surprised when I heard a few years ago that he had married again—this time to a princess of royal blood, a descendant of the great Moguls.

After Partition, the Latifis moved to Delhi. My father gave them a flat in the block next to mine. Dodging Danial became a game of wits: another thing endless talkers share in common is that they disdain making appointments. Once I told him that I was pestered by uninvited visitors. He got me a spy glass to put in my door so that I could see the visitor and if I did not want to be seen I need not open the door. Danial was the first victim of his own gift.

Danial did not change except that he began to drink in modest quantities. The last time I ran into him was at a French Embassy reception. It was a buffet dinner and guests had to line up for their drinks and food. The French make their guests as uncomfortable as they can so that they do not overstay their welcome. No chairs or tables were provided so you had to keep standing while you ate and drank. I ran into Danial holding a plateful of food in one hand and a glass of red wine in the other. The crowd of guests jostled us for attention. I greeted Danial and remarked how nice it was to see him drinking wine. That was enough for him to launch on a long explanation of there being nothing in the Koran or the Hadith declaring alcohol to be haraam for a Muslim. We were interrupted many times but Danial kept going till it was time to depart.

Another great talker I got to know was General Nathu Singh. He was a tall strapping soldier, proud of his aristocratic Rajput lineage and his martial exploits. He used to often stay with my parents, and after they died, with my elder brother. When they were out, the old General would drop in on me (unannounced) and keep me in thrall like the ancient mariner with the wedding guest. I protested to my sister-in-law. 'We've inherited him from your parents, so you must be patient and polite with him,' she admonished me. But she also warned me of his arrival in Delhi, 'General Sahib will be staying with us all next week. Don't complain I didn't tell you well ahead of time.' I had to tell my servants to tell anyone who came that I was not at home. Now that General Nathu Singh is no longer with us, I feel ashamed of myself because despite him being long-winded, I liked him.

I could not say that for Ranbir Singh, once in our foreign service. After retiring he settled abroad with his foreign wife. But every winter he came to Delhi and made it a point to call on his old acquaintances (unannounced). I was not an old acquaintance but was acceptable to him as I was a Sikh. This was strange as Ranbir was a Christian descended from the branch of the Kapurthala family which had converted to Christianity. (Rajkumari Amrit Kaur was his aunt.) Ranbir was proud of his Sikh ancestry, notably Jassa Singh Ahluwalia, the founder of the house of Kapurthala. Winter after winter, he would regale me with exploits of the Ahluwalia Misl and the feats of valour his ancestor, Jassa Singh, had performed. He would flex his biceps to convince me that he had inherited his bulging muscles from his forefathers. Like others of his ilk, he never bothered to find out whether I was free to receive him. After having my morning schedule upset many times, I put my foot down and told my servant to tell him that he should ring up before coming. He was outraged. I heard him shout at my servant to tell his master that he would never see me again. Thank God!

It was different with Nazar Hayat Tiwana. He is the eldest son of Sir Khizr Hayat Tiwana, the chief minister of Punjab before its partition and one of the biggest landowners of his time. The Tiwanas' estate included Hadali, the village in which I was born. I had great respect and affection for them. Nazar fell out with his father, married a Hindu girl and migrated to the United States. He got a job as an assistant librarian at Chicago University. Every winter he came to India and Pakistan. Since his father was long dead, he revived his affection for his Tiwana ancestors. He had his father's biography written; he set up an organization to promote Indo–Pakistan amity. He was, and is, a very lovable character. Also, an endless talker. Once he got started you never knew when he would run out of breath. He sensed I had begun to avoid him. The last time he came to see me, he was his old self, going on and on till my head was dizzy with his words. He paused for a second or two before he delivered the punch line. 'You know what my wife says? She says I lose friends because I talk too much.' I did not contradict him.

One man who loves the sound of his own voice is Joginder Singh, the retired head of the CBI. One evening I was in Lodi Gardens sitting on a ledge below the Bara Gumbad mosque. It is my favourite spot to take a short rest between my perambulations because I tire easily. It has become my chosen resting place for two reasons: the dome of the Bara Gumbad is the most sensuously perfect of all domes I have ever seen; and from where I sit I can see people striding along the paved footpath without them noticing me. I can watch the trees, birds and clouds without being disturbed. However, one evening I saw a family of three break away from the stream of walkers and head across the lawn towards me. As they got closer, I recognized Joginder Singh with a lady he introduced as his wife and a young girl who was his daughter. Joginder had a Walkman dangling on his side. He took out the earplugs to talk to me.

'I am listening to my recorded speeches,' he told me.

'Listening to your own voice?' I remarked, dumfounded.

His wife, who heads the publication division, came to his rescue. 'Yes, they are full of wisdom. He reads lots of books, gets the best out of them and puts them in his speeches. You should listen to them sometime.'

I did not rise to the bait. My lady companion diverted the dialogue to another topic. 'Are you writing another book?' she asked him.

'Yes,' replied Joginder Singh in a triumphant voice. 'Bofors! You'll see, I will reveal everything about it.' Joginder Singh was evidently very pleased with himself.

On my way back home, I recalled another man who was in love with the sound of his own voice. This was the late A.S. Bokhari, who was a professor of English at Government College, Lahore. He was a great wit; his *Patras kay Mazaameen*, a collection of humorous articles, is still widely read and acclaimed in Urdu circles. He was also an excellent after-dinner speaker and was applauded wherever he spoke. He became the director general of All India Radio, then of Radio Pakistan before he joined the UN as the head of the department of mass communications.

Professor Bokhari died in New York. Though he had a family, he lived alone in a spacious apartment attended to by an elderly female housekeeper and cook. My friend, Shafqat Mahmood, a retired Pakistani diplomat, who also lived in New York and visited Bokhari regularly, was informed. He immediately went to Bokhari's apartment and as instructed by the late professor's family in Lahore proceeded to make an inventory of his belongings.

When he had finished with the main rooms, the housekeeper told him about the attic where she said the professor spent his evenings and did not allow even her to enter. Shafqat went into the attic. He was surprised with what he saw. There was a hi-fi system; the shelves were lined with tapes of the professor's speeches. He spent most of his evenings in the attic sipping his Scotch and listening to his own voice. It was a kind of vocal narcissism.

The champion of all talkers whom I had to suffer was my security guard, Sita Ram. He was a Jat from eastern UP and a follower of Chaudhary Mahinder Singh. Sita Ram was into religion and was prone to deliver long pravachans on spiritual matters. Though a Jat, his fellow policemen addressed him as Shastriji. Once travelling with me and a film crew to Jaipur, he talked all the way from Delhi to the Pink City. It did not do him much good. While others who joined the police force at the same time became head constables and SHOs, Sita Ram remained a constable.

While on the subject of great endless talkers, it occurs to me that I have never encountered a female of the species. Long-windedness, like the prostate gland, is a masculine phenomenon.

POETRY WITH DAHI BHALLAS

Kishen Lal came into my life more than ten years ago. I knew
nothing about him till he told me he was the owner of Hotel
Rajdoot on Mathura Road. Thereafter he came to see me twice
every week. On both days he brought me food from the hotel:
dahi bhallas for lunch and fish or chicken for dinner. In the
afternoon, he would ring up and ask, like any good restaurateur
would, how I liked the food. His dahi bhallas are the best I
have ever tasted: a judicious mix of yoghurt with a couple of
bhallas, with bananas, ginger, saunth and other condiments. I
asked him why he always wanted to know how his food tasted.
'Because if you like something I reward the cook. If you don't
like something, I don't give him anything.' I made it a point to
praise every item of food he gave me.

The only other person he visited twice a week was Fali
Nariman, who had been his lawyer and had become a friend.
'You know I can't understand a word of what Kishen Lal says,'
Nariman confessed to me. It was true. His speech was a mixture
of mumbled gurgles. I had more trouble with it than Nariman
as Kishen Lal had a passion for Urdu poetry which he recited to
me with great gusto. He would usually come up with one line
and challenge me to come up with the next. I rarely passed his
test. His favourite poet was Bahadur Shah Zafar.

Kishen Lal was not well conversant with English but hated
to admit he had difficulty with the language. He insisted I give
him every book I wrote. On his next visit he would tell me

triumphantly: 'I've got to page so and so. I must say you must have been a rangeela.'

Kishen Lal was a self-made man. He started life with a small coffee shop, went on to become a military canteen contractor (among others, he served Lord Mountbatten) till he bought land on Mathura Road and built Hotel Rajdoot. It acquired quite a reputation for its cuisine and risqué cabaret shows. It made Kishen Lal a millionaire: he bought a farm and built himself a farmhouse.

Two years ago Kishen Lal had a fall and damaged one of his knees. Nevertheless, he kept up his bi-weekly visits. A few visits before the last, he announced to me in English: 'I am eighty.' Somehow eighty in English sounds like something one can crow about while 'ussee' in Hindustani or 'ussean da' in Punjabi has a tone of decline. 'You have another ten years to catch up with me,' I responded cheerfully. He threw his hands up in a gesture of despair and quoted lines from Zauq (oddly enough also my father's favourite poet):

Laayee hayaat, aaye Qazaa, lay chalee chaley
Apni khushi na aai hum, na apnee khushi chaley.
(Life came to me, death now stands at my door,
I came not of my pleasure, I go not at my leisure.)

On the morning of Monday, 7 June 2004, my daughter called me in Kasauli from Delhi to tell me that somebody from Hotel Rajdoot had rung up to say that Lala Kishen Lal was dead and his cremation would take place that day. No more dahi bhallas for me till we meet again.

On Religion

Have you seen God? No, I have not. Nor do I believe that anyone, at any time, past or present, has seen Him. As for me, even if I come face to face with Him, I would not recognize him. Were He to give me His visiting card and say, 'I am God', I would say in utter disbelief, 'Tell me another'.

However, there have been, and are today, people who claim to have seen Him and can give graphic descriptions of Him. I am not talking of people who give airy-fairy answers like, 'God is everywhere; you only have to have eyes to see him', or as is more common now, 'God is within you'. No X-ray of the human body shows the presence of anything resembling God. 'God is truth; God is love,' say many others, as did Bapu Gandhi. I do not know what truth and love look like—one is a principle of social behaviour, the other an emotion.

In our country most people believe in gods taking human form. There is, of course, the trinity of Brahma, Vishnu and Mahesh (creator, preserver and destroyer), but that is more of a concept of divinity than people who are visible. To many Hindus, Rama was, and is, God. To others it is Krishna. Many believe Satya Sai Baba is God incarnate; others believe Osho was bhagwan. All were and are mortals, some have gone, others are on their way out. Yet everyone insists that God is immortal. I am baffled.

For whatever they're worth, some people have given vivid descriptions of what God looks like. He is invariably portrayed as a patriarch with a flowing snow-white beard, in His sixties or seventies. Did He age over the years or was He always an old man? Perhaps by depicting Him as old the artist meant to convey wisdom and experience.

Some of the Old Testament prophets claimed to have seen God. Ezekiel describes Him thus: 'Above the firmament that was over their heads was the likeness of a throne, as the appearance of a sapphire stone: and upon the likeness of the throne was the likeness as the appearance of a man above upon it. And I saw as the colour of amber, as the appearance of fire round about within it . . . and it had brightness round about. As the appearance of the bow that is in the cloud in the day of rain, so was the appearance of the brightness round about. This was the appearance of the likeness of the glory of the Lord.'

Daniel added his own description: 'The Ancient of days did sit, whose garment was white as snow, and the hair of his head like the pure wool: his throne was like the fiery flame, and his wheels as burning fire.' The poet-painter, William Blake, painted God as the venerable father of humanity.

Our sacred scriptures do not venture to depict God. Even Krishna's self-portrait in the Gita, extolling His omniscience and omnipotence, does not describe His physical features. The one thing that all descriptions of divinity have in common is light at its most dazzling.

There is also a charming description of God in Bhai Bula's Janamsakhi (life story) of Guru Nanak, which scholars have spurned as spurious and written much after the guru. It describes God as a long-bearded old man draped in white clothes, sitting on an ornate charpoy, and surrounded by fat buffaloes bursting with milk—a peasant's concept of a rich Punjabi zamindar.

Right from the time life began on earth people have been asking themselves who or what made us, what was His, Her or Its purpose, where do we go, when do we die. Nobody has yet been able to give satisfactory answers to these questions. It seems no one will ever be able to do so. All we have are assertions about a God who one fine day decided to create life, gave different creatures different names, different spans of life and then made them disappear for ever. At first they conjectured that the elements that created life—the sun, rain, earth, air, etc.—were their creator's and therefore worthy of worship. They raised temples in their honour. Sometime later people thought there must be hundreds of thousands of creators who looked after different aspects of life; others argued there should be one creator. They called it God. Still later came philosophers and prophets. Philosophers speculated on the origin and purpose of life; Prophets asserted they knew the ultimate truth. In the Middle East we had Zoroaster, Abraham and Moses, Jesus Christ and Mohammed. Then: followers banded themselves into separate groups and sought to impose their views on others. In India we had Mahavir and Gautam the Buddha. Neither really accepted the existence of a God but laid down norms of societal behaviour and acquired large followings. Their predominance was challenged by Adi Shankara who was able to re-establish Hindu predominance.

Different religions, though they preached love and brotherhood of mankind, fought wars against each other. In India the inroads made by non-Indian religions like Christianity and Islam posed serious challenges to the caste-ossified Hindu society. These challenges were met in battlefields as well as in attempts to come to an understanding between each other. From the Hindu side they were the Bhaktas (notably Kabir and Nanak); from the Muslim, Sufis, notably Farid, Muinuddin and Nizamuddin of the Chishtia order. The process of coming to an understanding between contending faiths has continued.

Perhaps the most quoted lines to prove that Islam accepts the validity of other faiths is: 'To you your faith, to me mine.' Nevertheless it cannot be denied that the two religions most engaged in converting other people to their beliefs are Islam and Christianity.

They assume they have more viable answers to vital questions— the existence of the Creator, the purpose of life, the codes of conduct to be observed towards our fellow creatures, life after death if there is any—than other religions. Whether or not this is so remains to be established.

At some time or the other in their lives, all humans ask themselves these questions. Most often it happens when they lie on their backs on moonless nights gazing at the countless stars that stretch across the black sky. 'Where have they come from?' they ask. 'Where have I come from?'

Most often it is people who live in deserts, undisturbed by electric lights and city noises, and sleep in the open under the deafening silence of the stars, whose minds are triggered off to ponder over these problems. That is why so many of the prophets were people of deserts or waste lands.

All Semitic religions believe that God is one: so do Sikhs and Arya Samajis. Most Hindus believe in the multiplicity of gods and goddesses but give the trinity of Brahma, Vishnu and Shiva supreme status; Jains and Buddhists discard belief in God.

Most religions that subscribe to God make Him the creator, preserver and destroyer of life. They also believe in life after death—either in the form of the day of judgment or as rebirth. However, though Islam preaches belief in one God and in the day of judgment, Muslim poets do not hesitate to express their disbelief in either the genesis of life or in the day of judgment.

To quote Omar Khayyam:

Into this world and why not knowing
And like water willy-nilly flowing.

He admitted that he did not understand the mystery of life and death:

There was a door to which I found no key,
There was a veil beyond which I could not see;
Talk awhile of thee and me there was
Then no more of thee or me.

Ghalib, Zauq and other Urdu poets expressed similar beliefs. Azim Jahanabadi put it succinctly—*Na ibtada ki khabar hai, na intihaa maaloom*—we know not the beginning, we know not the end.

Although we have to concede that if the earth exists, somebody or some force must have created it and maintains it for whatever it is worth. As Voltaire said, if there is a watch, there must be a watchmaker. The analogy is misleading because while we can trace the watchmaker, the world-maker remains as elusive as ever. To wit:

Tu dil mein to aata hai
Samajh mein nahin aata;
Bas jaan gayaa yehi hai pehechaan teri.
(The heart believes You are there
The brain does not comprehend You;
That perhaps is the only way of knowing You.)

Why not be honest and admit we don't know whether God exists or not?

Epicurus (circa 300 BC) was a Greek philosopher who denied the existence of God and emphasized that since we do not know why we were born, for what purpose and know nothing about what would happen to us after we die, we should enjoy life as best as we can. Epicureanism was later summed up as a motto: eat, drink and be merry, for tomorrow we may die. It is also known as hedonism, the philosophy of good living.

We have been very unfair to Epicurus by equating his beliefs with an amoral way of living. In rejecting the existence of God, he made a series of assertions, for which I cannot find the answers. All God-believers (theists) affirm that the world was created by God (exactly when, we do not know), that He is omnipotent (sarvshaktimaan) as well as merciful (raheem), just (aadil) and has compassion (karuna). Epicurus argues as follows:

If God is willing to prevent evil, but is not able to
Then He is not omnipotent.
If He is, but not willing
Then He is malevolent.
If He is both able and willing
Then whence cometh evil?

If He is neither able nor willing
Then why call Him God?

The logic cannot be refuted. But it leaves an important question unanswered: What is the entire world about—the earth, sun, moon, stars, seas, mountains, humans and beasts? I admit I don't know and hence call myself an agnostic. I reject theism as well as atheism which answers this question with either a positive 'yes' or a positive 'no'.

India has a long and hallowed tradition of questioning the existence of God. Debiprasad Chattopadhyayay's *Indian Atheism: A Marxist Analysis* traces the questioning back to 6 century BC when Charvaka questioned both the existence of God and the sanctity of the Vedas. Later, Indian atheists questioned the Upanishads as well. Jainism and Buddhism put more emphasis on right thinking and right conduct than on the existence of God. It was evidently a society that was more open-minded and able to accept criticism than ours is today.

Since I have often questioned the existence of an omniscient (all-knowing), omnipotent (all-powerful), just and merciful God, I get a lot of letters from believers who denounce me as an ignorant, self-opinionated man ever bent on mischief-making and provoking controversy. They quote religious texts, founders of religions, savants and scholars' theology to me. Most of these letters are in the form of assertions without reasons to back them up. I pity and envy them for having a blind faith that God exists.

Some time ago I received a longish article on the subject from T. Gopal Iyengar of Hyderabad. It made a lot of sense to me. He was logical, lucid and examined the subject from different angles. He spelt out his doubts and wrote to the sankaracharya of Kanchi and the head of the Ramakrishna Muth in Belur. From both of them he received terse replies brushing aside his queries and advising him to read this or that. Evidently they did not have the answers.

Iyengar starts by asserting that we are nurtured on religious beliefs from day one as we start imbibing our mother's milk.

By the time we are old enough to think for ourselves, we are thoroughly brainwashed into accepting the existence of God and are incapable of questioning it. The very few who ponder over the matter try to define God. How do you define someone or something you can't see, hear, touch or smell? Nevertheless the feeling persists that there must be someone or some power that created the earth and life on it, and then takes it away, we know not where.

Two distinct approaches to the problem of defining God are available; the Hindic comprising Jain, Buddhist, Hindu and Sikh, and the Judaic (Jewish, Christian and Muslim). A good example of the Hindic approach is in the Vishnu Purana: 'O! Who can describe him who is not to be apprehended by the senses; who is the best of all things and the Supreme Soul, self-existent, who is devoid of all distinguishing characteristics of complexion, caste or the like, and is exempt from birth, vicissitude, death or decay; who is always alone; who exists everywhere and in whom all things here exist; and who is thence named Vasudev—the resplendent one in whom all things dwell.'

Right from the Vedic times to the advent of Sikhism, the pattern of the definition of God, with minor variations, has been the same. It should be noted that in none of them are justice, benevolence and mercy attributes of God as they are in Judaic religions where benevolence and mercy are important attributes of the Almighty. Indeed, in common Punjabi parlance, God is often described as 'vadda beparvaah'—the Great One who could not care less about human suffering.

That makes sense to me. Or how do you explain catastrophes like earthquakes and cyclones that take as heavy a toll on the innocent, upright and the God-fearing as they do on others? Why are so many children born blind, retarded or stricken with cancer? When there is so much injustice and cruelty in the world, why does the Almighty God not punish tyrants and the corrupt? Explanations like 'paying for deeds done in past lives' or 'punishments to be meted out in lives to come' have no provable rational basis and should be rejected.

So what is the answer? Iyengar does not give one. But from the way he argues I am inclined to conclude that we do not know whether or not God exists or ever existed. I go one step further and hold that his existence or non-existence is of no consequence to human beings.

Why do the innocent suffer? The question was put in different words by a Jewish rabbi whose only child was afflicted by terminal cancer. He and his wife were a god-fearing couple who had never harmed anyone. So why were they being punished by having their son taken away from them? The rabbi wrestled with the problem and put down his thoughts in a highly readable little book, *Why Bad Things Happen to Good People*. For inspiration he turned to the classic on the subject: the Book of Job in the Bible. I have read the Book of Job over and over again because it is beautifully worded but remain totally unconvinced with the arguments set out. Job was a good man without blemish. He was prosperous, had many sons, daughters, daughters-in-law and sons-in-law. Also, land, vineyards and herds of cattle. He was a man of conviction and believed that he owed his good fortune to God. Satan took on a bet with God that if Job was deprived of his family and possessions, he would lose his faith in God. Job assured himself, 'Whoever perished being innocent? Or where were the upright ever cut off ? Even as I have seen those who plough iniquity and sow trouble reap the same . . . God will not cast away the blameless, nor will He uphold the evil-doers.'

Job lost everything: his children, lands, herds of cattle and was himself afflicted with body sores and thrown out of his home. His wife pleaded with him, 'Curse God and die.' Three of his friends (Job's comforters) tried to argue him out of his faith. 'Man who is born of woman is of few days and full of trouble. He comes forth like a flower and fades away; he flees like a shadow and does not continue.' Job held fast to his faith but longed to present his case to God as his mouth was full of arguments. 'Great men are not always wise, nor do the aged always understand Justice.' God appeared before Job and reminded him that it was He who created everything on earth. He was all-knowing and all-powerful. God won the bet against Satan and Job was restored to good health and got back his family and property.

Does an unshakable faith in God really explain why the innocent suffer? Not to me; it is no different from accepting what happens with good grace: *Tera bhaanaa meetha laagey* (What You [God] ordain tastes sweet). It does not. More often it leaves a bitter taste in the mouth and in the mind.

The fact of the matter is that we have as little comprehension of why the innocent suffer as we have of why the wicked prosper. Can anyone give rational answers to these questions without resorting to theories about karma, evil deeds committed in previous births, and punishments to come in lives hereafter? They are absolute hogwash, unworthy of consideration by people with serious minds.

One of the most cherished myths that mankind has clung to from time immemorial is that everyone pays for his misdeeds: as you sow, so shall you reap. People cite instances of individuals who acquired wealth by corrupt means, were later brought to book, or were afflicted with some incurable disease or their progeny turned out to be bad. For every such instance of an evil person paying for his sins, I could adduce twenty where they went unpunished. They did not suffer from pangs of guilt, remained in good health, ate well, lived well, enjoyed life and the esteem of their fellow citizens, sent their children to the best schools and colleges and saw them settled in plum jobs, married into rich families which ensured their future prospects. 'There is a just man who perishes in his righteousness, and a wicked man who prolongs life in his wickedness,' says the Bible.

When faced with hard evidence that more often evil persons get a better deal in life than good people, upholders of the myth resort to inane explanations like 'honesty is its own reward', 'in the end, truth always triumphs'. They have even more devious explanations when confronted with cases of suffering inflicted on the good and the god-loving such as their children being born blind, mentally deficient or spastic. 'It is karma. They are paying for the sins they committed in their past lives.' And they explain the prosperity of evil-doers with 'They will surely pay for their sins in their lives to come: may they be reborn as snakes, pigs or vermin'. Such explanations are offered in the assurance that no one knows anything about past lives or the lives to come. As Ghalib said about paradise, I say about past and future lives: *'Dil kay behallaney koyeh khayaal accha hai'*. My friends don't suffer from the delusions that people suffer from for their misdeeds. How many paid the penalty for the crimes they had committed in November 1984? How many were punished for the destruction of the Babri Masjid? Far from being punished, three of them became members of Atal Bihari Vajpayee's cabinet and the man who soured the wind by his mischievously conceived rath yatra from Somnath to Ayodhya and spread the whirlwind of communal violence, which has not abated to this day, is the man-in-waiting to be the next prime minister. Do J. Jayalalithaa and Laloo Prasad Yadav feel guilty for squandering public money on weddings in their families? Do stockbrokers who fiddled with public money to the tune of thousands of crores, Pandit Sukh Ram or Ravi Sidhu, have sleepless nights for what they did?

I don't think so. They must have explanations which give them peace. No, my friends, there is no justice in the world. To succeed in life you have to be the three Cs (or chalakis in Hindi): chaalak (cunning), chaaploos (sycophant) and chaar-sau-bees (a cheat as defined under Section 420 of the Indian Penal Code).

God has no place in Jain theology. Instead, Jains believe in 'enlightened' human beings because escape is only possible in human form. Jains also reject the Vedas, the priestly order of the Brahmins and the caste system.

The Jain influence in India is largely due to the comparative affluence of the community. Some of India's biggest industrial houses are Jain—Dalmia, Sarabhai, Walchand, Kasturbhai Lalbhai,

Sahu Jain. The proportion of literacy among them is also high. Mahatma Gandhi, who was greatly influenced by the doctrine of ahimsa (non-violence), elevated it from a personal and ethical creed to a programme of national and political policy.

Despite ten years in Delhi's Modern School, an institution founded by the Jain family of Lala Sultan Singh, his son, Raghubir Singh, and currently controlled by Raghubir Singh's son, General Virendra Singh, I knew nothing about the Jain faith. Even in college I had some friends who were Jains, but I never got to know anything about their religious beliefs except that they were strict vegetarians. I also learnt that Mahatma Gandhi was profoundly influenced by Jain tenets, and the Jains were among the richest in our country. Also, their temples are among the most beautiful in India.

It was only in the 'sixties when I had to teach a course in comparative religion at Princeton University and later at Swarthmore College and the University of Hawaii that I read books on Jainism in order to pass on the information to my American students. I was deeply impressed with what I learnt. I admitted if I had to choose a religion to subscribe to, it would be Jainism. It came closest to agnosticism and the code of ethics to which, as a rationalist, I subscribed.

In the 'seventies, when I was the editor of the *Illustrated Weekly of India*, then the largest and the most influential weekly journal in the country, I wrote to the chief ministers of all the states that if they imposed a blanket ban on shikar in their states in honour of Jain Mahavira, I would give them all the publicity they wanted. Eight chief ministers responded to my appeal and banned killing for sport. I might mention that at the time, the Jains who owned the Times of India group of papers, including the *Illustrated Weekly of India*, had been deprived of control of the company and it was run by the government. The Jains had nothing to do with my anti-shikar crusade. As a matter of fact, when the Jains regained control of the Times of India group, they sacked me.

The word 'jain' is derived from 'jina', one who has conquered himself. Jains believe that their religious system was evolved by twenty-four tirthankaras (or makers of the river crossing), three of whom, Rhishabha, Ajitnath and Aristanemi, systematized their religious doctrines. Most of the Jain hagiography is legendary. But we do have reliable historical evidence of the existence of Parshvanath (877–777 BC), the twenty-third tirthankara, and Mahavira, the twenty-fourth (599–527 BC). There is reason to believe that in its formative phase, Jainism was a reaction against Brahminical Hindusim.

Vardhamana Mahavira was born in 599 BC in Kundagrama, a town north of Patna. He was the second son of a nobleman and was reared in the lap of luxury. The Jains love to enumerate everything. According to them, the child Mahavira was cared for by five nurses and enjoyed five kinds of joy. When he came of age, he was married and his wife bore him a daughter. But neither his wife, nor his child, nor the affairs of the state occupied his mind. On the death of his parents (according to one version, by suicide), he took the permission of his elder brother to retire to the jungles. He was then thirty years old. For twelve years he fasted and meditated 'in a squatting position, with joined heels, exposing himself to the heat of the sun, with knees high and the head low, in deep meditation'. In the midst of abstract meditation, he reached kevala (total) omniscience. He became nirgrantha—without ties or knots.

Mahavira discarded his clothes and spent the next thirty years of his life wandering from place to place. He spoke to no one, never stayed anywhere for more than one night, ate only raw food and strained the water he drank. He allowed vermins to feed on his body and carried a broom to sweep insects away from his path lest he trod on them. People scoffed at him and often tormented him. But he never said anything to them. He died in 527 BC, or, as the Jains put it, at the age of seventy-two, he cut asunder the ties of birth, old age and death.

Everything, animate or inanimate, has jiva (life-force). No one has the right to take another's life. The way of deliverance, said Mahavira, is in the pursuit of three gems (tri-ratans): right faith, right knowledge and right conduct. Right conduct prescribes five principles: sanctity of life (non-violence is the supreme law); truthfulness; respect for property; chastity and abandonment of worldly possessions.

Religions have had a renaissance in the form of belief in the irrational and kowtowing to superstitions. It is not a subject to be dismissed as a matter of academic irrelevance. What faith can you impose on a party that ruled us for six years and is the most important element in the Opposition—when it changes the entrance to its office from one side to the other because a Vaastu expert advises it that that would bring it better luck? And what do you think of an otherwise acceptable leader who wants the number of the house allotted to him to be changed from number 8 to 6A because the former is inauspicious? Or a Jayalalithaa and a Shobhaa Dé adding another 'a' to their first names because they believe it will improve their fortunes?

People who watch games on their TV sets must have noticed how many players attribute their achievements to God who, they presume, lives up in the clouds. Tendulkar, Ganguly, Dravid, Laxman and other batsmen, as soon as they score fifty, 100, 150 or 200 runs, first take off their helmets to raise their bats in order to acknowledge the cheering of spectators, then look briefly upwards to give thanks to the ooperwala. And this is not only the case with cricket players. Before the start of a hockey match, you will notice rival teams huddle together at either end of the field, put their heads together and say a short prayer for victory. Likewise, tennis players like the Amritraj brothers and Leander Paes may be noticed kissing the crucifix they wear around their neck to lend more punch to their services and smashes. I've noticed players of some other nations perform similar gestures in honour of their deities: Pakistanis, Sri Lankans, Africans and Latinos. I have never seen Englishmen, Australians, New

Zealanders or white Africans take much notice of the God of Sports. And in one interview in *Savaal Aapkey,* cricket celebrity Harbhajan Singh parried all the flattering comments hurled at him by attributing his success to bhagwan.

Nor I do think going on a pilgrimage makes one a better person. On my TV set, I've watched pilgrims gather in Jerusalem and Bethlehem, at Bodh Gaya, Prayag and Hardwar, at Mecca and Medina, at Amritsar, Hemkunt and Patna.

I have met people who had been on pilgrimages: they looked very pleased with themselves. But I did not notice any changes for the better in them. If they were prone to lying, cheating backbiting, scandal-mongering, using bad language before they left for their holy cities or rivers, they came back and resumed lying, cheating, backbiting, scandal-mongering and using bad language.

Truly had Guru Nanak spoken: *Ath sath teerath nahaaie utrey nahee maeil* (You may bathe at the sixty-eight places of pilgrimage, it will not wash the dirt off your body [and mind]). That does not deter the Guru's followers from doing precisely what he had castigated as a useless practice, or from going to pilgrim centres.

Some years ago, a film called *Nanak Naam Jahaaz* (the Holy Name is a ship that will take you across the waters of life) was shown in cinemas across northern India. Its theme was a man blinded in an accident visiting gurdwaras all over India. When he came to the sanctum of the temple and restored his vision, hundreds of thousands of people saw the film and were convinced that it was the truth, when in their hearts they knew it was a lie.

The Kumbh Mela at Allahabad is a pilgrimage on a scale grander than any ever seen in the world; as if the entire population of a country the size of Australia was packed into a few square miles of land surrounding the sangam (confluence) of three rivers; two, the Ganga and the Yamuna, are real, the third, Saraswati, mythical. The bandobast required to organize road, rail and air transport, housing, feeding, sanitation and maintaining law and order boggles the mind. One small mishap and the consequences would be disastrous. Is it worth taking such risks?

The people who go to the mela certainly think so. It is always a never-to-be-forgotten spectacle of sight and sound: thousands of ash-smeared Naga sadhus marching in processions from their ashrams and encampments to plunge into the waters of the Ganga and the Yamuna, hundreds of pandals with saffron-clad swamis chanting mantras or expounding the essential tenets of dharma.

And what about prayer? When I was a child of about four living in a tiny village with my grandmother, she taught me my first prayer. I was scared of the dark and prone to having nightmares. She told me that whenever I was frightened, I should recite the following lines by Guru Arjan:

> *Taatee vau na laagaee, peer-Brahma saranaee*
> *Chowgird hamaarey Raam-kar, dukh lagey na bhaee*
> (No ill-winds touch you, the great Lord your protector be
> Around you Lord Rama has drawn a protective line.
> Brother, no harm will come to thee.)

Being young, innocent and having infinite trust in my granny's assurances of the efficacy of these lines, I found they worked like magic. Later, I discovered that most Sikh children were taught the same lines even before they learnt other prayers. The hymn had four more lines:

> *Satgur poora bhetiya*
> *Jis banat banaaee Raam naam aukhad deeya.*
> *Eka liv laayee Raakh liye tin raakhan har, sabh biaadh mitaayee*
> *Kaho Nanak kirpa bhaee, Prabhu bhaye Sahaaee*
> (The true guru was revealed in his fullness, the one who did all create
> He gave the name of Rama as medicine, in Him alone I repose my faith.
> He saves all who deserve to be saved, He removes all worries of the mind.
> Sayeth Nanak, God became my helper, He was kind.)

Mark the Hindu terminology in this short prayer: Peer, Brahma, Raam-kaar, Raam-naam, and Prabhu. As a matter of fact, a painstaking scholar counted the number of times the name of God appears in the Adi Granth. The total comes to around 16,000. Of these over 14,000 are of Hindu origin: Hari, Ram, Govind, Narayan, Krishna, Murari, Madhav, Vithal and so on. There are also a sizeable number of Islamic origin: Allah, Rehman, Rahim, Kareem and so on. The Sikh term 'Wahe Guru' appears only sixteen times.

All religions borrow a lot from the others with which they come into contact; there is not a single religion in the world that has not borrowed some concept or the other from another: some borrow vocabulary and even rituals. In the Judaic family of religions—Judaism, Christianity and Islam—there is plenty of evidence of wholesale borrowing. A good example is Islam. Its monotheism (belief in one god) also exists in Judaism and Christianity. Its five daily prayers have roughly the same names as those of Jews; its greeting 'salaam aalaikum' is a variation of the Jewish 'shalom alekh'; turning to Mecca for namaaz is based on the Jews turning to Jerusalem; their food inhibitions (regarding pig's meat as unclean; halaal is the same as the Jewish kosher), the custom of circumcizing male children (sunnat) is also Jewish.

There is a lot of emphasis on what one should eat or drink in our religious traditions which has neither logic nor any bearing on health. For some beef is forbidden but pig meat is okay; in others beef is okay but pig meat is haraam (forbidden). Some insist that animals meant to be eaten must be beheaded at one stroke (jhatka); others insist they should be bled to death before they can be certified as edible (halaal). Vegetarians have kitchen fads of their own: some will not eat vegetables like onions, garlic, carrots or radishes because they are polluted by contact with the soil. But even they make an exception in the case of potatoes. How can anyone relish a vegetarian meal without spuds?

A couple of weeks ago I learnt of another eccentricity. The wife and daughter of a senior Bengali IAF officer told me that in

Bengali homes no chicken or chicken eggs are eaten: they prefer to eat duck and duck eggs. I asked them why? Their answer was amusing. Because, they said, Muslims relish chicken, so Hindus decided that eating chickens was un-Hindu. By that logic Bengali Hindus should be consuming ham and bacon which Muslims abominate.

Among Punjabis the kitchen fads are equally mind-boggling. Though both Hindus and Sikhs strictly abstain from eating beef (the Namdhari sect of Sikhs gained popularity for murdering Muslim cow butchers, and were later blown up by cannons to be acclaimed as martyrs), there is little enthusiasm for eating pig meat. At the most they take pickled pork (achaar), preferably made of wild boar meat. Ham and bacon, introduced to India by the English, can only be seen on the tables of the westernized Punjabis. And far from not eating chicken because it is relished by Muslims, chicken is the non-vegetarian Punjabi's favourite food. Chicken tandoori is the Punjabis' national bird.

Religious people who like to drink do so no matter what their scriptures say against drinking alcohol. On the contrary, taking wine is a part of Catholic and Anglican religious ritual. Only later sects like the Mormons who practice polygamy, the Jehovah's Witnesses, the Christian Scientists, the Quakers and the Plymouth Brethren disapproved of imbibing liquor. There are lots of references to the joys of drinking in the Old Testament.

The attitude towards drinking underwent a change with the advent of Islam. Scholars still disagree over whether the Quran forbids it as haraam (unlawful) or only censures it as something undesirable. So drinking in public is forbidden in most Muslim countries except Turkey, Tunisia, Algeria and Egypt which are comparatively westernized. In the more conservative Muslim countries like Sudan, Iraq, Iran, Afghanistan, Pakistan and Bangladesh despite prohibition people manage to get alcohol. A friend who had lived in Riyadh, the capital of Saudi Arabia, the most orthodox of all Islamic states, assured me that he had little problem getting his required quota of Scotch and wines.

The Hindic family of religions—Hinduism, Jainism, Buddhism and Sikhism—took a more tolerant view of drinking. Our gods drank somras; on many religious festivals drinking hard liquor or bhang (hashish) is de rigueur. My Sikh friends who disapprove of my drinking quote passages from the Granth Sahib to prove drinking is forbidden by the Sikh faith. Nevertheless, next to the Parsis (Zoroastrianism does not forbid drinking), the Sikhs are the biggest tipplers in India. The strong disapproval of drinking is a later development among certain Hindu reformist movements and was given religious sanction by men like Mahatma Gandhi and Morarji Desai.

The intermingling of faiths is much more in evidence in the Hindic family of religions: Hinduism, Jainism, Buddhism and Sikhism. All share a belief in karma, the cycle of birth-death-rebirth, meditation and so on. Needless to say, they also share much of their religious terminology.

Since Sikhism was the last of these major religions to emerge and the only one to come in contact with Islam, it is the only one which, coming in contact with the Bhakti cult, took a lot of the terminology of Islam from the sufi saints. When the thekedars (contractors or purveyors) of religion claim that their faith owes nothing to others and is therefore the purest of the pure, they make me laugh at their ignorance.

But to come back to prayer, I have memorized the principal power mantras of Hindus, Christians, Muslims and Sikhs but have not been able to work out why the followers of these religions endow them with powers above other mantras. It is generally agreed by all Hindus that the Gayatri Mantra is regarded as the most powerful invocation. I have translated it into English and often recited it while half asleep lest it escape my memory. I also know passages from the Gita and the Upanishads by rote which read as well but are relegated to secondary importance because the Gayatri Mantra is the maha-mantra.

If the most popular shabad among Sikhs is the one my grandmother taught me, for Christians, it is the twenty-third psalm:

The Lord is my shepherd; I shall not want. He maketh me to lie down in green pastures. He leadeth me beside the still waters. He restoreth my soul; He leadeth me in paths of righteousness for his name's sake. Yea, though I walk through the valley of the shadow of death, I will fear no evil; for thou art with me, thy rod and thy staff they comfort me.

The two most popular verses of the Koran that appear in Muslim mausoleums, including the Taj Mahal, are Sura Yaseen (which festoons the entrance gate) and Ayat-ul-Kursi, the throne verse. Of the two, Ayat-ul-Kursi is the more popular. Many Muslims wear it in their amulets. I have one in bidri and silver on my wall. I got a gold medallion from Tehran which my daughter, Mala, and then her daughter, Naina, wore in their necklaces while taking their examinations. Neither knew what it meant but felt reassured because their Muslim friends told them it was very powerful. It was as follows:

There is no God, but Allah, the living, the self-subsisting, the eternal. No slumber or sleep can seize Him. His are all the things in heaven and on earth. Who can intercede in His presence except as He permits? He knows the past, the present and the future. He cares equally for all. He in his knowledge grades his creations. His kingdom extends over the heaven and the earth. He is the guardian, He is the preserver. He is the highest. He is Supreme.

I am far from being a devout Sikh. But the first thing that I did when I set out to write about the religion and history of the Sikhs was to translate the Japjee, the Sikh's morning prayer. It was the earliest translation of the morning prayer rendered by a Sikh to be published abroad. Even while working on the translation, my literary inspiration was the Bible whose language I believe is most suited for the translation of scriptures of other religions.

There is one God.
He is the supreme truth.
He, The Creator.
Is without fear and without hate.
He, The Omnipresent,

Pervades the universe.
He is not born,
Nor does He die to be born again.
By His grace
shalt thou worship Him.
Before time itself
There was truth.
When time began to run its course
He was the truth.
Even now, He is the truth
And
Evermore shall truth prevail.
Not by thought alone, Can He be known
Though one think,
A hundred thousand times;
Not in solemn silence
Not in deep meditation.
Though fasting yields an abundance of virtue
It cannot appease the hunger for truth.
No, by none of these,
Nor by a hundred thousand other devices,
Can God be reached.
How then shall the Truth be known? How the veil of false illusion
torn?
O Nanak, thus runneth the writ divine,
The righteous path—let it be Thine.

No doubt, it is the simplest vocabulary, unambiguous and
well-worded. I know many other passages in the Koran which
read as well but I have not understood why the throne verse is
endowed with more power than the others.

The importance of the Japjee for the Sikhs cannot be overstated.
Besides being the morning prayer to be recited at amritvela (the
pre-dawn ambrosial hour), it forms the opening statement of the
Sikhs' scripture, the Granth Sahib, and is regarded as the essence
of Sikh theology.

We are not certain about the time when it was composed but
inner evidence points to the conclusion that it was in the later
years of the Guru's life and he took several days to finalize it.

It is the only piece in the Granth Sahib that can be read as one sustained piece where the Guru spells out his vision of God as the ultimate, timeless and truth and the path a seeker must take in order to achieve salvation. He was evidently inspired by the Upanishads: many theologians subscribe to the view that Sikhism is the essence of Vedanta.

The Japjee is the only part of the Granth Sahib that is meant to be recited, preferably in silent meditation and not set to the ragas of classical music like the other nearly 6,000 hymns of the Granth Sahib. The compiler, the fifth guru, Arjan, gave it the first place as it contained everything that is cardinal to Sikhism.

The founder of Sikhism, Guru Nanak, was born in 1469 to Hindu parents in a village north-west of Lahore, now in Pakistan. He was a wayward child who spent a lot of time talking to itinerant holymen. In his mid-twenties he left home with a Muslim family retainer and minstrel. They visited Hindu places of pilgrimage along the Ganges, went south to Sri Lanka and then west to Mecca and Medina. Nanak carried a notebook in which he wrote hymns in praise of God and set down his dialogues with men of religious learning.

There are not many references to historical events in Nanak's writings, but he does mention the invasion of northern India by the Mogul conqueror Babar in 1526 and the havoc it caused. Nanak was imprisoned for some time. He acquired a sizable following among both Hindus and Muslims. When he died in 1539 there was a dispute among his followers: the Muslims wanted to bury him because they thought he was one of them; the Hindus wanted to cremate him in the belief that he remained a Hindu to the end.

Nanak's teachings were a blend of Hinduism and Islam. He rejected Hindu polytheism and idol worship and accepted Islamic monotheism. He rejected the Hindu caste system and asceticism. 'Be in the world but not worldly,' he said. He emphasized the duty to work and earn a living.

It is clear that Nanak wished to set up a community apart from Hindus and Muslims. He appointed his closest disciple as the second guru, and the second guru appointed his closest disciple to be the third. Thereafter succession remained restricted to one family. The fourth guru founded the city of Amritsar in 1574. His son, Guru Arjan, raised the Harimandir (the temple of God) in the city. Later rebuilt in marble and covered with gold leaf, it became the Sikhs' most important place of pilgrimage.

Guru Arjan complied the Granth Sahib, the sacred scripture of the Sikhs. It comprises more than 6,000 hymns, all meant to be sung to the tune of the different ragas of Indian classical music. Besides presenting the writings of the gurus, it includes the compositions of Hindu and Muslim saints.

By Guru Arjan's time the Sikhs had become a sizable community, which alarmed the Muslim rulers. Arjan was summoned to Lahore where, after days of torture, he died. The same fate met the ninth guru, who was arrested, brought to Delhi and executed in 1675.

His only son, Gobind Rai, took up arms in defence of the community. 'Where all other means have failed, it is righteous to draw the sword out of its scabbard,' he wrote to the Mogul emperor. He called the Sikhs to gather at Anandpur and baptized five into a new fraternity called the Khalsa, or the pure. They vowed never to cut their hair or beards and always to carry a sword. He gave them a common surname—Singh, or Lion—and changed his own name to Gobind Singh.

Gobind Singh fought Hindu rajas and Muslim Mogul armies. He lost all four of his sons and was assassinated by two of his Muslim retainers. The Punjabi peasantry eventually rose and ousted the Muslim rule in northern India. This paved the way for a Sikh kingdom under Ranjit Singh, who ruled over Punjab until 1839.

The Sikh history is a long saga of bloody conflicts with the Muslims. When the British partitioned the region, almost half the Sikh population found itself in Pakistan. The Muslims drove them into India, killing hundreds of thousands. In their turn, the Sikhs drove the Muslims out of towns and villages in northern India with as much slaughter. How ironic that Sikhs should be confused with Muslims in the aftermath of 9/11!

Having spent the best part of my life working on Sikh history and translating selected passages of the Gurbani, I felt I owed it to myself to read the Granth Sahib. Many questions rose in my mind. Knowing the bigoted, unintelligent approach of the self-appointed custodians of matters scriptural I will not start a public debate. But there are some historical and linguistic aspects of the Gurbani that need elucidation. To start with, I would like scholars to compare the hymns of Kabir and Namdeo as they appear in the Granth Sahib with those in Hindi and Marathi. How did they travel from Varanasi and Maharashtra to Amritsar where the fifth Sikh Guru, Arjan, compiled the scriptures? Kabir's dohas in Hindi are different from his language in the Granth Sahib. How could he have composed the acrostics based on Gurumukhi at a time when the alphabet had yet to be finalized?

The case of Namdeo's baani is equally puzzling. I recall the late P.N. Oak, then secretary to the information and broadcasting ministry, asking me to give him Namdeo's baani in the Granth Sahib. Oak was a Maharashtrian studying the writings of Maharashtrian saint-poets. He went through the material and said: 'It is Namdeo but the vocabulary is different.' Did Guru Arjan rewrite both Kabir's and Namdeo's works before incorporating them in his compilation?

That reminds me of another work whose origin still intrigues me. Some years ago I translated Bapu Gandhi's favourite hymn, 'Vaishnav jan to tainay kahiye', said to be the compilation of Narsi Mehta who lived in the nineteenth century. When my translation was published, Swaran Singh, the editor of the *Sikh Review* in Calcutta, drew my attention to one of Guru Arjan's hymns on which Narsi Mehta's was based word for word. It could not have been a mere coincidence that Mehta had the same message for humanity that the Guru gave almost three centuries earlier.

There are things in our scriptures which we accept as the gospel truth without ever questioning their veracity. Two such truisms are 'the truth always triumphs' (Satyameva Jayate) and 'honesty is the best policy'. There are good reasons for accepting them at face value but when I begin to ponder over them, I begin to wonder how much of it is wishful make-believe and how much of it is proven reality. I concede that truth should always prevail and honesty should be the best policy, but is it, in fact, so?

The scriptures answer the question in the affirmative. 'Great is Truth, and mighty above all things,' says the Bible (Apocrypha 4:41). It might be recalled that the words are taken from Esdras, which tells the story of King Darius of Persia who asked three young Jewish scholars: what was the strongest thing in the world? The first one replied that it was wine, the second said the king was the strongest, the third said women were strongest and added a postscript: 'But above all things, truth beareth away the victory.' It became an article of faith, its Latin form being *'Magna est veritas, et praevalebit* (Great is truth and it prevails)'. Its shortened form MVP was often used as a motto on the flags and shields of countries claiming that they were fighting for the truth.

Guru Nanak equated truth with God. So did Mahatma Gandhi. Nanak put truthful conduct on an even higher pedestal:

Sachhon orey sab ko
Osper sachh aachaar.
(Truth above all
Above truth, truthful conduct.)

Gandhi went along with the guru in as much as he also made truthful conduct the central principle of his life. It should be evident that regarding honesty to be the best policy is a part and parcel of his concept of truthful conduct. 'To think good thoughts is one thing, to act upon them is another,' he wrote.

So convinced are we with such truisms that we also believe that anyone who transgresses the moral code pays a heavy price. *Haraam ki kamaayi kabhi hazam nahin hoti* (what is earned illicitly can never be digested). As a matter of fact we all know a lot of people who live very well with illicit earnings and do not have problems with their digestion. They also do not suffer from insomnia—sleeplessness. I know a few contemporaries who lied about their educational achievements, claimed that they had a first or higher second division, when actually they had thirds, did well in their interviews, landed good jobs and retired on fat pensions. No indigestion, no insomnia, they lived in good health into their eighties, respected by those not aware of the untruthful beginnings and envied by those who did. We have innumerable cases of wanton murders and deaths caused by drunken drivers where the culprits have got away by bribing eyewitnesses to retract their statements and tell lies under oath. Now turn your critical eye on your own lawmakers—MPs and MLAs. How many of them are 'tainted' (the word includes cheating, incitement to violence and murder)? They may not all be respected but their success in life cannot be denied. So what exactly does Satyameva Jayate mean?

According to our ancient scriptures, both Hindu and Sikh, krodh (anger) is as serious a shortcoming as kama (lust), lobh (greed), moh (self-love) and ahankaar (arrogance). They exhort us to overcome them in order to achieve moksha (salvation). They do not tell us how to go about getting the better of them. As far as anger is concerned, people have their own formulae: 'when roused to anger, count to ten before answering' or 'swallow the insult and keep your mouth shut'. There is no doubt that a person who loses his cool loses the argument. Another school of thought is that it is better to let off steam and get it over with because if you contain your anger, your blood pressure will rise and you may get peptic ulcers. I have evolved my own formula to get anger out of my system. I say nothing to the person who has insulted or snubbed me but when I narrate the incident to my friends later, I let loose a torrent of the choicest abuse in Punjabi and Hindustani—I have a large repertoire of filthy words in four languages—and purge myself of my anger. I even feel exhilarated for having scored over my traducer by saying nothing to him or her and I cleanse my system by letting out all the accumulated venom in front of third parties who thoroughly enjoy my outburst.

For many years, when I was young and believed in resolutions to improve myself, my New Year's resolve used to be to not run people down behind their backs. I was in the habit of doing so and hated myself afterwards. Whatever I said somehow reached the ears of the person I had maligned. When confronted by him or her, I had to deny what I had said and had reason to feel low in my self-estimation. I was able to check myself from indulging in vilifying people behind their backs for a few days. I resumed the bad habit, but somehow it got less and less on its own. I came to realize the truth of Guru Nanak's admonition:

Nanak, phikka boleeai
Tan manplukka hoi.
(Nanak, if you speak ill of the people
Your body and mind will fall sick.)

The Guru's words can also be interpreted as applying when saying nasty things to people to their faces. Many people make it a point to say hurtful things to others and justify their doing so. When in return they get more than they gave, there is a slanging match in which both participants get hurt while others enjoy the spectacle.

As for forgiveness, all religions counsel it. My father had a short temper; his father was even more ill-tempered. His pet word for me was bharwah (pimp) and since I went to a school that had lady teachers, rann mureed—disciple of a slut. My father never used bad language but being overworked, he was impatient and inclined to snap at everyone. We were terrified of him and kept out of his way as much as we could. In the later years of his life, he mellowed a great deal and I looked forward to joining him in the evenings for a sundowner. However, I could never get over my allergy towards people with short tempers. Incidents of people snubbing me still rankle in my mind. I have no forgiveness. Once somebody loses his temper with me, I write them off forever and no amount of their trying to make amends makes any difference in my attitude towards them.

In his own way Guru Nanak was also regarded as the dispeller of the darkness of ignorance, superstition and hate and the prophet of light and understanding among people.

The theologian, Bhai Gurdas, described Nanak's achievements in the following words:

> The true guru, Nanak, was then born;
> Fog and mist evaporated
> And light shone on the earth.
> As the rising sun dispels the dark and outshines the stars,
> As flee the herd of deer when a lion roars
> Without pause, without turning back for assurance.
> So fled evil from the world.

Nanak believed that the ideal was to achieve godliness while performing one's worldly tasks—*raaj meinjog*, that is, without renouncing the world or turning into an ascetic.

> Religion lieth not in the patched coat the Yogi wears,
> Not in the staff he bears,
> Nor in the ashes on his body.
> Religion lieth not in rings in the ears,
> Not in a shaven head,
> If thou must the path of true religion see
> Among the world's impurities, be of impurities free.

And again:

> The lotus in the water is not wet
> Nor the water-fowl in the stream.
> If a man would live, but by the world untouched,
> Meditate and repeat the name of the lord Supreme.

Nanak preached a crusade against meaningless superstition. During his time (and even today) the higher castes attached exaggerated respect to the sanctity of the kitchen: who may enter it, who may cook, what kind of food is pure and what is polluted. He wrote:

> There are worms in wood and cowdung cakes,
> There is life in the corn ground into bread.
> There is life in the water which makes it green.
> How then be clean when impurity is over the kitchen spread?
> Impurity of the heart is greed, of tongue, untruth,
> Impurity of the eye is coveting another's wealth, his wife, her comeliness.
> Impurity of the ears is listening to calumny.

He believed in the cleansing and purging qualities of prayer, naam. In the morning prayer, Japjee, he wrote:

> As hands or feet besmirched with slime, Water washes white; As garments dark with grime, Rinsed with soap are made light; So when sin soils the soul The Name alone shall make it whole; Words do not the saint or sinner make. Action alone is written in the book of fate. What we sow that alone we take; O Nanak, be saved or forever transmigrate.

Nanak equated God with truth. Truth is not an academic concept but something that has to become a principle of living. Guru Nanak was more conscious of nature than the gurus who succeeded him. His baramasi has some beautiful descriptions of natural phenomenon. The chirping of sparrows at the break of dawn, the drone of cicadas in forest glades and, of course, black clouds, thunder, lightning and rain during the monsoon. I give one example: *Mori runjhun laya, bhainey savan aya* (Raga Vadhans):

> Sweet sound of water gurgling down the water-spout
> (The peacock's shrill, exultant cry)
> Sister, it's Savan, the month of rain!
> Beloved—thine eyes bind me in a spell
> (they pierce through me like daggers)
> They fill my heart with greed and longing;

For one glimpse of thee I'll give my life
For thy name may I be a sacrifice.
When thou art mine, my heart fills with pride,
What can I be proud of if thou art not with me?
Woman, smash thy bangles on thy bedstead
Break thy arms, break the arms of thy couch;
Thy adornments hold no charms
The Lord is in another's arms.
The Lord liked not thy bangle-seller
Thy bracelets and glass bangles.
He doth spurn
Arms that do not the Lord's neck embrace
With anguish shall forever burn.
All my friends have gone to their lovers
I feel wretched, whose door shall I seek?
Friends, of proven virtue and fair am I
Lord, does nothing about me find favour in Thine eyes?
I plaited my tresses,
With vermilion daubed the parting of my hair
And went to Him
But with me He would not lie.
My heart is grief-stricken, I could die.
I wept, and the world wept with me.
Even birds of the forest cried,
Only my soul torn out of my body shed not a tear,
Nay, my soul which separated me from my beloved shed not a
tear
In a dream He came to me
(I woke), and He was gone.

Prabhat pheris—going around singing in the early hours of
the dawn—are customary at Hindu and Sikh religious festivals
in the plains of northern India. Behind the block of flats where
I live, there is a small gurdwara. A week or so before the birth
anniversary of Guru Nanak (this year it was on 11 November)
a loud cracker is exploded in the gurdwara courtyard at 4 a.m.
We are rudely shaken out of our slumber; most doze off again.
About a dozen men and women assemble in the gurdwara and
form a procession. The only music accompaniments are the chimta

and the dholak (drum). They go around the block singing Bhai Gurdas's eulogy, '*Satgur Nanak pragatya, mitti dhund jag chaanan hoya* (The true Guru Nanak made his appearance; dust and mist evaporated from the face of the earth).' This is followed by some hymns composed by the guru. The singing is not very melodious, but it is a manifestation of the singers's faith in their guru.

One prabhat pheri that still haunts me was the one I heard on my first day in Santiniketan in 1933. The monsoon was in full swing. From the window of the train to Bolpur, it was a vast expanse of water on both sides. 'Shamudro—it is like the sea,' remarked the ticket collector, who happened to be the only other person in the compartment. The Bolpur railway station looked drenched and desolate. I asked the station master how I could get to Santiniketan. 'Take a jutka,' he said.

I did not know what a jutka was. I found a small bullock-cart with a thatched roof, asked the owner if he could take me to Santiniketan. 'Baitho,' he replied, 'do taaka' (two rupees). I hopped in. We drove through a flooded countryside.

He dropped me off at the office. I was expected. I signed the entry register and was conducted to a room I was to share with a Buddhist bhikhu from Sri Lanka. Then I was taken to the dining hall where I had a plateful of rice and maachher jhole (fish curry). I got to my room and made acquaintance with my roommate. The room had no furniture of any kind. The bhikhu had a hurricane lamp by his pillow and read late into the night. I spread my bedding roll at the other end of the room. I had never slept on a hard cement floor. I was tired and dozed off before Bhikhu Manjushri blew out the hurricane lantern.

I slept fitfully, uncertain about what I had let myself in for. I must have fallen asleep because I began to dream. I heard the voices of an angelic choir at a distance, coming towards me. I realized I was not dreaming; it was for real. I groped my way in the dark and opened the door. The soft moonlight of the waning moon filtered through the mist of a gentle drizzle. I saw a dozen boys and girls dressed in white, carrying lanterns and candles, walking in a procession, singing as they went around the campus. Later I learnt it was the varsha mangal (the welcoming of the rains).

I envy other people's faith and religious fervour. I regret I will forever remain an outsider, sceptical of all pilgrimages save the one in one's own heart.

To quote Fitzgerald:

. . . Pilgrim, pilgrimage and Road
was but myself towards myself, and your
Arrival but myself, at my door.
Came, you lost atoms to your
Centre draw
Rays that have wandered into darkness wide
Return, and back into your Sun subside.

In the days left to me, I have come to the conclusion that I've been an imposter all my life. I have written several books on the religion and the history of the Sikhs, published translations of selected hymns from the Gurbani without having ever read the Guru Granth Sahib from cover to cover. Nevertheless when people refer to me as a scholar of Sikhism, I protest so mildly that they think I am being modest.

I am now trying to fill up the gaps in my knowledge by devoting my entire summer vacation to reading the Guru Granth Sahib in the morning; I devote my afternoons to reading Urdu poets, from Meer and Ghalib to Faiz Ahmed Faiz, Kaifi Azmi, Javed Akhtar and others. So the mornings are devoted to reading about praises of the Lord, the importance of the Guru for spiritual elevation, the need to conquer lust, anger, desire and arrogance by squashing one's ego and renouncing wine and women. The afternoons are spent reading about the joy that drinking liquor, making love to women and boys with rosy cheeks and rounded bottoms provide.

In short, it is the temple in the a.m., the tavern after p.m. I have become a split personality. By the time my vacation is over, I would have finished my first complete reading of the

Guru Granth Sahib. I would have also gone through the diwans of Urdu classical masters and modern poets. I fear I will end up as a schizophrenic in need of psychiatric help.

I comfort myself by believing that Mirza Asadullah Khan Ghalib must have faced the same dilemma. His Muslim friends who followed the Shariat law strictly must have chided him for not saying his prayers regularly and for his indulgence in wine. A man who had known want, woe and fear, a man who begged for a pittance from the king, I wonder, how he could decide so quickly to change his ways and give up drinking.

To wit:

So have I lived and passed my days
How can I bring myself to say that God exists.
God the Bounteous Giver,
God the Beneficent?
For God's possible for those who lead happy
sheltered lives,
And know God's grace and His loving care.

Sauda, another great master of Urdu verse, was even more outspoken about the joys of drinking:

Saaqi gayee bahaar, dil mein rahee havas
Too minnaton sayjaam dey
And main kahoon kay 'bas'.
(O Saki, gone is the spring of youth,
Remains but one regret in this heart of mine
That thou has never pressed the goblet in my hand,
And I protested 'I've had enough wine'.)

By the time the day is over and I turn indoors for my sundowner, I am a thoroughly confused person. I pour myself a hefty slug of Scotch 'n' soda and put on my cassette player. I refrain from putting on kirtan in respect for people who would consider it a sacrilege and instead listen to Bach, Beethoven or Mozart. I come to the comforting conclusion: 'imposter' is too strong a word for me, but 'humbug' fits me to a tee.

PROTIMA BEDI

Protima Gupta was born in Delhi in 1948. Her father, a small- time trader, was thrown out by his bania father for marrying a dark, Bengali woman. He tried his luck in different cities of India, flopped everywhere and rejoined his family business. He had four children, three daughters and a son. Protima was their second daughter and the least loved. Being a loveless child turned her into a rebel. She was a bright girl and did well in studies. The two words missing from her life's lexicon were 'no' and 'regret'; she could never say no to a man who desired her and grew into a very desirable and animated young woman whom most men found irresistible.

And she did not regret any of the emotional and physical experiences she had. She also felt that keeping secrets was like lying; so she told everyone everything, including her husband and the succession of lovers who entered her life. She broke up marriages but remained blissfully unaware of the hurt she caused people. She had to get everything off her ample bosom. She told nothing but the truth about everyone she befriended.

Death caught her unawares. She was killed in a landslide while on a pilgrimage to Badrinath. And on the same day, in Mumbai, died Persis Khambatta, India's first beauty queen and the one-time mistress of Protima's husband, Kabir Bedi.

I first met Protima in the home of Gopi Gauba in Mumbai. Kabir, whom I had known as a child in Lahore, was with her. I had little reason to like them as he had just ditched Amba, my friend B.C. Sanyal's daughter, to whom he had been engaged.

He was living with Protima, then only nineteen years old. I did not exchange a word with either of them. When Protima became pregnant they decided to get married. Pooja was their first child. But neither marriage nor the child made Protima change her ways.

Next I saw photographs of Protima running stark naked on a beach. It shocked middle-class society—exactly what she wanted. One day (I was editing the *Illustrated Weekly of India* at the time), I.S. Johar asked me to come over with a photographer as he was getting engaged to Protima.

I called him an ass on the phone, but I went. I even published a photograph of them exchanging rings. That's all they wanted: publicity. Protima later assured me that she had not so much as kissed Johar. I believed her because Protima never lied.

I did not see Protima blossom into an Odissi dancer. Nor did I see the dance village, Nrityagram, that she created. She came to Bangalore to invite me. I accepted. But when I discovered it would take me four hours on the road to get there and back, I cried off. She was very angry and swore she would never see me again. Her anger did not last long.

When her son committed suicide, she shaved off her long hair and renounced worldly pursuits. On her return to India, she asked me to let her stay at my villa in Kasauli for a few days so she could be near Sanawar where her son had been at school for a while. She spent four cold winter days walking about the hills all alone. She returned refreshed and full of smiles.

Protima Gauri (as she renamed herself) had a zest for living. She loved her men, liquor and drugs. She had an enormous appetite for sex and admitted to enjoying it as many as six times a day. She had a large range of lovers.

Protima hated humbugs and hypocrites. She wrote, 'Every woman I knew secretly longed to have many lovers but stopped herself for many reasons. I had the capacity to love many at a time and for this had been called shallow and wayward and a good-time girl.'

She also had a puckish sense of humour. Once, she arrived in Mumbai with an electric vibrator. A very scandalized customs officer refused to let it pass. She gave him a dressing-down, 'My husband is out of town most of the time, what do you expect me to do? I am trying to be faithful. Are you encouraging infidelity?' She got away with it.

M.A. JINNAH

From the time the British consolidated their empire in India, their Hindu and Muslim subjects began defining their attitudes towards each other and their rulers. The Hindus felt that it was time to reassert their religious identity, settle scores with the Muslims who had lorded over them for centuries, and when the time came for the British to leave, take over the ruling of the country. After the Mutiny of 1857 was crushed, the Muslims realized there was little chance of their becoming rulers again and that they had to come to terms with the British, and the Hindus who formed the preponderant majority in the country. One section, led by the founder of the Aligarh Muslim University, Sir Syed Ahmed Khan, was of the opinion that they were safer under British hegemony than under a renascent Hindu domination. Another section felt that they had nothing to fear from the Hindus and that they should join them in pressing the British to concede democratic rights to Indians and grant them dominion status. The one man who was able to reconcile these two groups was M.A. Jinnah (1876–1948).

To understand Jinnah's role as an ambassador of Hindu–Muslim unity, a title conferred on him by Sarojini Naidu, one needs to know his background. He was born in Bombay in an Ismaili Khoja family, regarded by orthodox Muslims as 'beliefless'. They were traders and merchants who had more dealings with Parsis and Hindus than with fellow Muslims. In 1897, he converted to the Shia faith. What the conversion entailed is not clear because he never conformed to any religious trends. In 1892, he proceeded to England to study law at Lincoln's Inn. During the four years he was in England, he made it a point to go to the houses of Parliament to listen to debates. He was deeply impressed by the speeches made by Dadabhai Naoroji, the first Indian to be elected to the House of Commons, and John Morley. Both men were liberals. Jinnah accepted them as his role models and liberalism as his political creed. Back home in Bombay, he befriended Sir Pherozeshah Mehta, Gokhale and Badruddin Tyabji. He was determined to pursue the careers of law and politics. He regarded both as gentlemanly professions. Although he married a Parsi girl, Ruttie, many years younger than him, his professional occupations left him little time to discharge his domestic obligations. He was also dour, unsmiling, tense and a chain-smoker. After some years, Ruttie left him with their daughter, Dina (the mother of Nusli Wadia of Bombay Dyeing).

Jinnah was quite clear about the role of Indian politicians. They must never mix religion with politics: one was a private matter, the other public service. Political differences should be settled by debate and not taken to the streets to create mob hysteria. The right to vote should be restricted to the educated taxpayer and not extended to the illiterate and those who do not contribute to the cost of administration. Primary education should be compulsory. What is truly amazing is that he found many takers for his ideas and was acceptable to the Indian National Congress as well as the Muslim League. For some years, he straddled both parties and was accepted by them as their spokesman. He used his forensic skill to reconcile the Muslim League's demands and persuaded the Congress to accept them: separate electorates with weightage for Muslims in states where they were in a minority, and Muslim hegemony in Sindh, Punjab, the NWFP and Bengal where they formed a majority. He succeeded in bringing about political unity between Hindus and Muslims so that they could jointly pressurize their British rulers to hand over the governance of the country to Indians. In a speech at the Muslim League Conference in Lucknow in 1917, he urged Muslims not to look upon the Hindu majority as a bogey, saying: 'This is a bogey which is put before you by your enemies to frighten you, to scare you away from the cooperation with the Hindus which is essential for the establishment of self-government.'

Unlike most other Indian politicians, he was not overwhelmed by English Governors and Viceroys: he spoke his mind to them without mincing his words. He carried on verbal warfare with Lord Willingdon, Governor of Bombay and then Viceroy of India. In short, he was for a time India's top leader till Mahatma Gandhi arrived on the scene. Gandhi not only infused religion into politics but also took politics to the streets through his call for non-cooperation and boycott of government-run institutions, including schools. Jinnah found this distasteful and difficult to digest. Besides these, Gandhi showed a marked preference for Jawaharlal Nehru as the future leader of the country.

Gradually, Jinnah was pushed off the centre stage of Indian politics to become more and more a leader of the Muslims. In any event, he was elected to the Legislative Council from a Muslim constituency. He was among the Muslim delegates at the Round Table Conferences in London. He stayed on in England for a few years and toyed with the idea of fighting elections to the House of Commons. No party was willing to accept him as its candidate. It was not surprising. As the *Manchester Guardian* summed him up, 'The Hindus thought he was a Muslim communalist, the Muslims took him to be a pro-Hindu, the Princes declared him to be too democratic. The British considered him a rabid extremist—with the result that he was everywhere but nowhere. None wanted him.'

Reluctantly, he returned to Bombay to resume his legal practice and his political career—now as a spokesman of Muslim interests.

A Requiem for Domsky

Dom Moraes's interest in poetry started very early in his life. In his preface to a new collection, he writes, 'I was about ten years old when I started to read poetry . . . I had an instinctive feel, even at that age, for the shape and texture of words.' By the time he was fourteen, he began to write poetry himself. He learnt French in order to be able to read Villon in the original. Poetry became a lifelong passion. But for a longish break (1965–82), he continued to write till the end of his life. It would appear that the writer's block that had lasted seventeen years was finally overcome when he met Sarayu Srivatsa to whom he dedicated this collection.

Dom Moraes (Domsky to his friends) is not easy to read. While his prose was limpid and lyrical, his poetry tended to be somewhat obscure like the works of many modern poets. His words have resonance but you have to read every line two or three times before you can comprehend their meaning. People brought up on simple rhyming verse like 'Twinkle, twinkle, little star' will find Domsky's poems obscure. However, one can detect a few themes which recur consistently. He was obsessed with death. The hawk was his symbol of doom. His mother's insanity haunted him all his life. He sought escape from it in hard liquor and making love. He sums it up in 'A Letter':

My father hugging me so hard it hurt,
My mother mad, and time we went away.
We travelled, and I looked for love too young.

248

More travel, and I looked for lust instead.
I was not ruled by wanting: I was young,
And poems grew like maggots in my head.

With the arrival of Sarayu, he turned to writing about love, but death remained a permanent fixture. We are not told how and when he fell in love with her. The confession is made in 'Fourteen Years':

Fourteen years, the same mixture
As when first I met her:
. . . Her breasts always ready:
Mindmarks and handmarks on each other:
I study the landscape of her body
As architect, husband, and brother.
He confirms their love remained unabated.
Under our feet the harsh subcontinent
where you and I were born,
. . . Eight years I have inhabited your weather,
the clear and darker seasons of your mind.
We have been more than married. It was meant.
We've lived in each other. It was meant to be.

Domsky was stricken with cancer but refused to undergo chemotherapy. He almost wallowed in the prospect of an early end with the ghost of his insane mother hovering over him.

From a heavenly asylum, shrivelled Mummy,
glare down like a gargoyle at your only son.
. . . That I'm terminally ill hasn't been much help.
There is no reason left for anything to exist.
Goodbye now. Don't try to meddle with this.

Dom Moraes died in his sleep in Mumbai on the evening of Wednesday, 2 June 2004. He was only sixty-eight. With him died the best of Indian poets of the English language and the greatest writer of felicitous prose.

THE MASTER BUILDER

When we talk about the builders of modern India, we tend to restrict our list to eminent politicians and social workers: Tilak, Gokhale, C.R. Das, Gandhi, Nehru, Sarojini Naidu and a few others. Not many of the present generation of North Indians even know the name of one who deserves first place on the list of men who changed the face of India in more ways than one: he was Sir C.P. Ramaswami Aiyar. In the ten years that he was the dewan of Travancore he initiated the scheme of compulsory primary education; he was the leader of the movement to help Harijans gain entry into the Hindu temples; he was a builder of dams, canals, hydroelectric works, fertilizer plants. He was a member of the Viceroy's Executive Council, a close friend of Annie Besant, legal adviser to Moti Lal Nehru and many nationalist leaders. He was the vice chancellor of three universities, a delegate at the Third Round Table Conference. And much else.

I first saw him from a distance when he came to deliver the convocation address at Punjab University in Lahore. He was a strikingly handsome man, as fair-skinned as any Kashmiri, with acquiline features and large drooping eyes. Women fell for him because he also had the gift for words. It was rumoured that Lady Willingdon was besotted with him. He took adoration in his stride. At the Lahore convocation, he raised a lot of laughter when he said that memsahibs who could not pronounce the word 'dewan' called him 'dear one'.

I had the privilege of having him over for dinner at my home in London some time in 1950. By then he was an old man and had to be escorted by his son. But he was as lively as ever. I got to know four generations of the family. In Bombay I met his granddaughter, Shakuntala Jagannathan, the director of tourism of the western and central regions, and the author of books on Hinduism. Then Shakuntala's daughter, Nanditha Krishna. The last time I was in Chennai she invited me to lunch at their ancestral family mansion, 'The Grove', standing among sprawling acres of ancient trees. Both mother and daughter had inherited their looks from Sir C.P. Nanditha is a ravishing beauty and the author of several books. Brains and beauty make a lethal combination.

Shakunthala Jagananthan has written about her grandsire: *Sir C.P. Remembered*. It is not a biography in the strict sense of the term but a collection of reminiscences of the adoring grandchild of this great patriarch. She tells us that 'Thatha' (Tamil for 'Dadaji') was born on Deepavali of 1879 at Wandiwash. His father had his horoscope cast by a European and an Indian astrologer. Both predicted that he would not pass any exams. Thatha proceeded to top the list in every examination he sat for and came to be known as the 'Prize Boy'. He was a voracious reader. Tamil, Sanskrit, English and French were grists to his all-devouring mill. He also loved Mathematics. He did not want to be a lawyer but his father coaxed him into the legal profession. Tamilian superstition stated that no new venture should be undertaken on a Tuesday. Thatha chose to join the Madras Bar on a Tuesday. All he made in the first year of his practice was Rs 104. Six years later he was earning more than any other lawyer. He was offered a place on the bench. He turned it down with contempt. He wrote: 'I prefer, Mr Chief Justice, to talk nonsense for a few hours each day than to hear nonsense everyday and all day long.'

His rise was meteoric. His most creative years were in the service of the maharaja of Travancore. Kerala owes its 100 per cent literacy rate to moves initiated by Thatha. Also, the agricultural and industrial prosperity that came to the state and its neighbours was through the schemes initiated by him. He was fiercely loyal to his maharaja, and on the eve of Independence pleaded for an independent Travancore. His favourite hero was Hanuman and he often quoted Milton in his support: 'Unshaken, unseduced, unterrified/His Loyalty he kept.'

Thatha wanted to retire in Ooty. That was not to be. He was sought after by Nehru for advice and sent to the UN to argue India's case on Kashmir. If Krishna Menon had let Thatha do so instead of hogging the limelight himself, we would not be in the predicament we find ourselves in today.

Once, when Thatha returned to Travancore, the citizens turned out in thousands to welcome him and an attempt was made on his life. Shakunthala does not tell us what the motives of the would-be assassin were or what happened to him. My friend P.R. Krishna Narayanan, retired press officer of Lakshadweep, in an article 'The Omniscient C.P. Ramaswami Aiyar' (*New Swatantra*, November 1988), was of the opinion that it was not an attempt to kill him but to disfigure him. The man failed on both counts. Thatha recovered from his injuries without a scar on his handsome face. He died in London at the ripe age of eighty-seven.

ALI SARDAR JAFRI

The day Ali Sardar Jafri died in Bombay (1 August 2000 at
8.30 a.m.), an ironic death in this season of troubled détente, I
made it a point to watch Pakistan Television to find out what
it had to say about him. Jafri was not only in the front rank of
Urdu poets in recent times but was also the spearhead of the
movement for a rapprochement with Pakistan. PTV made a
passing reference to Jafri's death as a poet who wrote of the need
for love and understanding between people. I was disappointed.
I was also dissapointed with the coverage given by the Indian
media, both print and electronic. There was a lot more to Jafri
than the hastily written obituaries and collages put together to
meet deadlines.

I had known Ali Sardar and his beautiful wife, Sultana, for
over thirty years. During my years in Bombay we met each other
almost every other week. Despite his commitment to communism,
he liked the good things in life: good Scotch, good food and
comfortable living. He lived in a pokey little three-room flat
off Peddar Road. Apart from his wife and three children, who
often stayed with him, he had two widowed sisters in the same
apartment. There was not much room to move about. Many of
his books were stacked under his bed on which he read, wrote
and slept. I would arrive armed with a bottle of Scotch. He would
send for soda and biryani from a restaurant, Allah Beli, facing
his apartment. I sought his company because he was one of the
most erudite Indian writers I had met.

Ali Sardar also had a phenomenal memory. If I quoted one line by any Urdu poet, he would come out with the rest of the poem. And explain every word by referring to Persian poets—from Rumi, Hafiz to Ghalib and Allama Iqbal. When I set about translating Iqbal's 'Shikwa' and 'Jawab-e-Shikwa', I went all the way to Bombay to seek his assistance. For two days Ali Sardar and Sultana came to my hotel in the morning; we worked till lunch time when Rafiq Zakaria and his wife, Fatma, joined us to find out how it was going. After they left, we resumed our labours till it was time for our sundowners.

I often needled Ali Sardar about his communism. He had been a cardholder and had been expelled from Aligarh Muslim University (which later gave him an honorary doctorate) and spent eighteen months in jail during the British Raj and again after Independence under Morarji Desai's government. Although he had ceased to be a cardholder, he stoutly defended Marxist ideology. What was beyond my comprehension was that despite professing atheism, during the month of Muharram he often wore black and attended Shia majlis and abstained from alcohol. During a TV interview with me, while he expected to be questioned about Urdu poetry, I confronted him with his contradictory beliefs in both Islam and Marxism. He was visibly upset and fumbled for words. He took it out on me after the interview was over. He called me everything under the sun and stopped just short of calling me a bastard. I am sure if he had not been so obsessed with communism and social problems, he would have made a greater poet.

I saw him often when he came to Delhi to record Kamna Prasad's series, *Kahkashaan* (Milky Way), on contemporary Urdu poets. And later to participate in the Jashn-e-Bahaar mushairas organized by Kamna to bring Pakistani and Urdu poets together on one stage every year. He presided over the last one a few months before he died. He had an imposing presence: he was a lean, tall man with a mop of untidy, tousled grey hair, sparkling dark eyes and an ever-smiling face. His voice held his audience spell-bound. His message to Pakistan at a time when Indo–Pak relations were at their worst was one of peace:

> *Tum aao gulshan-e-Lahore se chaman bardosh,*
> *Hum aayen subh-e-Banaras ki roshnee le kar*
> *Himalay ki havaaon ki taazgee le kar*
> *Aur iske baad yeh poochein ki kaun dushman hai?*
> (You come from the garden of of Lahore laden with flowers,
> We will come bearing the light of a Benares morning
> With fresh breezes from Himalayan heights
> And then, together we can ask, who is the enemy?)

Ali Sardar was an incorrigible optimist. Inspired by Rumi's line, '*Hum cho sabza baarha roeeda aym* (like the green of the earth we never stop growing)', he summed up his life story (*Mera Safar*) in a few memorable lines:

> I am a fleeting moment
> In the magic house of days and nights;
> I am a restless drop travelling eternally
> From the flask of the past to the goblet of the future.
> I sleep and wake, awake to sleep again
> I am the ancient play on the stage of time
> I die only to become immortal.

Ali Sardar, who was born into a zamindar family in Balrampur (Uttar Pradesh) on 29 November 1913, won numerous awards for his poems, short stories, plays and articles. They included the Iqbal Sammaan, the Soviet Land Nehru Award, the Jnaneshwar award and the Jnanpeeth award. More than all those it was the warm-hearted applause he won wherever he went, the respect and affection he received from people he knew, that sustained him during his difficult days. He returned the love he got in full measure. In a collection of his poems that he gave to Kamna's four-year-old daughter, Jia, he wrote the word 'pyar' in Urdu five times on each line down twenty lines. That was his parting message to the world.

YE OL' LADY OF BORI BUNDER

Seth Ram Kishen Dalmia bought Bennett, Coleman & Co., the publishers of the *Times of India* and its other publications, in 1947. He wanted to have a subservient press to propagate his brand of Hinduism with cow protection and vegetarianism as top priorities. He hated Nehru's agnostic socialism; in return Nehru hated his guts. I had a very brief meeting with Seth Dalmia. I had applied for the post of the editor of the *Illustrated Weekly of India*. He asked me one question: 'Do you know Sanskrit?' I replied, 'No, sir, I don't.' He dismissed me curtly: 'Go and learn Sanskrit, then come to me.' I got the job twenty years later, without a word of Sanskrit added to my vocabulary.

If Dalmia had his way, Bennett Coleman's publications would be devoted to propagating his brand of Hindutva. Fortunately he got into severe financial trouble and had to give the publishing house to his son-in-law, Shanti Prasad Jain, the husband of his eldest daughter by Rama, the first of his six wives. It was Shanti and more so his son, Ashok, who put Bennett Coleman back on its feet. Today Ashok's widow, Indu, and her two sons, Samir and Vineet, run the company. The driving force behind its spectacular success as India's leading group of newspapers is Samir.

I took over as the editor of the *Illustrated Weekly* in 1969 and held the post for nine long years. I got an insider's view of the organization. It ran like a well-oiled machine. The editors were well-paid, provided a house allowance, a new car and fringe benefits. We sat in red swivel chairs, and were served tea and coffee and a sumptuous vegetarian lunch. We were given a key each to open the doors of the lavatories reserved for editors. To have a pissoir of one's own was the ultimate in editorial prestige.

I was fortunate in being left to re-shape the *Weekly*. The Jains had been divested of control of the company because of some financial hanky-panky. A benevolent retired Justice K.T. Desai was the officiating chairman. An able and non-interfering Ram Tarneja was the general manager. I lasted out till the company was restored to the Jains.

The Times group has every reason to crow over its achievements. There are newspapers which enjoy more credibility and provide better reading. But the *Times* reigns supreme. The credit goes largely to Samir. He sensed that if print had to survive TV, it had to radically alter its content. While a weekly relies heavily on the personality of its editor, a daily does not. Three-fourths of its content is taken from the wires or foreign agencies (strip cartoons and crosswords, for example); the rest comprises correspondents' reports and readers' contributions, leaving the editor and his deputies a third or even less of the editorial page to comment on world and national events. Not many people read editorials. The *Times'* first Indian editor, Frank Moraes, was much respected for his forthrightness but not much read. His successor, N.J. Nanporia, was neither admired nor read. Sham Lal was lauded for his erudition but few people read more than his opening paras. Likewise, Girilal Jain, regarded as a perceptive political analyst and the first proponent of Hindutva, had few takers. His successor, Dileep Padgaonkar, failed to convince his proprietors that next to the prime minister he was doing the second most important job in India.

So we have the ironic situation that while we can name the editors of other dailies, no one knows the name of the editor of the most widely circulated paper in the country. Samir Jain (rightly?) concluded that editors were dispensable. From his great grandfather he has inherited the uncanny gift of making money: the Times group has become a major money-spinner. The trinity who run it know what is and what is not dispensable.

R.K. Laxman is not dispensable (he is worth three editors). God and religion are not dispensable: so we have articles on God, yoga, meditation and quotes from the scriptures. Scantily clad starlets are not dispensable: male readers need some titillation every morning. Books and book reviews are as dispensable as editors. That is the secret behind the longevity of the old lady of Bori Bunder. That along with the periodical injection of life-giving drugs by the Jain trinity. A reasonable way of discovering this secret is to compare its Sunday supplements with those of other national dailies. It has a string of contributors who command readerships of their own.

The one lasting contribution Bennett Coleman has made to Indian journalism is to cut to size editors who had grandiose notions about their positions. The roll of honour of those unceremoniously shown the door includes Frank Moraes, Girilal Jain, A.S. Raman, Kamleshwar, Inder Malhotra, Prem Shankar Jha, Dom Moraes and Dileep Padgaonkar. I don't feel too bad about being named among them.

OF GODMEN AND THEIR LEGACIES

Of the many godmen I have met, the one I found most incomprehensible was Harbhajan Singh, popularly known as Yogi Bhajan. He died in Espanola, New Mexico, on 6 October 2004 of heart failure at the age of seventy-five.

Harbhajan was born on 26 August 1929, in a small town now in Pakistan. After Partition, the family migrated to India where he was schooled in Dalhousie. After graduating in economics, he was posted as a customs official at Palam airport. Physical fitness and sports were his abiding passions. He also practised yoga and became a master of Kundalini, which he taught others.

When a departmental inquiry was instituted against him, he migrated to Canada in 1968 and became a yoga instructor in Toronto. From Toronto he moved to California. Wherever he went he taught an odd mixture of Sikhism and Kundalini yoga. He called it 3H—health, happiness, holiness. For some reason he chose the fourth guru, Ramdas, the builder of Amritsar, as his role model.

His 3H Khalsas were vegetarians. Soon a sect of Yogi Bhajan American Sikhs evolved. They were distinctly white: men in white turbans, long, flowing blonde beards, clad in kurta pyjamas; women put their hair up in a bun and wrapped it with white cloth. They took Sikh names with the suffix 'Khalsa'. Within a few years, their numbers swelled to thousands. They set up gurdwaras of their own, recited the Gurbani and sang kirtan. At times, Yogi brought his white disciples on chartered planes on pilgrimage to Punjab. Indian Sikhs were greatly flattered to see the message of their gurus taking root in foreign lands. Yogi, later given the honorific 'Singh Sahib', was the first to plant the Khalsa flag on foreign soil.

Yogi Bhajan also had a keen eye for business. He opened a chain of vegetarian restaurants where only 'organic' food was served. His Yogi Herbal Tea, based on Punjabi recipes, is about the tastiest tea I have ever had. However, some of his products have amusing names. A chewing gum bears the name 'Wahguru Choo'. His latest venture was to provide guards to the US government's high security installations.

I met Yogiji at a dinner party at the home of the multi-millionaire Nanak Kohli in Washington. He arrived with his entourage of Amazonian white lady disciples. I was surprised to see that the man who assiduously practised yoga was pot-bellied. Also, for one who practised the joys of simple living he wore a lot of gold rings studded with precious stones on his fingers. He also had a voracious appetite: one of his Indian lady disciples cooked his favourite bhindi for him. I had taken two American journalists from the *Washington Post* with me. They were not impressed.

Yogiji was an enigma. When fleeing from India, he borrowed Rs 10,000 to pay for his air ticket to Canada. Twenty years later, when he was on one of his visits to India, the daughter of the man from whom he had borrowed the money reminded him of the debt. She expected to be repaid with interest because Yogiji was, by now, a very rich man. Instead of getting her father's money back, she was snubbed: 'You are in your forties but are still caught in maya's jaal (the web of illusion),' he said, and blessed her.

No one can deny that Yogi Bhajan was the Sikh religion's pioneer in the West. His death at seventy-five, not a great age to go for a health-food faddist and a yoga preacher, will be mourned by the Khalsa Panth by flying their flag at half-mast for a long time to come.

Another godman I have got to know is the late Acharya Rajneesh (known to his disciples as Osho). I try to read everything written or spoken by him. His speeches were taken down by his followers and printed in the weekly *Osho Times* and then there are the innumerable books containing his sermons. I am currently reading his autobiography, *Autobiography of a Spiritually Incorrect Mystic*. I do so because I regard him as a propounder of new ideas on existence. He was an iconoclast who held nothing sacred, questioned the veracity of religious dogma and cleared the cobwebs of confused thinking from people's minds. He was one of the most erudite of the world's religious philosophers, but did not wear his learning on his sleeve; he was witty and humorous and often ended his sermons with a dirty joke with four letter words. He was a rare phenomenon.

Rajneesh was lucky to have broad-minded parents. Although they were Jains and his father did his best to conform, his mother rejected it all and encouraged her son to question his schoolteachers and the preachers of religion, and to think for himself. It is in childhood that parents start brainwashing their children.

Writing about his mother, Rajneesh says:

Now I can say that woman was really great, because as far as religion is concerned, everybody is lying. Christians, Jews, Jains, Mohammedans—everybody is lying. They all talk of god, heaven and hell, angels and all kinds of nonsense, without knowing anything at all. She was great, not because she knew but because she was unable to lie to a child.

'Nobody should lie—to a child, at least, it is unforgivable. Children have been exploited for centuries just because they are willing to trust. You can lie to them very easily and they will trust you. If you are a father, a mother, they think you are bound to be true. That's how the whole of humanity lives in corruption, in a very slippery mud of lies told to children for centuries. If we can do just one thing, a simple thing—not lie to children and confess to them our ignorance—then we will be religious and we will put them on the path of religion. Children are only innocent; leave them not your so called knowledge. But you yourself must first be innocent, unlying, true.

Rajneesh thought for himself. He rejected all religions as false. He rejected conventional notions of man–woman relations, love and marriage as based on false promises and preached the gospel of free love. His disciples shed their inhibitions as they shed their clothes. He came to be maligned as a preacher of promiscuity and as a sex guru. Although I had vast admiration for Rajneesh, I did not accept all his ideas as he often said contradictory things. He believed in rebirth after death, for which there is no scientifically provable basis, and practised meditation which I regard as a waste of time.

Once I visited Osho's commune in Pune. I was charmed by the happy atmosphere that prevailed: greenery, flowers, music, meditation combined with a large library, reading rooms and people going about their daily chores with smiling faces. I did not see Rajneesh; he was unwell. I wondered how long his commune would last after he was gone. It had become big business with 750 meditation centres across eighty countries including 200 in India, along with 1,500 books published in forty languages with 3.5 million copies sold every year; also, tapes of music and sermons.

I got to know some Osho disciples, notably his most attractive lady secretary, Ma Neelam, and Chaitanya Keerti, who looked after his press relations. Neelam was then living in the commune, before she rented a flat nearby. She spent most mornings in the meditation hall. Chaitanya Keerti looked after the publications in Delhi. Both of them have now been banned from entering the Pune commune.

The Osho empire is split down the middle. The cause is greed. A group based in New York and Zurich has laid claims to the copyright of all of Osho's works as well as his techniques of meditation. I could understand Americans trying to grab patent rights over Basmati rice and neem products—where they mercifully failed—but how can anyone patent thought and meditation? It sounds preposterous. The attempt is also contrary to what Osho stood for. In his book, *Om Shantih Shantih Shantih,* he wrote:

> I have told Neelam, my secretary, to write to them. Things can be copyrighted, thoughts cannot be copyrighted, and certainly meditations cannot be copyrighted. They are not things of the marketplace. Nobody can monopolize anything. But perhaps the West cannot understand the difference between an objective commodity and an inner experience. Maharishi Mahesh Yogi has copyrighted transcendental meditation and just underneath in a small circle you will find written TM—that transcendental meditation is neither transcendental nor meditation—just a trademark. I have told Neelam to reply to these people: 'You don't understand what meditation is. It is nobody's belonging, possession. You cannot have a copyright. Perhaps if your country gives you trademarks and copyrights on things like meditation, then it will be good to have a copyright on stupidity. That will help the whole world to be relieved . . . only you will be stupid and nobody else can be stupid; it would be illegal.'

How can you catch the sea breeze in a net? The slogan of true Osho disciples is 'Osho, everybody's birthright; nobody's copyright'.

KABIR

Without doubt the most popular saint-poet of northern India was, and is, Bhakta Kabir. Almost everyone, be he Hindu, Muslim, Sikh or Christian, educated or unlettered, rich or poor, will know a doha or two by Kabir by heart. And yet we have no definitive biography of the man. The popular cherished belief is that he was born in Benaras, of Brahmin parents, but was adopted and raised by a Muslim weaver's family. I find that hard to accept. My own reading is that he was the son of a Muslim weaver who was influenced by the teachings of Hindu bhaktas and rose above considerations of caste and religion. In his writings, he always referred to himself as a julaha (weaver).

There are two distinct compilations of Kabir's poems, his granthavali which is an anthology of his dohas known by rote by millions of Indians, and his slokas, incorporated by Guru Arjan in the Adi Granth, that are known to those familiar with the Sikh scriptures. Though the message that comes through is the same, the two read quite differently. While the former have been rendered into English many times, the latter have only been rendered by scholars like Macauliffe, Manmohan Singh, Gopal Singh and Talib as parts of their translations of the Adi Granth. For the first time, the Kabir of the Sikh scriptures has been published in translation in a separate book, *So Spake Kabira*, by Kartar Singh Duggal. He has taken the trouble to render Kabir in poetic form and his translation makes pleasanter reading than the translations of his predecessors. If he had presented

264

the opening lines of the slokas in Roman script, it would have made identification easier.

Duggal is among the top three or four writers in Punjabi; his output of novels, short stories and poems would fill a couple of shelves of a library. Rather late in life he realized that Punjabi could take him only that far but no further. So he switched to English. He is equally prolific in both languages. I can't think of another person who could have done more justice to Kabir than Duggal. He is a devout Sikh; his wife is Muslim.

Kabir (1398–1448) was by no means the founder of the Bhakti movement as stated by Duggal. The movement had started more than a couple of centuries earlier in Tamil Nadu and spread northwards. A popular couplet describes its advent and increase:

Bhakti Dravid oopjee, Uttar Ramanand
Pargat kiyo Kabir nay sapt dweep nav khand.
(Bhakti was born in Dravidian country; brought north by Ramanand;
Kabir spread it over the seven seas and nine continents.)

Kabir's message in the simplest words is the total rejection of religious bigotry of any kind. He mocked the pretensions of mullahs and pandits with equal relish, pointed out the futility of erecting mosques and temples for a God who is all-pervasive, and scorned the arrogance of the rich and the powerful who like the poor and the destitute must go into oblivion. He asked, 'What is the point of putting bricks and stones together or raise a minaret for the mullah to shout the call for prayer? Has god become hard of hearing? And why bother about the mighty and the rich? They are no better than the date palm which casts a very small shade for the weary traveller and its fruit is far beyond reach.' Kabir accepted the Semitic version of the origin of life and the casteless fraternity of humans:

Avval Allah noor upa ya
Qudrat ke sab bandey
Ek noor te sab jag upjea
Kaun bhaley kaun mandey.
(At first God created light,
We are creatures of nature;
From one light came the entire world
Who then is high and who is low?)

He summed up what the aim of life should be in four memorable lines:

Jab ham aaye jagat mein,
Jag hassa ham roey;
Aisee karnee kar chalen
Jab ham jaayen jagat say
Ham hassein jag roey.
(When I was born everyone rejoiced but I did cry
Fill your life with such deeds that
When you die
You have a smile on your lips while others cry.)

HIMACHAL'S WILLIAM TELL

He came, he saw, and after conquering, was himself conquered; that could be the veni, vidi, vici version of the life of Samuel Evans (renamed Satyanand) Stokes. A more colourful character would be hard to find in the annals of recent times. He was an American Quaker who came to India in 1904 to work among lepers, spread the message of the Gospel and convert us heathens to Christianity. He ended up marrying a pahaaran (hill woman), by whom he fathered a brood of American–Indian children and, having converted scores of Hindus to Christianity, himself embraced Hinduism.

There was a lot more to this renegade Christian missionary. He became a follower of Gandhi, wore handspun khadi and was the first and only American to be gaoled in the Indian freedom movement. However, his real claim to fame is the prosperity that he brought to the people of Himachal Pradesh. He introduced American apples to India. He bought land in Kotgarh where he planted the state's first orchard. He gave apple saplings free of charge to farmers used to raising only rice, maize or vegetables, which gave them immediate returns, to plant on the boundaries of their fields; he taught them how to look after the saplings, wait patiently for five or six years and thereafter reap golden harvests in autumn.

I never met Stokes but during my vacations spent in Mashobra I used to see long caravans of mules laden with crates marked HH going along the Hindustan–Tibet Road to Simla railway station or the bus stand to transfer their cargo to far-flung destinations across the subcontinent. During moonlit nights in October, I heard the tinkling of the mules' bells and the plaintive notes of the muleteers' flutes till the early hours of the morning.

I did not know what HH stood for. Somebody told me they stood for Harmony Hall. It was the name of Stokes's family mansion in Philadelphia. He built a large house in Kotgarh and named it after his ancestral home. He stocked it with books and antique furniture. His two sons, Prem Chand and Pritam Chand, were in St Stephen's College during my time. Both looked like goras, but wore Gandhi caps and khadi kurta pyjamas.

Stokes must have been a very eccentric person. He came from an affluent family and could have lived in comfort all his life. Instead he chose to come to India to work among the disease-stricken and the poorest of the poor. For a while he lived the life of a sadhu in a cave. Then he agreed to an arranged marriage with a Christian pahaari girl much younger than him. His lifestyle changed. For his honeymoon he took his bride to Bombay; they stayed in the bridal suite of the Taj Mahal Hotel. They travelled first class to America to stay with his family. Back in Kotgarh he built a large house where they raised their children.

He came under the influence of Mahatma Gandhi, and changed from Western clothes to khadi. And then decided he could serve God better if he identified himself with the people among whom he lived and converted to the Arya Samaj faith. He must have known he would cause embarrassment to the Christian missions in India but his granddaughter and biographer, Asha Sharma, insists that too much should not be made of his conversion because he believed Christianity and Arya Samaj had much in common. If so, why convert?

Stokes was amongst the handful of Whites, like Annie Besant, Nellie Sen Gupta, Reverend C.F. Andrews, Mira Behn Slade, B.G. Horniman and others who were tried in the Meerut conspiracy case, who joined India's struggle for freedom. He was the only one among the distinguished lot who brought prosperity to the poverty-stricken region of Himachal.

JACK WILBERFORCE BURKE PEEL

His name will mean nothing to my readers. It means a great deal to me. He was my closest English friend for more than seventy years. He died on 3 April 2004 at the age of ninety-five. I read of it in the *Independent* (London). It was a two-column obituary with his photograph. Despite my closeness to him, I did not realize his greatness because like most Englishmen of breeding he never spoke about himself. It was from the obituary that I learnt that Jack Peel had in his time met Stalin, Tito, Eisenhower, Churchill, Attlee and many other world figures and helped them to communicate with each other. He was not a politician, a minister of the government or a diplomat. He was a humble clerk with a gift for languages. He was fluent in half a dozen European languages and spoke them with the fluency with which he spoke his native English. Although he never went to a university, he was widely read and was an accomplished pianist.

I met him when I was a student and had taken lodging with Professor F.S. Marvin in Welwyn Garden city, some 40 miles north of London. Our first encounter was on the tennis courts during the inter-club tournaments. He was better at the game than I. Gradually, a friendship developed and I was invited over for tea to meet his father who ran a small private school, his sister, Nancy, and his wife, a very pretty Estonian girl named Dagmar Hansen. I recall him telling me once, 'I don't have much reason to be the friend of a Sikh. The last time I made friends with one he walked off with my girlfriend. His name was Gurdial Singh. He was in the Indian air force doing some kind of course at Hatfield. Do you know him?' I had not heard of Gurdial Singh. I replied, 'You better beware of all Sikhs; you have a very pretty wife.'

On days I had no college, I often went to a particular café to have a cup of coffee because Dagmar worked there as a waitress. Jack had a clerical job in the London branch of the National Bank of India and their home needed two incomes. Dagmar spoke very little English. I suspected that apart from her looks Jack had married her for her knowledge of the languages she spoke: Estonian, Russian and German. He was a quick learner. By the time World War II broke out, he had full command of these languages. In 1943, the Royal Air Force took him on its staff to monitor what passed between the pilots of the German Luftwaffe carrying out air raids over Britain. The authorities soon found that Jack was as fluent in Russian as he was in German. So he was made a liaison officer in a department dealing with Soviet pilots' training to handle British air fighters. He became an interpreter for the Soviet minister, Vyacheslav Molotov, and the Soviet ambassador, Ivan Maisky. He was seconded to the British Foreign Service and posted as Second Secretary at the British embassy in Moscow. There he met Josef Stalin. Unlike the popular image of Stalin as a cold-blooded dictator of little learning, Jack found him to be a warm, fatherly figure with a sharp memory. His English colleagues who looked down on him as an upstart tried to cut him down to size by asking him to play a piano piece by Prokofiev at an embassy reception. Jack did it with panache, unaware that the composer was standing behind him.

Jack resigned from his Moscow job in 1947 to return to Welwyn Garden city to be close to his wife who was seriously ill with tuberculosis. She died in 1947 leaving behind a son.

I lost track of Jack Peel during the war years. But no sooner had it ended and I found myself a job in India House, London, than I resumed contact with him. By then I had a wife and two children. Jack was a widower. He held a senior position in the Imperial Chemical Industries and because of his mastery over various languages, was put in charge of their operations in Eastern Europe. Largely because of him, I shifted my family from London to Welwyn Garden city. We met almost every day.

I quit the service in 1951 and returned to India. We wrote to each other. The same year Jack married an Austrian girl, Erika Fischa, through whom he had another two sons. One winter they came to Delhi and stayed with us. He had then developed an arthritic knee and walked with a limp. Whenever I needed medicines not available in India—as I did when my father and later my mother were taken ill—I could rely on Jack to send them without doctors' prescriptions which were mandatory. He kept track of my ventures into the writing world by reading my books and writing to me about them. Besides languages and classical music, he had an abiding interest in literature from his school days in Scarborough (Yorkshire).

During the last few years, instead of Jack, it was his wife, Erika, who responded to my letters. When my wife died two years ago, Erika wrote to me; Jack added a paragraph at the end of the letter. I was barely able to decipher it. Erika's last letter to me was about Jack's rapidly declining health. He was confined to his bed but he added three words to his wife's letter. It took me some time to decipher them: 'How are you?'

MIR TAQI MIR

Did you know that at one time Urdu novelists and chroniclers used to have appendices to their works in which they included their favourite jokes which had nothing whatsoever to do with the themes of their books? I discovered this after reading Mir Taqi Mir's autobiography, *Zikr-i-Mir*, translated from Persian into English by C.M. Nairn, professor of Urdu at Chicago University.

Mir Taqi Mir (1723–1810) lived through turbulent times as the Mogul empire began to disintegrate after the death of Emperor Aurangzeb (1707). The Persian invader, Nadir Shah, dealt it a near-death blow in 1738. He was followed by the Afghan, Ahmed Shah Abdali, who invaded India nine times and laid waste the whole of northern India. The Marathas, Jats, Rohillas, Pathans and Sikhs did their share of pillaging and looting. Mir gives vivid descriptions of the havoc caused by these unruly elements. He was particularly harsh in his judgment of the Sikhs. He wrote:

The arrogance of these people (the Afghans) had crossed all limits; and so God, in his Justice, decided to humiliate them at the hands of the Sikhs—men of no consequence, highway robbers, peasants, lowly men of no means, name or place; mean, destitute and disreputable people of that area. Some forty or fifty thousand of them came together and challenged that mighty army. Sometimes they boldly attacked and fought, and did not run away despite getting severely mauled. Other times, they attacked them, withdrew in different directions, pursued by small bodies of (Afghan) soldiers, whom they later slaughtered. Every morning they created some new mischief, and each evening they attacked from every side. They sent the soldiers of the Shah scurrying every which way, desperately trying to make an escape. Sometimes they suddenly appeared and pounced upon the baggage train and the people who followed the army. Other times they came in large numbers, and resolutely attacking some town, turned it into ruins. With tangled hair or a piece of cloth wrapped around their heads, they penetrated the camp itself. There was noise and tumult all night long, and all day long there was a hue and cry. Their foot soldiers attacked the Shah's horsemen with swords and filled their saddles with blood; and their retainers pounced upon the Shah's archers and tortured them to death. In short these unworthy wretches (be-namusan-i be-daulat) humiliated those vain-glorious brutes (be-hagigatan-i be-muravaat) to such an extent that the chief of the region, on hearing of what had been happening also stopped showing the Afghans any respect.

Mir Taqi Mir had a keen eye for detail. Having led a life of near starvation for most of his years, he was most impressed by a feast laid out by the nawab of Awadh for the British Governor General. He writes:

As for the types of breads at meal times: nan-i-badam (almond bread) of utmost delicacy; shirmal and bagar-khani, both coloured with saffron on the top that would put the sun to shame; nan-i-javan (youthful bread), so soft and warm that if an old man were to eat it he would act like a youth, nan-i-varaqi (paper bread) of such a quality that I could fill a whole book with its praise, nan-i-zanjabi (ginger bread), so flavourful that taste itself grows happy thinking of it. In the middle were placed varieties of qaliya and do-piyaza such rich stews of different kinds that the guests were all delighted and satisfied. And the kababs that were laid out on the long table-cloth; kabab-i-gul (flower kabab), full of bloom and flavour, perfectly salted kabab-i-hindi (Indian kabab) stole every heart; kabab-i-gandhari attracted all and sundry to itself; kabab-i-sang (stone kabab) brought relief to those who were tired from the hardships of the journey; kabab-i-varaq (paper kakab) was of such an amazing recipe that it delighted everyone; and all the more common kababs, spicy and flavourful. Ten large plates of food were placed before every single guest. Then there were pulaos of all kinds and wonderful soups of every type. 'Praise be to One, who is Bountiful and Generous!'

I was not impressed by Mir's sense of humour. Many of the anecdotes quoted by Professor Nairn are outrageously ribald and would not be acceptable to editors of today. A borderline joke goes as follows: 'Two men were close friends; they were also engaged, each to the other's sister. By chance the astrologers also set the same date and time for the two weddings. Mulla Muhammad Baqir Majlisi was invited to perform the weddings but, due to another obligation, he excused himself. Instead he sent his nephew, Mulla Muhammad Ashraf, who had a jocular bent of mind. Ashraf came and performed the weddings. Then he turned to the two grooms, and said, "Why are you still sitting here? Go and start poking into each other's sisters."' A repartee I found acceptable runs as follows: 'Once, in the Pavilion of Pleasure, the Shah asked Mirza Sahib to have some wine. When the Mirza declined, the Shah asked for a reason. "It takes away one's intelligence," the Mirza replied. The Shah didn't accept that and pressed him even more. Finally the Mirza gave in, and became so drunk that, by midnight, he had to be removed from the gathering. The next morning, when he again came to the court, the Shah said to him, "You made quite a mess of yourself last night. No one should be so shallow when it comes to holding his liquor." The Mirza said, "I humbly told you that wine takes away one's intelligence." The Shah retorted, "But then didn't I drink too?"

"May I die for you, sir," the Mirza replied, "but the reasoning concerned losing one's intelligence—you had none to begin with."'

AVEEK SARKAR

My association with the *Telegraph* is as old as the *Telegraph* itself. I started writing for it the day it was born and continue to do so till this day. It began with the Malice column that I wrote for *Hindustan Times*. The proprietor of that paper, K.K. Birla, was generous enough to allow me to offer the column to the *Telegraph*. Later, when *Hindustan Times* started publishing in Calcutta, he quite rightly withdrew his permission. That did not break my association with the paper as it took over my other column, '. . . This Above All'. So I remain a part of the *Telegraph* parivar.

As a matter of fact, my relationship with the Sarkar family goes back more than forty years to when I was the editor of the *Illustrated Weekly of India* in Bombay. M.J. Akbar was amongst the earliest trainees on my staff. So was Mallika who later married Akbar. I was nominated godfather for their first born.

Aveek Sarkar, now the editor-in-chief of the Anandabazar group, used to drop in to see me whenever he was in Bombay. When I was fired from the editorship of the *Illustrated Weekly* and rendered jobless, he and Akbar offered me the editorship of the fortnightly, *New Delhi*. I was given a swanky office in the PTI building on Parliament Street, a staff of my own choosing and a brand new car. I was on cloud nine.

The euphoria did not last very long. There were strikes in the Anandabazar Patrika's press and the printing schedule went haywire. *New Delhi* often became a monthly. I threw in my towel. The Sarkars understood and folded up the journal. Our friendship remained unimpaired. On the contrary, Arup Sarkar loaded me with expensive gifts: a terracotta Ganpati of massive size and a large lithograph of Lord Harding receiving captured Sikh artillery in Calcutta following their victory in the first Anglo–Sikh War of 1845. It's a rare piece. The Anandabazar family, of which the *Telegraph* is a member, has done more for art and literature than any other publishing house. Many Bengali writers including Sunil Gangopadhyay and the Bangladeshi Taslima Nasreen have been published and honoured by it. Rakhi Sarkar, Aveek's wife, has personally taken the works of artists from Calcutta to other Indian cities. I don't know of a government academy of arts and literature that has done so much.

Arup's gifts were followed by an invitation to my wife and me to attend the twenty-fifth wedding anniversary of Aveek and Rakhi at the Grand Hotel. The programme was kept as a surprise for the couple till they arrived at the banquet hall. It was a memorable feast. They also made me an adviser of Penguin/Viking (India) in which they acquired substantial shares. My home is flooded with books, thanks to the Sarkars.

The *Telegraph*, ever since its inception, arrives in Delhi in the evening. When it was first published and was delivered to me after sunset, I used to merely glance at it as in the morning I had to plough through half a dozen papers. But very soon I realized, despite my cursory glance at the *Telegraph*, that it was a more professional product than any of the Delhi morning dailies. It was professional in production, in printing, in layout and in its selection and placement of news. I began to read it more carefully and began enjoying it. Now it has become my staple evening read. I look forward to it with my sundowner.

There are certain features of the *Telegraph* that I would like to pick out for special mention. One is that the paper does not believe in gimmicks. There are no special columns devoted to religion and spirituality; I find such columns immensely irritating. It also doesn't reproduce risqué jokes from *Playboy* or the Internet. In a newspaper such jokes are in bad taste. It is only from the

Telegraph that I get detailed news of eastern Indian and the North-East. No other newspaper provides me with this.

The *Telegraph*, since its inception, has had a nose for controversy. I appreciate this even though I was once a victim of it. When I made some critical comments about Gurudev Tagore, the *Telegraph* was the only paper to splash it on the front page. As a result of this I became the subject of a censure motion in the West Bengal legislative assembly and in the Rajya Sabha.

I am absolutely addicted to the *Telegraph* crossword. I find it to be about the best in the country. Neither too difficult like the one in the *Statesman* nor too silly like the ones in other papers. The *Telegraph* crossword is the perfect companion to my evening Scotch whisky.

In my long life of nienty-three years I have worked in many government departments and edited several journals, official and privately owned. I can say without hesitation that I have never served in another business house where I received as much respect, affection and high wages as I have from the Anandabazar group, now officially named ABP Private Ltd.

Aveek has a few eccentricities that I find charming. He used to like to smoke Cuban cigars. He lighted one after every meal. 'How many do you have everyday?' I once asked him. A little hesitantly he replied, 'Only four.' I worked out the cost of Romeo y Julieta: Rs 150 each. 'So you blow up six hundred rupees everyday in smoke!' He smiled sheepishly.

· He still likes to entertain friends in restaurants, never at his home. Like a pukka Brit his home is his castle, impregnable. I breached its bulwark by provoking him. 'You Bengalis don't have a cuisine. Besides maachher jhol, rasgollas and mishti, you have nothing to offer. In Calcutta you can find gourmet French, Italian, Chinese, Mughlai and Marwari restaurants. Not one where you can have Bengali food.' At the time there were no Bengali restaurants in the metropolis or anywhere else in India. He gave me a very tame answer: 'We Bengalis are not restaurant-goers. We prefer to eat at home. And eat very well.'

'I have never been invited to a Bengali home,' I replied. 'In Bangladesh yes—and enjoyed the best hilsa I've ever tasted. Never in Calcutta.' That got me an invitation to the Sarkars' citadel. Rakhi went out of her way to prove there was more to Bengali cuisine than I thought.

Another of Aveek's eccentricities is to number everyone in order of merit. If I mention the name of a singer, dancer or artist, he will place them in the order of merit. 'So and so is number one, so and so number two, so and so number three.' There is no point contradicting him because he exudes so much self-confidence.

And lastly, his habit of never answering letters. David Davidar, then the head of Penguin Books India, who had to write to him officially, once said to me in a tone of exasperation, 'He has a shredder installed in his office. It can separate envelopes that contain cheques from those that do not. The chequeless envelopes and their contents go straight into the shredder without Aveek having to open them.'

On Death and Dying

'Have you ever thought about death?'

This was the second time he was asking me this. S. Prasher, retired commissioner of income tax, the moving spirit behind the Save Kasauli Society, has this disturbing habit of tossing questions at me to which I have no answers.

'Indeed I have,' I replied. 'I think about it all the time. I've read as much about it as I could. I found no answers.'

I quoted my favourite lines on the subject:

> There was a door to which I found no key
> There was a veil beyond I could not see;
> Talk awhile of thee and me there was
> Then no more of thee or me.

'Omar Khayyam!' he said triumphantly. 'But surely there is more to it than just admitting that you do not know?'

'The body goes, perhaps with it the mind as well. Your memory remains in some people's minds while they are alive. After them even that is gone. You may leave charitable trusts in your name, you may write books that may be read after you are gone.'

'That is not what I mean,' Prasher said. 'What about consciousness?'

'Consciousness of what?' I asked. 'Where does it survive? It has to be something more tangible than the notion of consciousness.'

He proceeded to explain at great length. Most of it was beyond my comprehension. I tried to bring him down to earth. 'Most thinkers play with words, some talk of death as an integral part of life. I agree. Some compare life as a journey on a train; some get off at one station, others continue a little further. Bhola Nathji in his *The Secret of Death* writes, "One can deny the existence of God, but one cannot deny the existence of death . . . Life is that which must go, and death, that which must come." I entirely agree, but does that tell us where we go when we die? Does anything of us remain when we are gone?'

Most people who have written on the subject have dwelt more on the inherent fear of dying rather than death. They give false assurances that death is nothing to be scared of. For example, John Donne (1572–1631) describes it as 'merely a form of rest and sleep':

Death, be not proud, though some have called the
Mighty and dreadfull, for thou art not so;
For those whom thou think'st, thou dost overthrow
Die not, poore Death, not yet canst thou kill me.

For Donne, death was:

One short sleepe past, wee wake eternally,
And death shall be no more; death, thou shalt die.

John Keats (1795–1821), who died at the young age of twenty-five, had no such illusions of something surviving after he 'ceased to be'. He knew that he had a lot more to give but felt he was a 'fair creature of an hour' after which love and fame would sink to nothingness.

The key word, I told Prasher, is 'nothingness'. Death erases our bodies, our minds and everything our bodies or minds may have achieved in our lives. Prasher was not satisfied with my answer. But he had no answers to offer besides conjecturing that consciousness remained. He exhorted me to think more deeply on the subject. I promised to do so, fully aware it would get me nowhere.

Neither I nor anyone else has the slightest clue of what remains of us after we die. Many claim to have an answer, going round and round the same theme: the body perishes but the soul (atman) survives. I don't buy that. What does the soul look like? If it survives, where does it reside? One letter I received on the subject ran into six pages from one Munish Markan of Sangrur who claims to have all the answers. He starts by saying he never reads the rubbish I write and calls me an ignoramus for asking silly questions. Then he elaborates on the theme of death. I quote him at some length because he is typical of the verbosity used by subjantawallas. He fails to provide any answer but bombards me with a lot of gratuitous advice. He writes: 'I should tell you that your very thinking is stopping you from encountering death while alive in this body. As far as I can judge, your interests seem to be only intellectual. Had it been possible for the humans to know, experience and transcend death by reading and contemplation, majority of the humanity would have gone beyond death and had known the secret of death.'

I pondered over the statement for a while. Without any intellectual pretences, I could not see what other faculties besides reasoning I could use to find answers to my questions. He proceeds to caution me: 'We all are riding high up on the ladder only in the end to find that our ladder was inclined on the wrong wall. Probably, in temporal matters, you have enjoyed considerable prosperity and now at the fag end of life, you seem bothered about the "journey beyond" if there is any. One thing you must admit that nothing is known beyond death and before birth. No knowledge of these areas, nowhere is it taught in schools, colleges and universities.'

If nothing is known about life and death, how can they be taught in schools and colleges?

He advises me to switch off 'this instrument called mind'. At times nature does the switching off when we fall into a deep, dreamless sleep (sushupti). He asks: 'Where do we go when we are in dreamless sleep? Try to find the answer to this question existentially, not intellectually.'

Honestly, my answer would be: 'I go nowhere. I just wake up to realize I had a sound sleep.' I don't know how one answers simple questions existentially.

He proceeds to say: 'If I may analyse, your whole knowledge is your enemy. The answer to the question, "who am I?" will provide all answers about life and death as Ramana Maharishi always used to say.'

I don't care what Ramana Maharishi had to say; to me death is the end of life. He gives an analogy of how electrons cannot be seen unless a ray of light is beamed at them. That may be so. Also, that time seems to take much longer to pass for one in distress than it takes for one in a joyous mood. True, but what does it prove?

He advocates meditation and suggests different techniques for emptying the mind. I find meditation a sterile concept productive of nothing except peace of mind—which in turn produces nothing but peace of mind. I would prefer to have a mind constantly engaged in finding answers to questions. He recommends *The Autobiography of a Yogi* by Paramhansa Yoganandaji. I went halfway through it, found it boring and gave up. I do not accept kriya yoga as a science and find the talk of a 'subtle body' a meaningless play with words.

'Logic has its limitations,' he asserts. I agree. But I do not understand what is meant by experiencing something at 'the existential level'. Again, another pointless analogy.

Reading books on swimming does not enable one to swim. Or learn to balance oneself on a bicycle without riding on one. He continues: 'Similarly, anything and everything you read and listen to about death is not of much consequence. At best it can point the direction in which you have to move. But contemplation on death has never helped anyone to know death. Direct jumping is required.'

Must I kill myself to solve the mystery of death? No, thank you. 'Why is man fearful of death? One reason is that we are accustomed to live in future, in tomorrow, and when death comes, it says no tomorrow, only today. Now that is what we fear. Life is a sum total of todays . . . That is why it is said that we should enjoy the small things in life.'

He recommends Japanese tea meditation. I sat through one: a kimono-clad lady went on endlessly cleaning a tiny cup with a brush while a tea-kettle was on the boil. The end result was a thimble-full of bitter, undrinkable tea.

He ends his long letter with another clever play on words. 'You know how habits are formed: doing an act repetitively over a period of time unconsciously. It becomes one's nature. Another sutra for experiencing bodilessness is to become aware; in this context live and read Osho. Stop reviewing and reading novels of others. Enough of it you have done throughout your life. You did a lot for the literary world. Now, live for yourself. I know it takes great courage to break off from the habits of past, because of habit I have heard:

If 'H' goes, a bit remains
If 'A' goes bit remains
Even if 'B' goes it remains.'

What does it prove? To me, nothing. Don't bamboozle me with words. If you don't know the answer, be brave enough to admit it.

But I think too much is made of facing death bravely. My friend Preetam Giani of Abbotabad (Pakistan) wrote me a letter soon after an earthquake which he survived without a scratch. 'There seems to be a qualitative difference between living bravely and dying bravely,' he wrote. 'While the latter is admirable enough and certainly not easy, the former appears to me not only much more but also more difficult.'

Allama Iqbal lauded it in a Persian couplet:

Nishaan-e-mard-e-momin ba too goyam?
Choon marg aayad, Tabassum bar lab-e-ost.

(You ask about a man of faith?
When death comes to him, he has a smile on his lips.)

Unfortunately, death often overtakes one without giving one a chance of displaying one's courage. For example, in an earthquake or a tsunami; in a plane, train or car crash, one may be struck by lightning, crushed under a tree. Or go into a coma as my mother, a cheerful soul did, many days before she went into the deep slumber from which there is no awakening. Even more difficult is it to keep a brave face when you are in acute pain. Not even the bravest of the brave can smile if he has a throbbing toothache or earache.

Perhaps the show of bravery is most evident on the battlefield. But it's valour in a spirit of revenge or fanaticism that these fighting men show. Muslim Ghazis (present-day jehadis) who form suicide squads rarely think of the consequences of their acts. Maharaja Ranjit Singh's nihang troops were equally religiously motivated and fortified with bhang (hashish).

On the other hand, being brave in life is altogether different. It can be a life-long battle. Your parents, teachers and childhood friends mould your way of thinking. They fill you with racial, religious and patriotic prejudices before you begin to think for yourself. You are told to strive for success, make lots of money, win popular acclaim. Most of this requires scoring over others by means foul or fair, compromising your principles, double-crossing friends and indulging in all kinds of skulduggery. You have to decide whether you want to be regarded as a success in life or as a man with a clear conscience. It is tough to opt for the latter.

As far as I am concerned, I would like to go the way my ninety-year-old father went. He was enjoying his evening drink. He felt a little uneasy and lay down on his bed to let the uneasiness pass. It was one for the long road to the unknown. He rose no more.

The main concern of all the world's religions is how to overcome the fear of dying. We coin words to lessen its impact: gone to his heavenly abode, passed away, marched on, became beloved of God, ended life's journey, etc. We have different customs to distance ourselves from the dead: some bury them, some cremate them. We have periods of mourning and we have prayers on their death anniversaries. The most important thing to keep in mind while performing rituals for the dead is that you too must die—memento mori.

'We are not afraid of death but of dying' was the opening sentence of an article in Gurmukhi I received one day. After asserting that we are more afraid of dying than of death, the anonymous author goes on to say that there is only one way we are born but hundreds of millions of ways in which we can die. The dead far outnumber the living. We try all kinds of medicines to cure us of illnesses, whereas death is the final cure of all that ails our bodies. Death is the ultimate in democracy as it comes to everyone, the rich as well as the poor. No one can argue with it or persuade it to change its mind . . . it is nature's reminder to mankind that their time is over. Life is short. What is more important is how you live the life given to you and not how long you live.

People of different ages have different perceptions of death. Children do not understand it beyond thinking the dead person has gone to some other place. In youth they think it is still a long way away. It is only when people are in their forties that they seriously contemplate death and wonder if they will have enough time to complete the tasks they have undertaken. In their seventies, the possibility of impending death becomes a reality. As long as one has grandparents and parents, one does not think one also is mortal. It is after they are gone that a person realizes that his turn to go will be next.

Death is the basic element we all fear. We play hide and seek with it. It is better to confront it boldly. Don't count the years you have lived, but what you put in in the years you lived.

We have to be constantly reminded that it is not only other people who die. However much we try to put death out of our minds, other people's deaths will remind us of its inevitability.

Of all the gods of the pantheon, the one we cannot appease by prayer, bribery or flattery is Yama. Aeschylus wrote:

> Alone of gods death has no love for gifts
> Libations help you not sacrifice
> He has no altar, and he hears no hymns
> From him alone persuasion stands apart.

Unless you commit suicide or are hanged, you will not know when death will come to you. The prayer in the Psalms, 'Lord let me know mine end, and the number of my days that I be certified how long I have to live', remains unheard. The older we grow, the more we realize that our end is near. To wit Kingsley Amis:

> Death has got something to be said for it
> There's no need to get out of bed for it,
> Wherever you may be
> They bring it to you, free.

One way to overcome the fear of death is to make fun of it. On his seventy-fifth birthday, Winston Churchill was asked what he thought about it. 'I am ready to meet my maker. Whether my maker is prepared for the ordeal of meeting me is another matter,' he replied. Lord Palmerston on his deathbed told his physician, 'Die, my dear doctor? That is the last thing I shall do.'

One day in Calcutta, I was waiting for a taxi when a man who was about ninety years old looked at my suitcase and asked, 'Where are you going?'

'On a short trip,' I replied.

The old man said, 'I'll be going on a long trip soon.'

Touched, I said, 'Well, we all have to take that long trip one day. If I'm fortunate and live to be your age, I'll be very happy about it.'

His look changed from that of attentive listening to one of impatience. 'Young man,' he retorted, 'I'm going to my grandson in London!'

A Love Story: Dharma Kumar

She died in the early hours of Friday, 19 October 2001. She was in the intensive care unit of Apollo Hospital for over a month; so her end did not come as a surprise. What sustained a little hope in my mind was that women like Dharma did not die; they faded out of one's memory like a lost dream. She was seventy-three. Dharma was more animated than any woman I have ever met. I write about her because all of us have someone or the other in our lives who means more to us than we care to admit till after they are gone.

It must be over fifty years ago when I first met her and her husband, Lavraj Kumar, at a large luncheon party in a garden. He was an executive for Burmah-Shell; she was working on her doctoral thesis at Cambridge University. She was the centre of attraction, sparkling with wit and humour and mimicking celebrities. She had everyone in splits of laughter. I was completely bowled over. For the next few days I spoke about her to everyone I knew and tried to get as much information about her and her husband as I could.

Lavraj Kumar was from Uttar Pradesh, the only child of a well-known and rich family. He was also a very bright student. He won the Rhodes Scholarship to Oxford. Dharma was a Tamilian Brahmin and the only child of a well-known scientist, Dr Venkatraman, the head of the National Chemical Laboratory in Pune. They met in England and got married. Lavraj answered all that Dharma wanted from a man. She had an exaggerated respect for academics; almost all her cousins had gained firsts in

Oxford or Cambridge; Lavraj had bettered them. She married him because he was brighter than any other of her many suitors. What she did not like was Lavraj joining Burmah-Shell and becoming a boxwallah and having to take orders from the white sahibs. Lavraj was a softspoken and self-effacing man.

Dharma was outgoing, garrulous and revelled in admiration. She was not the kind of woman I usually fell for. Her features were passable; she used no make-up or perfume. It was her animation that I found irresistible. Her eyes sparkled as she spoke: come to think of it, the only reason she responded to my overtures was because she was overwhelmed by my adoration. It was an entirely one-sided affair. I dedicated my second novel, *I Shall Not Hear the Nightingale*, to her. I don't think she bothered to read it.

Her favourite put-downers were about a cousin, Raghavan Aiyar. Like others in the family he was a topper: first in MA (philosophy) from Madras; first class first in Cambridge and elected president of the Cambridge Union. While at the university he acquired a group of admirers who assembled in his room periodically to hear him speak. He told them that the source of all human frailties was the ego. Unless one conquered one's ego there could be no peace of mind. One day a lady admirer asked, 'I agree with all you say about the ego, but how does one conquer the ego?'

'Good question!' replied Raghavan Aiyar. 'You will appreciate it poses a bigger problem for me than it does for you. For myself I have evolved a formula for self-extinction. Everyday I sit in padma asana (lotus pose), shut my eyes and repeat: "I am not Raghavan Aiyar who got a first class from Madras University; I am not Raghavan Aiyar who got a first class first from Cambridge University; I am not Raghavan Aiyar the most brilliant philosopher of the East. I am merely a vehicle of the mahatmas, a spark of the Divine."'

According to Dharma, when Raghavan Aiyar stood for presidentship of the union, he did not bother to canvass for himself but left it to his admirers. After the counting of the votes they rushed to his room to break the good news. They found him seated in padma asana on his carpet with his eyes shut: 'You've won! You've won!' they shouted triumphantly. Raghavan Aiyar raised one hand with his finger pointing to the roof and exclaimed: 'Victory's thine, O Lord!'

Dharma got her doctorate in economics. She became a professor at the Delhi School of Economics and wrote a couple of books which were very well received by economists. Her husband left Burmah-Shell to become Secretary of the petroleum ministry of the Central government. She was happy that she was no longer the wife of a boxwallah. But even as the wife of a much-respected bureaucrat, she refused to entertain ministers or befriend their wives.

Undeterred by her indifference I continued to long for her company. The break came unexpectedly. Lavraj had invited her closest friends for dinner to celebrate her invitation for a lecture tour abroad. Very light-heartedly I asked, 'Dharma, how did you wangle it?' She went pale with anger and burst out: 'I don't like that kind of insinuation. I am not a wangler.' The outburst of anger took everyone unawares. An uneasy silence descended. The party was ruined.

The one thing I cannot forgive or forget is people losing their temper with me. I swore to have nothing more to do with Dharma. She was the victim of an uncontrollable temper; I, of being unable to forgive. She did her best to make amends, but something within me had snapped which I could not join. After some months our families began to see each other again. But I was never relaxed in her company. I transferred my affection to her husband and even more so to her daughter, Radha.

When her husband died suddenly, I went to the crematorium expecting to meet Dharma and wipe out the uneasiness that had come between us. She was not there. I condoled with Radha and Lavraj's uncle, Dharamvira (ex-Governor, Punjab and Bengal). I told him, 'Dharma has all the gifts anyone would wish for except the gift of friendship.' He agreed.

None of us who cherished Dharma realized that her fits of temper may have been due to things going wrong inside her. She developed a brain tumour and had to be flown to London for surgery. It did not help. Another tumour developed. Then another. The only one left to look after her was her ninety-four-year-old mother-in-law. She told everyone, 'Dharma is not my bahu but my beti.' She was with her to the last.

It is hard for me to accept the fact that Dharma was a mortal. I will not see Dharma any more. She may not have cared for me but I will cherish her memory for the years left to me.

On the Emergency: The Diary
of a Bureaucrat

Bishan Narain Tandon was a Joint Secretary in Prime Minister Indira Gandhi's office for seven years (1969–76). He was witness to the events leading to the Indo–Pak war for the liberation of Bangladesh, the imposition of the Emergency on 25 June 1975, and its aftermath. He spent his days in the PM's office in North Block, Parliament house or, when summoned, at her residence. Back home, he recorded his impressions of the people he had met everyday. They fell in three categories: Indira Gandhi, her son and their coterie of advisers; cabinet ministers and senior politicians; and the author's colleagues in the PMO. He stripped the first two naked but spared his colleagues and himself. I will do that job for him.

The diary begins on 1 November 1974. The victorious Durga of the Indo–Pak war had shrunk into a mortal beset with imaginary fears of everyone plotting her downfall; she trusted no one besides a few untrustworthy, semi-literate minions, became short-tempered, impetuous, arrogant and unsure of herself. Serious charges of corruption had been levelled against Tulmohan Ram and L.N. Mishra. Hovering above her like a thundercloud was Jayaprakash Narayan, with another building up under Morarji Desai. Against advice, Mrs Gandhi was determined to defend Mishra without concern for moral principles: she simply wanted to prove to the country that she was the boss. Also, she was a little unsure of her ability to prove her point. Unlike her agnostic

father, she sought counsel from soothsayers and priests. Tandon
has the word of his colleague, N.K. Seshan, the PM's personal
secretary and principal purveyor of gossip, that L.N. Mishra 'has
sent a Swami staying with him to her residence to perform puja
. . . She keeps having such pujas. Even the time for the swearing-
in ceremony for ministers is decided after consulting astrologers.'
Tandon writes, 'P.N. Haksar once told me that the PM was inclined
towards sruti and not smriti. I was upset that people like Om
Mehta, who had very little understanding of any subject, told the
PM all manner of things merely because of sycophancy.' Similar
opinions were expressed about R.K. Dhawan 'who offers advice to
the PM on things about which he knows nothing. What's worse,
his advice and suggestions are taken seriously'. As rumours of
her one-time stenographer, Yashpal Kapoor, acquiring valuable
real estate in New Delhi's prime residential area and her son's
ham-handed attempts to manufacture a people's car became
public knowledge, Mrs Gandhi's attempts to stifle criticism and
punish her critics became more frenetic. She appointed a man of
her own choice as chairman of the Central Board of Direct Taxes
who took orders directly from her. 'The misuse of CBI, RAW,
etc., has become a topic of common discussion.' H.Y. Sharada
Prasad, her press adviser, was of the opinion that her distrust of
people and turning nasty towards those who had stood by her
was due to her loneliness from childhood: 'She looks at every
question solely from her own personal point of view. She lacks
generosity, lacks self-confidence and is somewhat arrogant. All
this has made her a very difficult person.' Her cousin, B.K. Nehru,
who had been high commissioner to the UK, and the Governor
of Assam and Nagaland, thought she had no understanding of
economic issues and even simple things seemed difficult to her.
She was only interested in slogans like 'garibi hatao'.

Having an innate distrust of her colleagues, she turned for
advice to people without knowing their background. One of
them was Rajni Patel whom she put in charge of the Bombay
Congress Committee. 'Like many other opportunists, he has

joined the Congress after it split in 1969. Unfortunately, he does not have a good reputation,' writes Tandon. He was a wheeler-dealer and made an agreement with the Shiv Sena. Another was Kishan Chand who was made the Lt Governor of Delhi at the recommendation of Sanjay Gandhi and R.K. Dhawan. On the last day of 1974, Tandon summed up his impressions of Mrs Gandhi: 'The main cause of the crisis is the PM's personality and character. I have always held that three qualities are needed to lead the country: character, ability in its broadest sense and tolerance. Unfortunately, the PM is deficient in all three. In fact, she is completely lacking in tolerance. As far as ability is concerned, she is very able when it comes to political manipulation. But she has no ability to think seriously and in an organised manner about serious issues. I have discussed various issues for hours on end with her. But I have always felt that I am talking to a person with very pedestrian intellect whose concerns are not with the substance but with the form. She is only concerned with the impact on herself and on politics. She is not at all interested in the values which her father had done so much to foster. She is outwardly civilised and decent but she totally lacks cordiality . . . She does not have the high moral standards expected of the country's leaders.'

Early in 1975, Mrs Gandhi's troubles began to mount—not in a single file but in battalions. JP's call for a total revolution began to gather strength. Morarji Desai became restive, then openly defiant; her election to Parliament was challenged by Raj Narain, and many people knew that she tried to fiddle with the records to disprove that Yashpal Kapoor was still drawing a salary from the government when he became her election agent; Sanjay's plan to manufacture Marutis in large numbers floundered. She sensed power slowly but surely slipping out of her hands. The usurper was her own son, Sanjay. She told her law minister, H.R. Gokhale, that 'she was unable to sleep at night and that Sanjay's behaviour was uncivilised and rude. The law minister said that he behaves rudely not just with him but with his mother also'. Goddess Durga was not astride a tiger but her own son, and could not afford to dismount lest he eat her up.

Mrs Gandhi began to crack. Her speech in the Rajya Sabha on the President's address was 'hollow and full of mistakes . . . whatever she said about corruption was completely without substance. For instance, a reply has been given today that the engine used in Maruti was not imported. This major act of corruption has been carried out only for the sake of the PM's son'. She suspected treachery where there was none. Most of all, she suspected Babu Jagjivan Ram and began to collect information against him. 'This is perfectly consistent with her style because she constantly worries about her senior ministers and keeps up secret activity against them,' records Tandon.

Mrs Gandhi vented her anger against people who could not hit back. One was Chedi Lal, the inspector general of police, Pondicherry. Another was the highly respected civil servant, Dharam Vira, then Governor of Mysore. She did not like some statement he had made and summoned him to Delhi. When he arrived, she had no time to see him and he returned to Mysore. 'She was livid.' She got annoyed with Pavate, then Governor of Punjab, and wanted to dismiss him. She summoned the industry minister, T.A. Pai, and gave him a severe dressing-down. A streak of sadism hitherto unnoticed began to manifest itself.

On 12 June 1975, Justice Jagmohan Sinha of the Allahabad High Court set aside Mrs Gandhi's election to the Lok Sabha on grounds of corruption and debarred her from contesting polls for six years. She lost her cool. While she consulted lawyers like Gokhale, Nani Palkhiwala and S.S. Ray, she encouraged Sanjay, Dhawan, Bansi Lal and Kishan Chand to organize mass rallies in her favour. To add to her woes, her party lost the elections in Gujarat. In her appeal to the apex court where Palkhiwala appeared for her, all she got from the vacation court judge, Krishna Iyer, was a stay order depriving her of the right to vote. She didn't want to resign and hoped that the mass rallies her son and his cronies organized would somehow vitiate the judgement. Mother and son ticked off the information and broadcasting minister, I.K. Gujral, for not publicizing the meetings. Sanjay, who little respected constitutional proprieties and understood how people feared the danda, took over the administration in his mother's name. On the night of 25 June 1975, a docile Fakhruddin Ali Ahmed signed the proclamation of Emergency. All leaders of the Opposition, including JP and Morarji Desai along with over 10,000 (the figure rose to 30,000) others, were put behind bars. The mettle of our leaders can be gauged from the fact that not one cabinet minister uttered a squeak in protest: Jagjivan Ram, who had shown signs of dissent, agreed to lead the motion of approval in Parliament, Swaran Singh argued for it like a mofussil lawyer, the Chhatrapati of yesteryears, Y.B. Chavan, lost all his valour. They were like a bunch of eunuchs (no offence meant to our hijda brothers/sisters) willing to dance and clap to any tune. The only ones to prove their manliness were two Parsis—Palkhiwala, who returned his brief, and Fali Nariman, who resigned as additional solicitor-general.

Tandon sums up his reactions quoting Harivansh Rai Bachchan's poem, 'Kaliyug ka Chorus':

On hearing of tyranny,
With fingers you plugged your ears,
And blindfolded your eyes,
On discovering a swindle spree,
Then sealed your lips,
Allowed a ruffian rule.
Oh, you Gandhi's monkeys three,
If there is some shame left in you,
Slap your face red—each one of you.

A postscript is in order. Tandon has praised his colleagues in the PMO—P.N. Haksar, P.N. Dhar, N.K. Seshan, H.Y. Sharada Prasad—all able and men of rectitude. Did any one of them do more than gnash their teeth at their luncheon meetings? While they accused others of cowardice, did any of them have the guts to resign?

Tandon got a taste of Mrs Gandhi's vengefulness after he was reverted to service in UP. He notes: 'Not only did she decide that I will not get a position at the Centre, the Uttar Pradesh government was unofficially and orally instructed not to give me even the due promotion.' All I can say to that is: serves you right!'